T0000115

BREATHING FIRE

BREATHING FIRE

FEMALE INMATE FIREFIGHTERS
ON THE FRONT LINES OF
CALIFORNIA'S WILDFIRES

JAIME LOWE

MCD 🜏 FARRAR, STRAUS AND GIROUX | NEW YORK

MCD
Farrar, Straus and Giroux
120 Broadway, New York 10271

Grateful acknowledgment is made for permission to reprint "Female Inmate
Firefighter Dies Following Injury in Malibu Blaze," by Joseph Serna and
Brittny Mejia. Copyright © 2016 *Los Angeles Times*. Used with permission.

Library of Congress Cataloging-in-Publication Data
Names: Lowe, Jaime, 1976– author.
Title: Breathing fire : female inmate firefighters on the front lines of
    California's wildfires / Jaime Lowe.
Description: First. | New York : MCD / Farrar, Straus and Giroux,
    2021. | Includes bibliographical references and index.
Identifiers: LCCN 2021007793 | ISBN 9780374116187 (hardcover)
Subjects: LCSH: Women fire fighters—California. | Women prisoners—
    California. | Wildfires—California.
Classification: LCC TH9118.W46 L57 2021 | DDC 363.37092/5209794—dc23
LC record available at https://lccn.loc.gov/2021007793

Designed by Gretchen Achilles

Our books may be purchased in bulk for promotional, educational, or
business use. Please contact your local bookseller or the Macmillan Corporate
and Premium Sales Department at 1-800-221-7945, extension 5442, or by
email at MacmillanSpecialMarkets@macmillan.com.

www.mcdbooks.com • www.fsgbooks.com
Follow us on Twitter, Facebook, and Instagram at @mcdbooks

10 9 8 7 6 5 4 3 2 1

Some of the names in this book have been changed.

Dedicated to Shawna Lynn Jones and Diana Baez

and

the women of California's Conservation Camps

There is no country where nature is more lavish of her exuberant fullness; and yet, with all our natural beauties and advantages, there is no country where human life is of so little account.

—The *Los Angeles Star* on Southern California, 1853

CONTENTS

PART IV
RELEASE

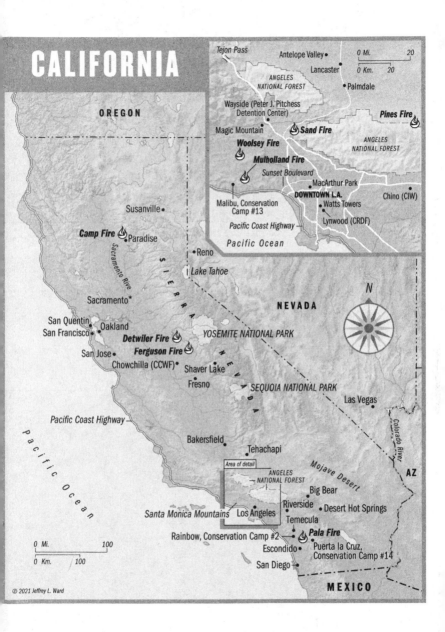

CALIFORNIA

OREGON

Susanville •

Camp Fire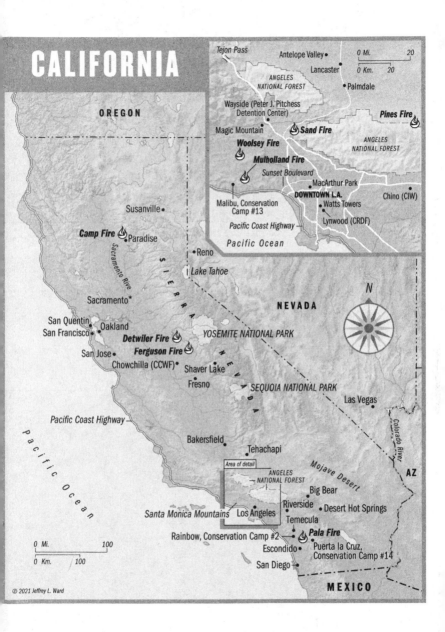
Paradise

Sacramento River

Reno •

Lake Tahoe

NEVADA

Sacramento ✳

San Quentin
San Francisco • Oakland

Detwiler Fire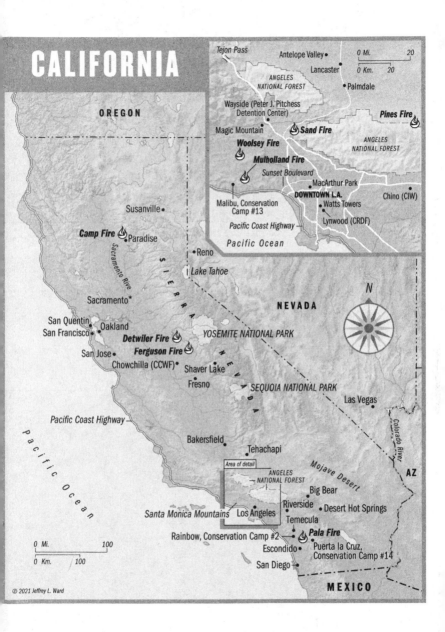

YOSEMITE NATIONAL PARK

San Jose •

Ferguson Fire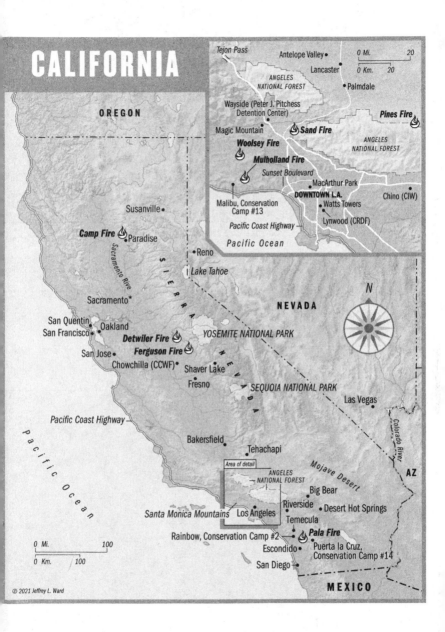

Chowchilla (CCWF) •

Shaver Lake •

Fresno •

SEQUOIA NATIONAL PARK

Las Vegas •

Pacific Coast Highway

Bakersfield •

Tehachapi •

Area of detail

ANGELES
NATIONAL FOREST

Mojave Desert

AZ

Big Bear •

Santa Monica Mountains

Los Angeles •

Riverside • Desert Hot Springs •

Temecula •

Rainbow, Conservation Camp #2 •

Pala Fire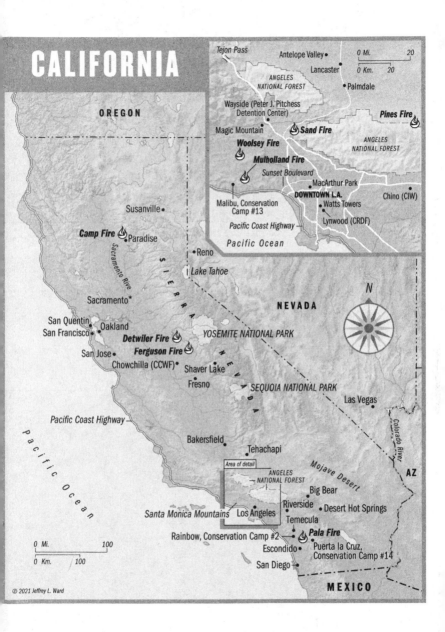

Escondido •

Puerta la Cruz,
Conservation Camp #14

San Diego •

Colorado River

Pacific Ocean

MEXICO

© 2021 Jeffrey L. Ward

0 Mi. 100
0 Km. 100

N

Inset map

Tejon Pass

Antelope Valley •

0 Mi. 20
0 Km. 20

Lancaster •

ANGELES
NATIONAL FOREST

• Palmdale

Wayside (Peter J. Pitchess
Detention Center) •

Magic Mountain •

Sand Fire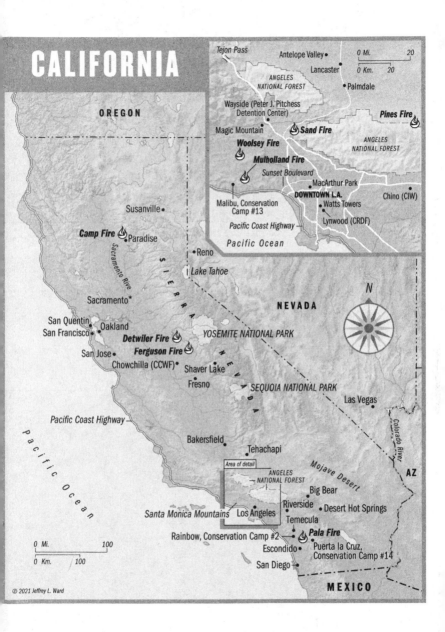

Pines Fire

Woolsey Fire

ANGELES
NATIONAL FOREST

Mulholland Fire

Sunset Boulevard

MacArthur Park •

DOWNTOWN L.A.

Chino (CIW) •

Malibu, Conservation
Camp #13

• Watts Towers

Pacific Coast Highway •

Lynwood (CRDF) •

Pacific Ocean

PART I

SHAWNA LYNN JONES AND THE WOMEN OF CREW 13-3

1.

THE MULHOLLAND FIRE, FEBRUARY 25, 2016

Shawna Lynn Jones heard the siren at 3:00 a.m., but refused to get out of bed. What she heard sounded like the school bells that pulsed to announce earthquakes. She could sleep through those. Those bells were drills, those drills were drop-and-covers. And everyone in California knew, if the big one hit, there's no way an Antelope Valley school desk would save you.

"Shawna, let's go. We've got to go out with another fire," Carla said, shaking her.

Shawna refused to get out of bed.

"Get up, Shawna."

Shawna groaned.

"Is it for reals this time?" she asked.

Carla nodded. "Yeah, get up. Come on. Bailey's gonna be pissed."

Shawna got up, and ran, groggy, to the buggy. Her shirt was stamped, in twelve-inch letters, "CDCR"—California Department of Corrections and Rehabilitation—so that underneath it all, under her NOMEX protective gear, she'd never be mistaken for a free world firefighter. At the buggy, Carla pointed at Shawna's feet.

"Where are your boots?" Carla's eyes widened. Shawna was shoeless. She had raced out in a dream state. Was she imagining the siren? Was she actually even running to the buggy? Was she in jail? Was she a firefighter? Was she back home in Lancaster? Was she at the biker bar her mom managed in Antelope Valley? Was she skateboarding? Was she jumping into Shaver Lake on a hot day? She didn't know what the fuck was going on. She groaned and asked again, "Is this a for reals fire?"

They had to treat every alarm as real. They had to rush to the buggy every time. It was their job. It was why they got paid the prison salaries of $2.56 a day and $1 an hour when they were out on the line, fighting fire. Shawna had barely seen flames before, but she was itching to. She kept saying she wanted to fight an out-of-county—when crews would travel across county lines and assist statewide efforts, sleeping outside for up to two weeks at a time, sometimes longer.

Shawna held her black, dirt-caked boots in her hands but hadn't yet pulled them on and laced them up. They looked just like the kind of shoes correctional officers favor: White's Smokejumpers. They were heavy black leather with winged wooden heels. New girls always complained about the boots and the blisters that came with them.

It was dark. Red and white lights flashed.

She made the crew late; the foreman, Don Bailey, was waiting. Shawna made the crew late a lot. She often came out of the barracks sloppy, shirt untucked, shoes untied, disheveled in a way that would often warrant punishment. The crew would get harder work the next day. But Shawna and Bailey had their own rapport. He wasn't as strict with her; everyone could tell he liked her. And anyway, it was his last day with crew 13-3. After this he'd be promoted to captain and transferred, and they'd have a new foreman. He told Shawna to hurry up.

It had been the third, fourth, maybe fifth alarm of their shift. Around 10:00 p.m., when inmates had to be on their bunks for final count, the crew had assumed it just wasn't their night to catch a fire. They toasted pizza pockets, got ready for bed, but stayed dressed in their oranges, just in case they caught a call. They went to bed in the open concrete-floored barracks. Bunk after bunk after bunk. They slept in the same order they walked as a crew. First, the sawyer, the woman in charge of handling the chain saw and cutting brush. Then, her bucker, the person who cleaned up whatever she slashed down. A second sawyer, and her bucker—that was Carla and Shawna. Then, the rest of the crew—the women in charge of tools, the girls who scraped the earth with McLeods and cut line with Pulaskis. And last in line, the dragspoon, the person who looked out for safety issues.

They lay down, thinking the calls had stopped. With only an eighth of their twenty-four-hour shift remaining, it was a good gamble. Some went to sleep hard; something deep. Others floated on the edge of consciousness, knowing another alarm might sound. Thing about fire camp, you were always tired. Always needing to catch up on sleep. And when you were on call, sleep was half a notion. Crew 13-3 had to be ready to get to the buggy in two minutes or less. So, they tucked into their cots, boots unlaced next to the cubbies. All day and into the evening, they laced their boots, raced to the fire buggy, and pulled on their turnouts, only to turn around after being told the fire call was canceled. Sometimes Bailey would pull the alarm just to test their readiness. They'd never caught an out-of-county with Bailey. Many of the fourteen women in the crew hadn't seen fire at all.

———

"Come on, Shawna, get on the buggy. I think we caught one."

Carla was not used to being responsible for other people, but Shawna was her bucker, which meant they were a team. If Carla had to cut brush on a cliff, it was Shawna who held her by the belt, dangling Carla's body closer to the dried-out grasses that blanketed the wild mountains of Southern California. For Carla, it had started in fourth or fifth grade with the feeling of powerlessness, the feeling that she couldn't trust the adults, or the kids, around her. She got picked on. Pushed around, bullied. She felt her size, small. It was easy to mistake small for weakness. Once she got to middle school, kids would wage all-out war on the asphalt. They'd put gum in Carla's hair. They'd pull her hair, scratch her face, punch her in the gut, the neck, the cheek, whatever was exposed. She'd fight back, straddle whoever was coming at her, one-two-one, fists clenched, leaving nail marks in her palms, not letting up until someone pulled her off or the school cops came to break it up. Sometimes she ran, sometimes she got caught.

When she was caught, police would drive her to the San Fernando courthouse where her mom was a clerk for a judge. Growing up, Carla had seen all the criminals lined up in cuffs and judges donning their robes. She knew some judges by name. When people in the courthouse saw her, they asked, "Carla, what are you doing here?"

She went through those metal detectors as a kid, on Take Your Daughter to Work days. Her mom never thought she'd have to teach her daughter to try to avoid the lock-up side of the courthouse. It just seemed obvious. *Don't end up like them. You are better than that. I am better than that.* The more Carla got in trouble, the harsher her mom punished her. *You won't go out. You won't eat. You won't live with me anymore. Go to your grandmother's. You're an embarrassment,* she'd tell Carla.

By high school, Carla had learned that the best defense was a good offense. She went to three different schools, got kicked out of each for fighting. She got into fights about dumb things, gossip or rumors. If someone started shit or lied about her or demeaned her, she would not back down. When one girl told Carla she couldn't wear the same Nikes, Carla thought, *That's bullshit, I'll wear whatever shoes I want.* And that was a fight. The fistfights continued, augmented by the hair pulling, spitting, scratching, bruising, bleeding. She didn't know how to walk away and didn't want to. She knew it was dumb shit, pointless shit, but it felt important. It felt necessary. She had to stand up for herself because no one else would.

Girls were getting jumped, girls were pledging gangs, and Carla's attitude remained the same: *I am not one to be fucked with.* Conflict was every day.

When she thought about it now, her crime seemed so dumb, but the whole system seemed dumb and rigged. It started as a fight. Money was owed, threats relayed through rumor, things Carla didn't talk about, even at Malibu. The confrontation that landed her in prison had quickly escalated from words to violence. A window was broken and the other girl was left beaten in front of her apartment. Carla had bruises and scrapes of her own. A week later, police officers arrived at Carla's door with a warrant and a report that had been filed, detailing the assault and much more. The report said there had been a burglary, a knife, things that Carla knew did not happen. *Why would I rob someone from the projects? I'd rob someone where there was actually something of value.*

Carla thought it was all settled on the street, that this girl wouldn't go to the police. Carla was wrong. That fight felt like a long time ago. And in many ways, it was.

Now, she was in the middle of Malibu, piling into a dirt-caked fire buggy, in the middle of the dry, brush-tangled mountains, dragging Shawna along.

Shawna groaned and asked again, "Is this a for reals fire?"

Shawna didn't think she'd see a fire. She had arrived at camp in November and hadn't caught a call. Her release date was April 10, 2016—just forty-five days away. Since it was February, and California's fire season was technically over, it seemed unlikely she'd be on a fire. But she wanted that experience; she'd trained for it. In the few months she'd been at camp, Shawna had worked her way from the back of the line to bucking. If you're a bucker, you have to be saw-certified so you're ready to take over if your saw gets tired.

Shawna turned to Carla.

"Car, I'm scared. An actual fire."

Carla told her to calm down and breathe. Most people called her Baby Carla, because she was only nineteen when she started serving her time. But this was her third fire season and second camp. First, she'd been at County, then Chowchilla in the Central Valley for processing, then the California Institution for Women (CIW) in Chino, then Rainbow, north of San Diego, then back to CIW, and then finally Conservation Camp #13 in Malibu. At Rainbow, the foremen were harder on the girls. They played favorites, bought Starbucks for the ones they liked best. At Malibu, Carla felt pressured by the running hikes in rocky terrain. But she liked the exacting work, cutting line and maintaining fire roads. Being on a fire crew here was just as hard as it was at Rainbow, but sometimes Bailey let them get away with shit. They could race to the fire buggy, orange shirts untucked, holding their boots, and lace them up on the way to a fire. It just depended on his mood.

She told Shawna everything would be fine, as long as she could breathe and stay calm. It was hard to stay calm. Outside the buggy, flashing lights flickered through the darkness, and inside the fire buggy, as it climbed up the curving mountain road, girls were getting nauseated and nervous. Malibu fire roads, built by generations of inmate crews, are serpentine. As the buggy negotiated the narrow, sharp switchbacks that hugged the steep inclines and dropped into valleys, it was hard not to look over the edge and imagine plunging.

Selena, the first saw and the woman who led the crew, was quiet and used to the roads. She didn't barf and she didn't hold her stomach and she didn't complain and she wasn't afraid of live fire. She was nonchalant about everything—the fires, prison, jail, juvy, the gang she used to be in, her love of animals. She spoke of it all with the same even keel. She was young and seasoned, not yet twenty-one. Sometimes Selena told jokes. She had been on so many fires, out-of-counties that required full fourteen-day assignments, that this one just a few miles north of camp seemed like a routine assignment. Tame compared to the wildland blazes she'd been on. She sat in front of Carla and Shawna on the buggy.

Carla stared through the fire buggy's windows as they approached.

"Oh shit, there's flames. We're fighting a fire today," she said.

"We're gonna get off the buggy now. Don't panic. You're going to feel like you can't breathe. Let your body naturally just breathe," Carla said.

Shawna nodded.

"I remember my first fire, there was so much smoke. You're just like freaking out and you start thinking, Oh shit, I'm going to die. Or, These flames are so big." But you're fine, Carla told her. "You're going to be okay. You know, just put your shroud on"—the draped face and neck covering for extreme thermal protection—"and just try to breathe. You know, just try to breathe like that. And if you can't breathe or you can't see—" Before Carla could finish, Bailey ordered everyone off the truck. They had loaded in so that they could exit the buggy in order: Selena first, Lilli second, Carla third, and Shawna fourth.

"I don't know. I'm, like, feeling it." Shawna seemed overcome by the claustrophobia, the heat, the smoke, the fire, all just down the canyon and up the ravine. She was feeling the rush, but also the terror of doing something for the first time. She knew how to run with a backpack and she knew she could do the burpees; they had trained her physically. But that's not training for flames. That's not live fire. They never trained with live fire. Not like the free world crews.

Bailey briefed them. There would be planes above, dropping retardant; there would be helicopters dropping thousands of gallons of water to stave off the advancing flames. Other crews would join them, but they—inmate crew 13-3 of Malibu—were the first to arrive on scene. He pointed northeast and said, "We're going to hike down that ravine, then up the hill, we're going to cut line around the fire so it can't advance. We're going to do what we've been training to do." Inmate crews are usually on the ground, executing grunt work, the first line of defense cutting circles to try to contain flames and stop the forward progress of a fire. They are the hand crews. To contain the fire, they establish a line, usually a few feet wide, by cutting through trees and shrubs and removing anything that could burn. Fuel. The sawyers, like Selena and Carla, take chain saws to growth; the buckers, like Lilli and Shawna, throw the cut growth down the steep hillsides, sometimes into sheer-drop canyons. Then, the inmate firefighters with smaller tools follow, grinding out the roots until the line is established. What's left is a swath of bare earth.

Selena stood in front of the flames, ready to hike in. She knew how to run. She was fast. She grew up in MacArthur Park. The thirty-five-acre park was the closest she got to nature before Malibu. As a kid, she knew which parts of the park to walk through and which parts to avoid. MacArthur Park, halfway between Koreatown and downtown L.A. and just north of south Los Angeles, was an area controlled to varying degrees by MS-13, 18th Street gang, the Wanderers, and Crazy Riders. Selena was in CRS, Crazy Riders—they protected her from rival gangs. They called her La Niña, because she was so young when she joined, just fourteen. Each gang fought for a corner of the park to control. Selena was not bothered by violence or drugs. Those, she could navigate. She worried about the cops and the foster care system, in that order. She thought she could outrun both.

At age thirteen, Selena was separated from her mom and brother and funneled into the system. Her mom was addicted to crack, and child services had been called on more than one occasion. Selena toggled between foster care, group homes, and juvy. At the time, California Department of Social Services paid foster parents $963 a month for expenses, but that was only if they could keep her in-house for the full month. Selena ran away from the first house she was placed in. A couple of months later, a social worker took her to a second house. Selena saw she'd have her own room, her own bathroom. She saw that it was a nice setup. But when she went to the bathroom, all she could see were the bars on the windows. She told her potential foster mom and social worker that she'd be right back and snuck out the back door, hopped the fence, and took a bus to a friend's house. "I never really had a stable place to live," Selena said. She didn't seem bothered. It just was. She ran from every foster care setup— family homes, group homes, short-term homes—about half a dozen in five years, until the last one. That one was more like a house for friends, a place run by slightly older women who had kids Selena's age. She was nearly eighteen and they'd all smoke weed together on comfy sofas and she thought it was chill.

Selena, first saw, got out of the buggy first. Thirty-pound pack strapped to her back, twenty-pound chain saw carried in front. This brush fire, off Mulholland Highway, in a barren and circuitous section of the road, was about two miles uphill from the Pacific Coast Highway. The only structures dotting

the immediate landscape were three enormous AT&T satellite dishes that connect Hawaii to the mainland. When crew
13-3 assembled outside its buggy, the women knew the terrain. They had hiked up and down the trails and cleared the
fire roads nearby. This time, the crew would have to establish
its own path, away from the maintained roads. The fire wasn't
predicted to be a particularly big one; dispatchers thought
it would be a ten- to twenty-acre blaze, but the terrain was
challenging.

Acreage doesn't matter when you're tasked with hiking
into a wall of flames in an attempt to control them. One lick of
fire can singe skin; one inhalation can choke a life; one acre can
turn into ten or twenty or a hundred or a hundred thousand.
When the women of crew 13-3 unloaded, they saw a ten-foot-tall
wall of orange-white-red flames curling up toward the fingers
of chaparral and beyond. Braided hot ribbons of fire were mu-
tating into plumes of black smoke. Smoke that blacked out the
already dark night.

Selena was meant to hike out first. She didn't spook easily.
But these flames were growing. Even when she was arrested at
age eighteen, she had calculated a clear path of escape and was
confident she could outrun well-positioned cops dispatched to
arrest her. She was confident because she had always been ath-
letic. Growing up, Selena's mom insisted that she sign up for
every after-school program available, including cross-country.
She went to a magnet school in Culver City for grades six
through eight, and at age eleven, Selena trained for and ran the
Los Angeles Marathon. Running was calming; it was a chance

to think. She parlayed her hobby into a useful skill; instead of running races, she ran from cops. She heard a voice yell over a bullhorn in front of her grandmother's apartment, "Selena, don't run, we've got units in the back." A couple of days before, Selena had held a small knife to a stranger's side, and took his fixie bike. When reporting the crime, the victim assessed the value of his bike to be $950. In California, any theft over $950—the exact value of the bike reported—meant the theft was an automatic felony. Selena didn't think much of taking the bike, but the guy she lifted it from was associated with a rival gang. He knew her brother. He could ID her, and did.

The LAPD got a tip informing them that Selena was selling drugs—she allegedly had a package—and that she was the female involved in the bike theft. When Selena heard, "Don't run, we've got units in the back," she thought they were trying to trick her. She ran to the back of the apartment and outside. "When I got to the back of the apartment complex, there were like six cops already trying to go in the back. And I kinda did this dodging move, it was like a movie," Selena said. "And then I ended up running down the alley. I was running. I looked back and I seen this fat, like, two-hundred-pound cop running after me. And I'm like, I got this, I got this. I almost ended up out the alley, but my dog wasn't there and I just stopped." Selena's puppy, Papi, a Chihuahua who was normally right at her heals, was nowhere. The cops had Papi, so they had her. Selena voluntarily turned herself in with the idea that Papi would be taken care of. She was cuffed and arrested. The cops gave her the name of the shelter where they would take Papi.

Because the robbery involved a weapon and the gang unit was already aware of Selena, she faced five years max for stealing the bike and ten more for gang affiliation. They never found drugs, nor was she charged with any crime related to distribution or use. Her first plea offer was twelve years at 80 percent, meaning at minimum she'd serve nine years and six months. She said no, "I'd rather take it to the box and fight it in trial." Her public defender came back with another plea of two years at 80 percent.

This time, she pled out.

It was her first felony as an adult.

Every day, from county jail in Lynwood, Selena called a friend and asked her to pick up Papi. The shelter refused to release the dog unless Selena came to the shelter in person and signed the paperwork. But, since the dog came from an LAPD arrest, the people who worked at the shelter knew Selena was already in Lynwood, likely on her way to Chowchilla, and that she'd never be able to sign for Papi.

———

At this point, Selena had cycled through County, Chowchilla, and CIW, and had been at Malibu for a full fire season. Selena had been on more fires than she could count, and she was two weeks away from her release date. She'd been dispatched for a month, sometimes longer, to national parks she didn't even know existed. Parks with trees like giants and rock formations that looked like delusions. This fire felt different. Usually, the crew was mop-up, stomping out and pounding remaining embers that might flare up. They would hunch low to the ground, carrying thirty pounds of food, water, and tools, and sift through charred earth, searching for a glow of orange, for heat. On this fire, Selena saw flames taller than the trucks and trees. She saw fire eating through the Malibu mountain, and she knew what they were supposed to do—they were supposed to climb toward that wall.

As he had anticipated, Bailey had to send them down a steep ravine in order to enter the canyon area. There were no established paths, so the women followed Selena, as they were trained to, in tight single-file formation. It was dark, and the terrain was uneven and jagged. The air was congested with blackened particles. The crew went down, then up, then down again, and up again, cutting, cutting, cutting along the way. Granite rocks embedded in the earth and small trees with stubborn stumps made forward progress challenging. They carved a line that would keep flames at bay. For most of these women, firefighting was their first introduction to hiking.

As the flames spread, helicopters dropped cherry red retardant. Some of the crew were overwhelmed by the thumping and shouting and crackling. The noise was deafening. Aircraft hovered. They could hear the fire snapping trees and chewing through plants and roots and grasses, growing bigger and louder the more fuel it consumed. And shouting: orders, warnings, conditions being relayed. In the best of circumstances, a controlled chaos. After all, wildland firefighting is concerned with one thing: controlling the uncontrollable.

When Selena spotted an ember catch just yards away, she called it back to the dragspoon, Maria, who relayed it to Bailey. The crew scrambled and RTO'd—Reverse Tool Order—changing direction and hiking away from the flames threatening their intended path. Up, down, curving around the ravine. A spot fire was put out by an engine crew who had arrived with hoses. Once the spot fire was out, crew 13-3 hiked down the ravine again. Then RTO'd out *again*, as another fire jumped the containment line. After the second RTO, Bailey called a bathroom break and Carla knew the question that was coming next.

"Did you pack paper, Car?" Shawna asked.

"Of course." Carla always had toilet paper in a Ziploc baggie stashed in her helmet; Shawna never remembered her toilet paper. Car would share, but she'd only share with Shawna, because Shawna was her bucker and because it was Shawna. The other girls on crew could fend for themselves. Crew 13-3 didn't always get along, but everyone liked Shawna. Shawna was a bridge.

Even on the ride over, when everyone realized they were heading to real flames, and tucking in their oranges and pulling on their turn-outs and getting nervous, Shawna kept it light. When they had gotten on the bus, it stank. Carla was cranky from being woken up; they were all in bitchy moods from pointless sleep deprivation and now their bus smelled toxic. The crew started shouting over one another.

"Put the fucking windows open."

"What the fuck is that smell?"

Shawna's seatmate, Nichelle, said, "Whoever did that is *nasty*."

Shawna moved away from Nichelle to the edge of her seat, until her butt was just inches from hitting the floor.

Shawna clucked. "It was you."

Nichelle shot back: "It was probably yo ass, shit."

And most of the people on the bus agreed with Nichelle, that the smell was coming from Shawna. Shawna paused long, acutely aware of comic timing.

"Nichelle," she said, making sure the whole crew could hear, "I felt the seat vibrate."

Nichelle went berserk. "It wasn't me, I swear, it wasn't me."

Shawna defused the tension. The farts were easier to focus on than fire.

Now, after two RTOs and the bathroom break, the fart incident was long since forgotten. They'd already had to piss and shit in the woods. Some had their periods and, if they were lucky, had tampons; others on the rag tried to figure out how to navigate prison-issue pads. It still seemed like this would be a quick fire. Because the crew arrived early and the fire was so close to camp, it meant they had more time to contain it by cutting line around the perimeter. Now, crew 13-3 was just waiting for the engine crew to put out that spot fire.

Bailey noticed Shawna helping the engine crew lay hose.

"Future forestry girl here," he said with a touch of pride. Shawna had already decided to go into forestry when she paroled. She liked the hikes; she liked the physicality. She liked the idea of doing something that could get her out of Lancaster. Every time she spoke to or visited with her mom, Shawna told her, "This is what I want to do. This is what I'm going to do."

Shawna Lynn Jones didn't grow up with dreams of being a firefighter. She wanted to be a cop, a K-9 cop specifically. As a teenager, Shawna couldn't sit still in class; she wouldn't. She didn't see the point of paying attention. School was never going to get her out of Lancaster. She looked around at her classmates' parents and saw the obvious. Top employers in Lancaster were Edwards Air Force Base, a naval weapons manufacturer, Lockheed Martin, and prison industries. You were either born into those jobs, or you were a member of the newly formed class of "working poor," living below the poverty line. Her mom, Diana Baez, was the latter, and by generational transfer-ence, Shawna was too. For as long as she could manage, Diana held on to department store jobs. But when the first recession hit in the early nineties, jobs became scarce. Then, with the second great recession of 2008, and Amazon's ascendance, de-partment stores like the May Company and Robinson's and Broadway and Bullock's ceased to exist. Diana cobbled together what she could by bartending dive bars, working Lancaster's KJ circuit—she was a karaoke jockey, similar to a DJ only fa-cilitating nights of full-throated singing. Shawna helped out by working at the mortuary owned by her boyfriend's family.

Shawna met Mike when she was sixteen; he was eighteen. Mike and Shawna were like any other high school couple, hik-ing out to Shaver Lake on weekends, baking on the rocks until it was so hot, the only choice was to plunge into the water. At first, his mom disapproved; she was a correctional officer and knew the kind of people that hung out at the Trap, where Diana worked.

Diana worried about Shawna and the dead bodies at the mortuary. One morning, Shawna was called in at 2:00 a.m. to wheel a dead baby out of a hospital. When Shawna got there, she couldn't put the cold small body on the gurney. She held it the entire way to the mortuary. It felt too impersonal to put the baby on wheels.

When Shawna got home, she showered and went back to sleep. Mike and Shawna stayed together for four years. To-ward the end of their relationship, they smoked a lot of weed. Diana knew because she could smell the stink of it—but it seemed innocuous, not unlike any other teenager.

Once, Diana walked by Shawna's room and opened the door.

"Shawna, what the hell is going on here?" she said.

Mike answered for both of them. "Everything's fine," he said.

"I asked my daughter the question. Can she even sit up right now?"

Diana, who was usually timid and seemed to shake from nerves even when she wasn't nervous, was more than concerned. She couldn't be angry, she let them smoke pot in her house, but what she saw worried her.

"Shawna, answer me."

She was passed out. So high, she couldn't. Diana tried to get friends from the Trap to talk to them. She tried to talk to them. Shawna and Mike went from smoking weed to trying meth, not a drug you try once and let go of. Diana didn't know where they got it; she didn't care. She just wanted it gone from Shawna. Mike and Shawna both still worked at the mortuary, collecting dead bodies in boxes, only to go home and lie half-dead on Shawna's futon. Diana tried to intervene; Mike's mom tried to intervene. Mike got clean. They broke up. The job ended when the relationship did.

By 6:00 a.m., the fire had charred seven acres of steep hillside.

"Sun's coming out. It's almost morning," Carla told Shawna. Night was finally meeting day. They were high enough above the charred footprint and far enough along in containing the fire that they could see the sun. "You know what that means."

"Only one more day until the weekend," Shawna said.

"Only one more day until we can see our family."

That was how they counted the days. How many days until visits? How many days until a day off? How many days until phone access? One of the reasons women apply for fire camp is not that they want to fight fire. It's that they want their family to see them in a nice place. A respectable place. A place that doesn't require inmate searches before and after a visit. A place that doesn't have sterile rooms with plexiglass dividers and guards who scream *Back the fuck off* if you attempt a hug or hold hands; a place where kids can visit their mothers without the backdrop of spiraling razor wire and watchtowers manned by correctional officers with shotguns. Conservation Camp Malibu 13 was covered in old coastal live oaks and eucalyptus trees. (Eucalyptus are oily and nonnative, the worst for Southern California fires.) Some of the firefighting camps even have cabins that inmates can rent for the weekend. Families can barbecue together in settings that abut fancy sleep-away camps and wineries. Families get to visit in the shade. They get to relax a little and inhale the same scents an aromatherapist might prescribe.

By 7:15, the fire had a name—the Mulholland Fire—and 13-3 was still working on burning stumps and branches, but the winds had picked up in the firefighters' favor. The fire was 35 percent contained, and water drops from helicopters continued. They drenched the flames, but also loosened the soil. A water drop from a helicopter can crush a truck.

Bailey stopped Carla and Shawna and told them to switch positions. He wanted Shawna on second saw and Carla to buck, even though Shawna had never held saw before in a fire. Since she'd only been cutting for about three hours, Carla protested. She'd cut through thirteen-hour shifts before, holding her twenty-pound saw the whole time. This was nothing.

"I'm not asking you," Bailey said. But Carla persisted.

"I don't want to give up my saw. Come on, Bailey. You know you're playing favorites."

Bailey had trained Carla on the saw. He knew she could do it and she felt like this decision was somehow insulting her ability. She wanted to fight but stifled the impulse. She also knew she shouldn't give him shit for the order; they were meant to get out there and execute. Putting up a fight was dumb. It was a pride thing. Shawna was her friend, but she didn't want to give up her saw for anyone.

It wasn't her choice. Carla knew Bailey could write her up if she didn't hand over the saw. A write-up would mean doing more time. That was the nature of camp. You were a firefighter. But you were also an inmate. Small things, like a messy bed or an irrational correctional officer, could mean added time. An infraction from a foreman could also mean more time. An attitude could mean more time.

"I'm sorry, Car," Shawna said, taking over the saw. She held it in front of her body, hands at two o'clock and eight o'clock.

"But can you do it?" Carla asked.

Shawna was already worn through. She'd been working her ass off hauling three-foot sections of trees, tossing them away from the flames, out of the fire's path. She'd been helping the crews lay hose. She was tired. But she was saw-qualified and Bailey wanted Shawna to practice hiking with a saw. This was going to be the only time he could supervise her.

"I think I got it," Shawna said.

Crew 13-3 set out down the ravine, and hiked the mountain again, to get back to the containment line and back to cutting brush. Shawna may have been new to the saw while fighting live fire, but she knew the machine. She could take apart a chain saw and put it back together effortlessly. She could handle the sudden thrust when it kicked back, sharpen the chain when it dulled, clean the clutch cover. The calluses on her hands came from working the saw in camp and when they would trim back brush on fire roads. But now they were here, in the middle of a mountain at daybreak, smoke dulling an early sun. They marched up, into the fire. *Hot, loose, fast.* She could feel the ground moving under her feet. She could feel that heat, that suffocation, that adrenaline. She could feel her calves burn, her muscles crying with each step. She knew that when she got back to camp, she'd feel zapped of energy, drained. The kind of tired that was so close to dead. She just needed to remove any and all kindling, the fuel for fire. She just needed to get to the containment line and start cutting.

"Bump it up," they yelled, moving forward.

"Oh my god, don't look down. It's so deep down there," Nichelle said. Selena, Lilli, Carla, and Shawna pushed ahead. The rest of crew 13-3 lagged behind.

Carla saw Shawna struggling with the weight of the saw. It was sandy ground. For every one step forward, she was slipping three steps back.

"It's fucking hard," Shawna said.

"Yeah, it's hard, and you still have to cut when we get up there."

Carla tried to push Shawna from the bottom of her pack, but nothing was getting her up that mountain with the added weight. She just wasn't used to it. All the training in camp meant little when carrying twenty extra pounds on a mountain incline pockmarked with embers.

Carla offered to switch back. And they did.

Carla was now carrying two instruments, the chain saw and her ax. They cut up the ravine partway, creating a rugged path. Then they stepped aside so the rest of the crew could re-move the chaos of slaughtered growth and dig a trench. They were establishing the line they'd walk.

With nothing left to cut, Selena and Carla waited in a small alcove, looking toward the edge of a cliff. A small bush was still hanging on, growing perpendicular to the mountain. They were fucking around, passing time until the crew could move on to the next portion of the containment line. They threw a pebble, watching it fall hundreds of feet down the cliff. Then they threw a branch. Then a rock. They watched how different weights were swallowed by the canyon.

They jawed back and forth and tossed shit until Carla stepped a little too close to the shrub and realized it was an-chored by sandy soil. One wrong step and they'd go flying with the pebbles and branches. Carla and Selena hovered at the edge until they realized their bodies would fall faster than anything they'd thrown. They stepped back.

"Boss, check this out, there's a cliff here," Carla told Bailey. "You gotta check this spot out."

"Stop throwing things, Carla."

"Yeah, boss. We got it. But look."

They stepped back into the alcove. Bailey and Maria, the dragspoon, walked each crew member past the sheer-drop cliff, one by one until they were back in hookline order, in single file inside the trench. Shawna was watching everything closely: the slow sunrise, the copters dropping water, the flames chewing up the mountains indiscriminately.

While standing on the cliff they heard catcalls coming from above.

"This is what I get for wishing for an out-of-county," Shawna said to Carla, rolling her eyes.

The women of crew 13-3 had caught glimpses of a male inmate crew working on a containment line about a hundred yards up the mountain, and just above them. Now, some members of that crew talked at Selena, Carla, Lilli, and Shawna. They asked what their names were. How they were. Anything to get their attention. Selena saw one throw a rock down the ravine. She heard them laughing. Bailey had already told their foremen that 13-3 would hang back and wait for the crew to finish before advancing. Inmate crews were not supposed to talk to each other. Men were not supposed to address women; women were not supposed to address men. But they were both supposed to fight the same fire. The male crew continued to call to 13-3. And 13-3 continued to ignore them.

Standing in the trench, Carla felt small rocks falling again. Pebbles or rocks, some the size of quarters, others as big as silver dollars. Carla felt one sting through her safety gear and gloves, then ricochet off her wrist. She couldn't tell if it was loose soil or what, but rocks were falling. It was just after 8:00 a.m., two hours after their shift was supposed to be over.

"Yo, that stings, Selena, can you move up?" Carla said.

But Selena wouldn't move, because she didn't want to wait on the uneven ground or be outside the trench. Even if she did move, it would be just around the corner from where they were standing. They would still be under the falling pebbles. Carla and Selena went back and forth, until Carla stepped out of line, closer to Selena.

"Why can't you move a little bit forward?" she asked. But she didn't push as hard as she might have. She didn't flash a bad attitude. She didn't want a write-up. She didn't fight. Selena flagged down the free world crew hiking out and asked if they could follow them, away from the pebbles. Their foreman said no, you have to wait for your crew boss.

Selena could see more pebbles falling in front of her now. They were coming down faster. They started getting bigger. She started cursing to the crew above.

"Hey, you guys are fucking throwing rocks down here. Stop fucking playing," she said. She couldn't actually see the crew. But she was pissed; they all were. It had been a long shift of false alarms, capped by a full night of cutting in live flames.

Then. There was a bang.

It sounded like a wood-chipper. Like a car crash, a gunshot. The bang was louder than the fire. Louder than the branches falling, the copters circling, the orders, the crackling, all of it. The bang echoed in the canyon. Carla had never heard anything like it and turned around.

Shawna had collapsed. Flattened on her back.

Carla was silent.

Crew 13-3 screamed.

Carla stood over Shawna. She wasn't moving.

She grabbed Shawna's backpack straps and yelled, "Get up!" At first, Carla thought it was a joke. Another one of Shawna's weird pranks. There was a boulder the size of a basketball next to Shawna's head.

"Get up," Carla said again.

But Shawna didn't move.

Carla always made fun of Shawna for buckling the chin strap of her helmet—she and Selena were the only ones who ever did that. But now, Shawna's helmet was tilted to the side. Blood leaked out of her ears and then her nose.

She lost color. Then she turned blue. She didn't look like Shawna anymore.

Bailey shouted to another foreman, "Get my crew down!" He called a rescue response team. Provided coordinates for their location. Maria ran up the incline and started giving Shawna mouth-to-mouth.

Everyone was screaming.

Everyone was crying.

Everyone was teetering on the edge of the cliff.

Carla refused to leave. She watched Maria cut open Shawna's orange shirt. Shawna was unresponsive. Shawna was hoisted up to an L.A. County Fire Department helicopter. The emergency helicopter stirred embers from the fire. They landed on Shawna's body. They landed on Carla. They landed on Bailey. They landed on Selena. The embers seared and burned and no one could feel a thing.

When Shawna arrived at critical care, she was handcuffed to the gurney.

2.

THE AFTERMATH

Around 10:00 a.m. on the morning of the Mulholland Fire, an unknown number flashed on Diana Baez's cellphone. It flashed again and again and again. Diana kept declining the call until it seemed like something she shouldn't ignore.

"There's been an accident."

Diana, immediately hysterical, asked, "Where is my daughter?" There were no details to relay; just that there had been an accident.

An hour later, when the Lancaster sheriff's office called with numbers and instructions, Diana scrawled as much information as she could on her bedroom mirror using eyeliner. The sheriff told her that Shawna was not admitted under her birth name, because of her incarcerated status. He told Diana that when she got to the UCLA hospital, she should ask for "Hawaii X." She arrived to find her daughter lying unconscious on a gurney.

The first thing she did after opening the curtain was wrap Shawna in a hug.

Diana said to no one in particular, though there were dozens of people filtering in and out, "You promised me."

Just two days before, the last time Shawna and Diana spoke, Shawna had said, "Momma, I'm coming home in six weeks." Whenever Shawna called her mom from camp, she told her about the training, about the exhaustion after sandbagging a hillside to prevent flooding, and about the weekend hikes through the canyons of Malibu. Shawna found something in this sort of work, something she liked.

Diana held her, and said again, "You friggin' promised me."

Diana hardly recognized her daughter. Her face was swollen; her eyes were taped shut so that they wouldn't dry out; her mouth was full of tubes; her head had been shaved because the doctors were trying to drain a blood clot. Diana crawled onto the gurney next to her daughter, but Shawna remained unresponsive.

The two police officers standing guard at the door to Shawna's room tried to explain what had happened. Captains and representatives from CDCR all tried to explain. But Diana could only cry and hold her daughter's hand. Diana wouldn't leave Shawna's side. A nurse had to force her to eat a snack of orange juice and graham crackers. Diana continued to hold Shawna's hand. Time was elastic. Diana didn't notice the hours passing, she didn't pay attention to calls from friends. She remembered she was scheduled for a shift at the Trap and called.

"What day is it?" she asked her boss.

"It's Friday, Diana," he said.

"I need to be at work soon, right?"

"What are you talking about? Stay there," he said.

The room was filled with people—doctors, nurses, representatives from CDCR and L.A. County Fire. They all kept asking Diana if she needed anything.

"Anything you need, anything you need, please let me know," one person said.

To which Diana shot back, "The next person that asks me what I need, I'm going to let you know what I need. I want my fucking daughter. I want her back. Get away from me. Stop asking me what I need. I don't even need to breathe right now. I don't care. I want my baby back."

Her daughter had been sent to the state prison; she was under its care. And look what had happened, she thought. What could these people possibly do for her now?

"Just go away. Go away."

A nurse told Diana to play Shawna her favorite songs. So she played "Love Is on the Way," by Saigon Kick, and "Temporary Home," by Carrie Underwood. She also played Matchbox Twenty. There was one Matchbox Twenty song that Shawna's dad had learned to play on the guitar before he went to prison. Diana used to tell Shawna that her real dad was Rob Thomas, the lead singer of Matchbox Twenty. Whenever Matchbox Twenty was playing on the jukebox at the Trap, Shawna would say, "Oh my god, it's my dad." Everybody would turn around and look at Diana.

"She knows he's not her father."

"What are you talking about? That's my dad on there."

Nurses came in, talking to the air, "Shawna, we're going to brush your teeth now." And they'd suction out trays of blood, sponge the area around her gums. They all said she had perfect teeth. Diana would tell them that Shawna never had a cavity.

An administrator pulled Diana aside and informed her that Shawna was an organ donor. He asked if she knew that.

"No," she said.

"Can you fill out the paperwork necessary?"

"No, I can't do it."

She froze up. She just wanted to keep her daughter in one piece. She was not ready to imagine Shawna's organs outside of Shawna's body. She was not ready to imagine Shawna's kidneys, her liver, her heart, her eyes, her lungs, her pancreas, her intestines distributed to other bodies. She could not imagine her daughter dissected. She could not imagine that this body in front of her was no longer her daughter, no longer Shawna. She could not see that Shawna's body was shutting down. That it had shut down before it even arrived at the hospital. After a while, Diana signed the paperwork.

Shawna's liver and heart and kidneys and lungs were preserved. Each organ was sold for about $20,000—the money was subtracted from the $100,000 hospital bill, a bill that was sent, itemized, to Diana months after Shawna's death.

On that February morning of the Mulholland Fire in Malibu, Conservation Camp Malibu 13's remaining crews—the ones who weren't on call—woke up to the 7:00 a.m. bell. They'd heard the false alarms and then the real one the night before. They heard Shawna run out without her shoes on. They knew 13-3 caught a fire and they knew, now, something was wrong. They could see the foremen across the CDCR stomp-and-shout dividing line, scattered, on their walkies. They could see them calling in whatever had happened. They could see a freneticism that translated to fear on men who tried very hard to appear fearless. Men whose haircuts alone calmed entire neighborhoods. There were rumors someone was injured. They didn't know who, they didn't know which crew. They knew the danger. Every fire they went on—big or small—there were risks. The ground could shift; a branch engulfed in flames could splinter and drop; a shelter-in-place might be unrolled too late to act as protection.

The camp was still, the trees were quiet. It was warm for February. A captain gathered everyone outside in the visitors' area. He told them, "It was Shawna." Shawna had been injured severely, flown by helicopter to a hospital, and had suffered cardiac arrest, but he didn't say anything more beyond those details. That was enough. Enough to warrant cries and hysteria. Enough to generate fear.

On the ride home from the fire, Carla was thinking, *Why couldn't I have had my fucked-up attitude that I always carry with me. If I could have just moved in front of Selena after the pebbles started falling and brought Shawna with me. If I had just had my bad attitude. If I could have yelled back at the crew above. At the captains. The foremen. At the other firefighters. Anything.* Carla wished she could have gone back and replayed that morning. Had a second take. There were so many times when she wished for a do-over. But this was different, this was Shawna. And last she saw Shawna, Shawna looked gone.

When Bailey pulled the buggy into the L.A. County side of camp and opened the back doors of the truck to let 13-3 out, the crews who were not on call gathered around. They went into the common room on the CDCR side and watched the local morning news quietly, waiting for any updates about the injured inmate. Some women who sign up for fire camp don't ever really believe this work could end in death. It was hard labor. It hurt. They complained about injuries and pulled muscles, about their feet and lower backs pulsating after clearing roads. But death seemed unlikely. They felt protected by the captains, their foremen, their crew. This seemed surreal. What they saw on the local NBC newscast was twenty seconds showing rescue workers maneuvering a stretcher into the cabin of a waiting L.A. County Fire helicopter. The stretcher held an unmoving, injured female inmate firefighter wrapped in a red blanket. Once the stretcher was strapped down inside, the rescue chopper lifted up and flew east over the hills. NBC cut to a talking head, who was quick to point out that this was "only" the third death in the program's history, perhaps a talking point on a CDCR press release.

Crew 13-3 sat in the rec room, still sobbing, still clutching one another, still in shock. Selena stayed behind in the buggy. She was cool and collected, even-keeled, joke-telling Selena. She didn't know what to do with this. She saw all the girls hugging each other as they climbed down. She didn't want to be hugged or touched. She wasn't really an affectionate person. She didn't let people in easily. She waited until it calmed down outside. When a friend came up to the buggy and asked if she was okay, Selena said she was fine, and didn't say much more.

Later that afternoon, they sat with the other crews around the TV, waiting. Carla looked at Nichelle.

"All right, Nichelle, now's the time. Now you have to say the truth, because Shawna's sick." Carla paused. "Was it or was it not you that farted on the bus?" Nichelle went crazy again, and said, "It wasn't me."

"All right, whatever. I think you did it. I'm gonna believe Shawna."

"It wasn't me."

They all laughed, they all cried. There wasn't anything else to do. They hadn't slept in twenty-seven hours. They weren't going to sleep anytime soon. They didn't want to eat.

A CO told the women that Shawna had regained her pulse, making it seem like she might pull through. But the women, all of them—whether they were on the fire or not—were exhausted. They had the wind knocked out of them. It could have been anyone. But it was the one person missing—Shawna Lynn Jones.

CDCR restricted any news of Shawna's death. The inmates at camp weren't allowed to talk to anyone. Carla kept replaying the scene and the circumstances. A stream of thoughts persisted. *How the fuck, we were just talking, and we're in jail, and she was about to go home, that noise, that sound, that bang, I hope she didn't suffer.* She kept picturing Shawna's head, beneath her helmet, split at the temple. She kept picturing her pale face with blood leaking. *What the fuck, it's not fair. No one should die, but not Shawna. She was nice. She was Shawna. I wish it was me. I wish I had done something, pushed us ahead.* She could picture Shawna's helmet with black skid marks where the boulder struck, gray scrapes and striations, but no dent. There was no dent in the helmet but Shawna's head split anyway. Her head split, blood leaked. Carla could not erase the image of the helmet and the blood.

By afternoon, news vans from channel 5, KTLA, and channel 7, KABC, had arrived at camp. Reporters were trying to break into the grounds. CDCR considered transporting the crews back to CIW so that they would be "protected." The crews could talk only to one another, and there wasn't much to say. The women of Malibu 13 were not allowed to make calls to family or friends. It was a no-work day at camp. A rare occasion.

Fire investigators in black suits and collared shirts arrived from L.A. County and CDCR. They interviewed each member of crew 13-3, individually. When they got to Carla, they asked a series of questions.

"Did Shawna have her helmet on?"

"*Of course*, she had her helmet on, why the fuck would she take it off?" Carla said. It felt like the investigators were trying to find a way to blame Shawna. They were trying to make it seem like she didn't have her chin strap on or follow the rules.

"She always had her chin strap on, none of *us* did. But Shawna always had her chin strap on," Carla said. For all of Shawna's wildness, she was a safety-first girl. Even when she was hanging out at the Trap she used to approach strangers and recite the slogan *Don't be silly, protect your willy*, and hand out condoms.

When the inspectors interviewed Selena, it seemed to her that they were trying to shift responsibility onto someone in 13-3. That they thought someone in the crew intentionally put Shawna in harm's way. That because they were inmates, they were somehow to blame, untrustworthy.

"Did anybody have tension there? Did anybody fight before the fire? Was anybody mad?" They separated out the girls who witnessed what happened, those who were at the front of the line. Selena, Lilli, Carla. They interviewed the back of the line, including Maria.

CDCR sent a mental health professional to talk with the crew. He validated the way they were feeling. He asked form questions about trauma and PTSD; they answered with feelings of fear and sleeplessness and hauntings and depression and anxiety. He said, "That is perfectly normal for what you've experienced."

Like, thanks, Carla thought. *I didn't need to know that feeling awful was normal, I wanted to know how to not feel awful.* Every time Carla went to clean her saw, she thought of Shawna. When she went to bed, she thought of Shawna. When she ran out of hygiene, she thought of Shawna. She remembered how Shawna helped her clean the chain saw, how when they were cutting roads, Shawna would dangle her over cliffs. Whatever Carla thought needed to come down, Shawna found a way for Carla to cut it. Carla trusted her with her life, and now Shawna was gone. No other bucker was going to be able to carry her in the same way. Even before camp, Carla never let anyone carry her like that.

For two days they weren't allowed calls or visits. They weren't even allowed to talk to Bailey. He had been their leader and no one told crew 13-3 why he wasn't communicating with them anymore. When their captain spoke with them, he broke down in tears and told 13-3 he felt responsible even though he wasn't on the fire. Bailey called his dad, John, from the buggy. John had retired from L.A. County Fire in 2009. Almost his whole family was in fire—Bailey's brother was a captain, his sister was in the Forest Service. His brother was a senior lead officer for the Los Angeles Police Department. John came down to camp, to be with Bailey. The girls knew shit was bad when they heard Bailey had to call his dad. After a couple of days of the communication blackout, someone—a foreman or a captain—talked with CDCR. *You know, these girls are human, they need to talk to people about what happened. Maybe let them have phone privileges? Maybe let them see their loved ones?*

A couple of days after Shawna's death, crew 13-3 was supposed to go back to work. The women of 13-3 were supposed to be cutting line, maintaining roads, running the trails. They didn't want to be together. When they were on the line, crew 13-3 went hard and functioned like a machine. But off-the-line friendships? They didn't really happen. Latina members of the crew spoke Spanish to each other and Black members resented it. Even before Shawna died, 13-3 had a reputation for being the hardest crew. Tension in crew 13-3 was high. Carla thought Shawna's death would either bring them together or tear them apart. The latter was true. Maria got into a fight that was so severe, CDCR transferred her back to CIW, where she eventually was sent to another camp.

Instead of having them return to work, one of the fire captains told 13-3 to get in the buggy with their lunch coolers. He took them to the beach. He sat them in a semicircle so they could see the waves and feel the sand. He led them in prayer. They listened to the ocean move, the rhythmic waves retreating, advancing, retreating, advancing, pulling each cycle of salt water out to sea, then spitting back another wave. They walked together along the shore and collected rocks for Shawna. The fire captain let them sit silently together at a nearby park. They mourned Shawna. Selena took her boots off and dug for sand crabs. Later, at camp, some sent letters to Diana explaining who Shawna was on the line, how she played her part.

Laurie knew Shawna from Lancaster, from the Trap. But they also went through forestry training at CIW together, then rode the transport bus to Malibu together. On Laurie's first hike, she cried and cussed the whole way up the hill. The pain from her blisters wormed its way into her head, stopped her from forward progress, made her doubt all her training. *Fuck this*, she thought. *I'm not doing this. I can't do this. I'm not going to make it.* Shawna killed it, running the hike like it was the only thing she cared about. When they took a lunch break after the first hike, Laurie told Shawna she was gonna quit, go back to CIW. If this is what they had to do, she couldn't do it. Shawna told her to just keep trying, maybe it would get easier. It was only the first hike, they needed bodies on crews and weren't sending anyone back on the first day. Before the next hike, Laurie put a whole box of moleskins on her feet, and tried again. And again. Once she could do a hike without getting dizzy, she thought, *I did that*. After two weeks, she pushed further than she thought she could, through the pain and doubt. Her body adjusted. It was . . . rewarding, an accomplishment.

Plus, Laurie was lucky. Because she was on Princess crew, their captain would let them do the work they were assigned and then stop if they finished. Other crews worked up until the time their shift ended, in the late afternoon. Princess crew took lunch under the shade of the oak trees while their nearly retired captain took "union breaks" to smoke cigars. After finishing their work, they could kill time at Malibu Overlook or Inspiration Point, sitting in the open air, breathing in salty breezes, looking at the mountains and vistas.

When crews would return to camp at the same time, they'd line up for a security check. COs would look through their lunch pails, pat them down, ask them why they had fresh cuts and bruises if they did. Sometimes, Laurie would see girls fighting in the trucks, when foremen and captains weren't paying attention. It was the only place to get shit settled. That, or behind the weights in the camp's back area. In a small camp filled with women, there were bound to be issues. Laurie had her face bashed in and her eardrum gouged. "We fought, we argued, we got over it. Then we were friends." If someone had visible wounds, the women would just say, "Oh, I fell down a mountain." COs knew the explanation was bullshit, but if they couldn't prove anything, they let it go. The wounds would just hold up the line to get back into camp, or hold up the shift change.

Shawna and Laurie would wait together, lying in the dry grass of the visitors' area, wrecked from the hike but full of dizzying adrenaline. They'd look at the sky, at the clouds, and announce the shifting shapes they saw.

"There's Minnie Mouse."

"I see Mickey."

"There's a penis."

"And balls."

"There's a smaller penis."

"And smaller balls."

"There's a heart."

They'd go back to the barracks, shower, and watch TV. Shawna would run across the rec room toward Laurie, sit on her face, and fart. She'd giggle in the cloud of stank. Shawna got along with most people, but Laurie was a slice of home. Shawna's uncle, not by blood, but a close friend, was friends with Laurie. They had their times at the Trap to relive. Their place that they would go back to, eventually. Shawna talked about the Trap all the time.

Shawna promised Selena, who was twenty when she arrived at camp, that when they were both out, they'd drink together at the Trap.

"When you turn twenty-one, come over to the Trap, I got you with the Irish trash can."

"What's that?"

"Vodka, gin, rum, triple sec, Blue Curacao, peach Schnapps, and Red Bull."

Shawna never lost her playful menace. Selena, who was going through some heartbreak, would play Sam Hunt's "Break Up in a Small Town" on loop. The crew grew to hate the song, but Shawna would egg her on, *Sing it again, play it again*, she'd tell her. Selena would sing it in the rec room, in the barracks, in the shower, on the bus, at the top of her lungs. The song was her only salve. Selena's boyfriend was a firefighter, a trained EMT. They'd been together for a year. She was incarcerated for half of their relationship. "Our worlds were nothing alike. I wanted to save him the trouble. He was a good boy." It was never going to work, she thought. He can't have an inmate bringing him down. She'd remembered the video, how Sam Hunt was singing and walking away from a house on fire. That's what she thought she had to do too, scorch earth and start over, let him start over. When Shawna sang the song, Selena howled with her. The whole crew would tell them both to shut the fuck up.

Though the work was physically grueling, Shawna was constantly learning, because she wanted to move up in the crew. She wanted to be saw. She wanted that experience so she could take it with her when she was released. On her first hike with a twenty-pound chain saw, Shawna felt the weight shift her balance. She tried to move forward with the hookline. She tried to keep pace, but her footing slipped; she braced herself, slipping again, and tumbled down a mountain. As she rolled, out of control, limbs flailing, her swamper yelled.

"If you just lay flat, stiffen your body, you wouldn't roll."

Shawna didn't know; she'd never fallen down a mountain with a chain saw before. The weight of the machine carried her, because gravity will do that.

When she injured her arm, they had her off work for a week. Any more than a week and she would have been sent back to CIW until she recovered. Every inmate avoided being sent back to CIW for health runs. She didn't want to get her captain in trouble, she didn't want to get stuck at CIW, she didn't want their version of health care. It was better to be in pain. Another time, a tree snagged her uniform and she fell on a heavy branch, and that tore her up a bit too.

Whenever she could, Shawna called Diana, but phone privileges were more restricted at camp than they were at Chowchilla or CIW—only two phone calls a week. Every Thursday night, all crews lined up for calls. It was first come, first served, based on a punitive points system. If one girl's hiking time was too slow, her crew got a point; if a girl's oranges were untucked, her crew got a point; if a bed wasn't made, another point. The crews' points were tallied by the COs, and the one with the highest total got the last choice of phone times. When Shawna told Diana about camp, about how much she liked it,

Diana could hear a lightness in her voice. Shawna sounded better than she did at Lynwood, she sounded better than when she was in Lancaster.

But the injuries worried Diana enough to plan a visit with Ashley, Shawna's younger sister, who was thirteen. They'd stay the night in Thousand Oaks so that Diana wouldn't worry about getting to the visiting hours on time. She was nervous about seeing Shawna at camp, in prison. She didn't know what to expect. When they arrived, Laurie was standing on the roof of the TV room, waving down at the picnic benches. It was like a Trap mini-reunion. Some of the other girls yelled, "Hey mama," to welcome her. They spent the full day together, eating Kentucky Fried Chicken and breathing the fresh air, and it was like they were having an actual picnic in a park. It didn't seem like prison at all. The cops in the front office took a digital picture of the threesome. Diana, Ashley, Shawna, all the same height, all the same long chestnut hair. It was clear Shawna had been training. She'd lost the County weight and gained muscle; she'd gotten with the program. Her oranges were tucked in, her belt buckled. She was fire ready and proud to show Ashley and Diana the camp. Shawna told Ashley they'd go to the beach and play volleyball when she paroled. Shawna said she couldn't believe Ashley made straight As. The trees behind them seemed endless, the ocean over the Santa Monica Mountains felt close and calming. Diana was relieved. Sitting and eating in the woods, they imagined the food they'd eat in the backyard of the Trap, the shots they'd drink, the pool Shawna would play in the free world, in only five months. Shawna hugged Diana goodbye, a big full-bore bear hug, the you-don't-want-to-let-go hug. Diana and Ashley drove back to Lancaster. In a few months, Shawna would be out, they reminded themselves.

The next month, on December 8, 2015, Shawna turned twenty-two. Her birthday outfit was the same as the day before and the day after: oranges stamped with "CDCR." Crew 13-3 ordered gifts from their catalogues and made her cards. They decorated her bed and her cubby—collages from dated magazines and cards cut from construction paper. They had leftover cake from dinner and toasted Pop-Tarts. They sang. They danced. Everyone celebrated their birthday, or tried to.

A few days after Shawna's birthday, an officer repeated her name over the loudspeaker. She was called to the main office. It was late, after dinner, but before final count. They said Shawna's dad, Roger, had been sick. She knew he was sick; he had cancer. When she could, she called to check up on him. Camp commanders didn't often call out names over the loudspeaker. Shawna knew something was wrong.

An officer told her, "Your dad died." Shawna was not allowed leave to see him or her family, or to grieve outside of camp. There are no days off in prison. They called Laurie down to the office and asked her to stay with Shawna and comfort her. They said the two of them could sit outside. It was cold, but outside was the closest place to feeling free. Suffocating from grief, Shawna hyperventilated and cried, the heaving kind. Laurie held her as they sat at the visitor's tables, a place her father had never sat. Because he was an ex-felon, he wasn't allowed to visit.

When Shawna called Diana, Shawna was sobbing.

"I know, sweetheart, I'm so sorry."

Shawna was kept busy with crew work, but after Roger died,

she got quiet. Sullen and guilt ridden, she felt like she should have been there for her dad on the outside. That she should have been able to say goodbye. That she should have been able to take care of him. That once he died, she should have been able to hug her mom, to grieve together. Instead, she was stuck in Malibu. For weeks after, Shawna wasn't Shawna. She sulked. Her energy was down. She didn't make jokes or fart on Laurie. She didn't want to listen to country music in the rec room early Sundays when no one else was in there. She slept whenever she could. She just barely got through the work. Laurie was worried about her, and thought Shawna was depressed. The COs worried about her for different reasons—they thought Shawna was a flight risk. Diana called camp because she was worried.

"Do you think she'd run?" one officer asked Diana. They saw Shawna's mental health deteriorating; they saw her depression affecting her ability to do the work. They saw her wanting to go home and eyeing the edges of camp.

"Let me talk to her." Diana knew that if Shawna's behavior persisted, she'd get sent back to county jail in Lynwood. Shawna had only four months left on her sentence; Lynwood was not an option. Diana remembered how Shawna sounded on calls from County. She couldn't go back.

"Shawna, you know that there's nothing you can do here, right? You can't bring your father back?"

"I know, Mom, I know. I'm not going to run." But it was the only thing on her mind. She wanted to be home.

Laurie worried about what she might do. On hikes, Shawna would tell Laurie, "I just really wish I was with my dad right now." Laurie took that to mean that Shawna wished she were dead.

For Christmas, all the girls in camp had secret Santas. They ordered gifts off their books. Some got dry food or candy or power bars, others got T-shirts or tank tops from the catalogue. The kitchen did it up. Turkey, ham, mashed potatoes, gravy, greens, more food than they could imagine, more food than they'd fantasized about when they were in CIW. Even the COs came in to sit and eat. Each girl got to take a picture and send it to her family. Some girls posed for group shots, but a CO intervened and deleted them—group pictures weren't approved. Even on Christmas, when there was no work, no fire, no PT, and a rare chance to celebrate, it was still made clear to crews where they were, what they were, who they were. They were in prison and they were inmates. New Year's passed without much notice, and 2015 bled into 2016.

For Laurie's birthday, Shawna returned the favor of a decorated bunk. She made her a fluorescent green card in the shape of a daisy. On the petals she wrote, "Happy B-Day, Love You, I wish we could have a real party but don't trip, I gotcha next year." She made a second card in the shape of a penis, with hairy balls and veins on one side, with this message on the back: "A big boy penis. LOL. Happy B-Day. Love, Shawna."

Laurie and Shawna talked about parole. Shawna still had a few months of camp, but she wanted to go into forestry in Big Bear. She was fixated on Big Bear. She told a friend from the Trap that she was going to work landscaping or fire when she got out. He heard what Diana heard and what Laurie saw every day—Shawna was thriving. He believed her—not a lot of kids he knew got out of the Antelope Valley. Most went to prison, drank, did drugs, or some combination of all three. Maybe this firefighting would help Shawna get out.

As soon as she could, which turned out to be a couple of weeks after her birthday, Laurie qualified for Custody to Community Transitional Reentry Program (CCTRP) in Bakersfield. She couldn't keep up with the Malibu hikes and the fire calls. Her body was tired. She thought getting a job would help after release. She'd be able to work, continue rehab programs, and live in one of the seventy-five beds available. All the women got jobs and wore ankle monitors. She thought minimum wage sounded good. Even Bakersfield, because it was anywhere-but-the-Antelope-Valley, had some appeal.

The rehab facility was beige, close to the correctional offices, and walking distance to Home Depot. The residence had all the same feeling of prison. The women there could apply for jobs and work, but they came home to isolation, strict rules, and punitive directives. Leadership at the home was dictated by political battles between the rehab director and CDCR counselors. Laurie felt like she was back in CIW, back in Chowchilla, back in Lynwood. She was punished for slight infractions—getting home from work after curfew, not cleaning the kitchen until the sinks were spotless, not making her bed with tight enough corners.

When she interviewed for a job at Home Depot, Laurie followed her counselor's advice and didn't tell the store manager she was a felon. She hid her ankle monitor under khaki pants or jeans, and made eleven dollars an hour stocking shelves. The women in CCTRP couldn't do anything but work and come back to the home. "They really showed me what not having any freedom was like." CCTRP was considered a privilege, but Laurie hated it. "It was so bad, it was a turning point for me, a nail in the coffin. I realized I could never go back to prison. I could never be treated that way again." When Laurie requested a transfer back to Malibu, she was told it was against regulations. All she wanted was to go back to camp.

Laurie was cleaning the kitchen of the rehab facility when one of the other residents ran in and said, "Something happened to your friend."

"What friend?" Laurie asked. There was a pause. "Tell me what the fuck is going on."

A counselor refused to elaborate or let anyone else talk about it until finally a third person pulled her aside and told Laurie, "Shawna died. She got hit in the head with a rock."

"Bullshit. Yeah, right," Laurie said. She didn't believe it. "There's no way she was hit. We know what to do if rocks are falling. It's got to be wrong."

The women in training at CIW were called out to the yard. Marquet listened to the CIW captain who called the meeting. Sonya, in her first day of Physical Fitness Training (PFT), listened too. News of Shawna's death had spread to CIW. It was now thirty-six hours after Shawna had been struck down. The captain described the scene. The women in the yard were in the process of learning their 10s and 18s in class: the ten Standard Firefighting Orders, developed in 1957 to prevent injuries and fatalities, and the eighteen Fire Watch-Out Situations (situations that warrant the shout "Watch out"). They were in the beginning of their training. They recognized what might have gone wrong, what he did not say explicitly. Maybe crew 13-3 shouldn't have been stopped, waiting down slope from another crew. Maybe there should have been more communication. More awareness of the surroundings. They were tired;

it was hard to know. None of the 10s and 18s seemed like it could have predicted a boulder the size of a basketball dropping from the sky. The captain made one point clear—this was dangerous work, deadly work. If anyone wanted to leave the program, she could. If anyone had doubts or fear, now was a good time to think about different work, or return to general population.

Everyone was in shock. Many dropped out of the program, thinking they couldn't do it, or wouldn't do it. No one took a three-year sentence at 80 percent just to die. Six months before, Shawna had been doing burpees on the same yard where these women were gathered. A lot of the girls knew her. They remembered her. The captain led them in a peace and quiet time. Then, the captain read her time of death, the moment when she was removed from life support. He also read her obituary, which ended with, "Shawna made the ultimate sacrifice on February 26, 2016, while working as an inmate firefighter for California Department of Corrections. While trying to overcome the mistakes of her past, Shawna discovered a new path in life through wildland firefighting. She was very excited to continue her career in wildland firefighting when she was done with her time with California Department of Corrections. Shawna had a passion for sawyer work on the fire line and wanted to pursue this job in the fire service. Shawna gave her life so that others may live."

3.

MALIBU CONSERVATION CAMP #13, FOUR MONTHS LATER

was born in California, at a time when extreme fires were once-a-decade events. The first time I heard about Shawna Lynn Jones and how inmate fire crews fought to keep my home state safe from increasingly frequent blazes was when I picked up the *Los Angeles Times* on the day after Shawna's death, on February 27, 2016:

Shawna Lynn Jones, who died Friday after being struck by a falling boulder in Malibu, is the first woman inmate in state history to lose her life while battling a wildfire, according to the California Department of Corrections and Rehabilitation.

Jones, 22, had joined the state's Conservation Camp program in August and was working fire lines near Mulholland Highway early Thursday when she was struck in the head by a large rock that fell 100 feet, authorities said.

She was helicoptered to Ronald Reagan UCLA Medical Center in critical condition, and her family removed her from life support Friday morning. Her organs were harvested for donation, "in keeping with her family's wishes," authorities said.

"Her death is a tragic reminder of the danger that inmate firefighters face when they volunteer to confront fires to save homes and lives," state corrections secretary Scott Kernan said in a prepared statement. "On behalf of all of us in the department, I send my deepest condolences to her family."

Jones, who was from the Lancaster-Palmdale area, was serving a three-year prison sentence for repeatedly violating probation for a 2014 drug offense, according to Los Angeles County Sheriff's Department jail records. She was scheduled to be released April 10.

Although the state uses thousands of inmates to battle wildfires each year, Jones is just the third conservation camp inmate to die since the program began in 1943.

Female inmates were incorporated into the program in 1983, according to the CDCR. Of the roughly 4,000 inmates housed in 44 conservation camps across the state, only a couple of hundred are women.

Typically, inmate firefighters are armed with such tools as shovels and pickaxes, and focus on fire containment lines in often rugged terrain. Inmates operate in crews of about 14 and under the direction of a fire captain. "They are, for all practical purposes, professional firefighters," said Bill Sessa, a corrections department spokesman. "They're trained to do the work that they do."

When not fighting wildfires, inmates work on fire-prevention projects. During the winter of 2014, women at the Malibu conservation camp where Jones was stationed helped to fell and remove diseased trees that would act as fuel for wildfires.

Inmates who work in fire camps are carefully screened and evaluated to ensure they have the right temperament and attitude. Anyone with violent tendencies or attitude problems is weeded out, Sessa said.

The Mulholland fire, where Jones was injured, had broken out shortly before 3 a.m. on Mulholland Highway about two miles north of Pacific Coast Highway, according to Los Angeles County Fire Inspector Randall Wright. The fire scorched 10 acres before it was halted early Thursday morning. No structures were damaged, although a voluntary evacuation had been put into effect temporarily.

The cause of the fire remains under investigation. In addition to the inmate fire crews, the blaze was battled by Los Angeles County and Ventura County firefighters.

The Sheriff's Department, as is standard procedure, will investigate Jones' death, officials said.

The article was on the bottom of the first page of the California section, below a story about two class action lawsuits filed against Donald Trump by students who had attended Trump University. Shawna's death was sandwiched between a memorial for a ninety-year-old philanthropist and an article about a KKK rally in Anaheim in which the organizers were hoping to communicate the message "White lives matter too."

Shawna's article ran with the headline: "Inmate Firefighter Dies in Malibu Blaze." The only picture of her was blurry, taken from afar, her horizontal body wrapped in a red blanket, strapped to a board and dangling from a rescue helicopter, ascending skyward. On the ground below, a couple of wildland firefighters were dwarfed by a Malibu rock formation. The earth they stood on was tilted, the land they protected was crisscrossed with roots from chaparral stands that rose up to ashen branches, the surviving carcasses of the Mulholland Fire. The article was continued eight pages into the B section of the newspaper, nestled under the day's weather report. The numbers in Southern California didn't seem especially high— seventies and eighties. But it was winter and dry, and the west winds were creating swells and rip currents. (On a previous page, a picture of a surfer, arms wide for balance, rode a wall of a wave in Redondo Beach. The caption noted a man had died there and a high surf advisory was in effect for San Diego, Orange, and Los Angeles Counties. The winds affect the waves; the winds affect fire.)

The picture of the Mulholland Fire showed two crews, specks on the landscape. One crew was in orange, an inmate crew; the other in yellow shirts and dark green pants, a wildland crew. I was struck that the article revealed only a few salient facts about Shawna Lynn Jones, bullet points of a person. She was twenty-two, from Lancaster, an inmate, serving time for a probation violation, and only six weeks from her release date. The article wrote of her death, offering so little of her life. She was defined by her crime.

The news of Shawna's death was tucked into a hierarchy of importance. Would Leonardo DiCaprio finally win an Oscar, for *The Revenant*? Would those who arrived on the red carpet be toned and painted and smiling broadly with fake, capped, glistening teeth? Would it matter that Marco Rubio called Trump a "con artist" during the final Republican debate before Super Tuesday? Would it matter that Trump's response was to make fun of Rubio's sweat: "Can you imagine Putin sitting there waiting for a meeting, and Rubio walks in and he's totally drenched?" Would Marmaduke enjoy his ride in a golf cart? Did anyone care that El Chapo agreed to extradition if he was guaranteed a stay in a minimum-security prison while awaiting trial? That the Lakers lost eight straight games while an injured Kobe watched from the sidelines? That millionaires were getting tens of thousands of dollars in lawn rebates for replanting their gardens? That there was a cease-fire in Syria? That a fourteen-year-old in Massachusetts was sentenced to forty years to life for a rape-murder charge? That a lost "unicorn—a six-hundred-pound Shetland pony with a prosthetic horn and fuzzy pink bridle"—was captured after a four-hour chase by the California Highway Patrol in the Central Valley? That Governor Jerry Brown won a court victory allowing allies to gather signatures for a measure to revamp prison parole policy? That the Chino Hills High basketball team destroyed Mater Dei, 102–54, with Lonzo Ball leading the charge? That Charcoal opened in Venice and, though it was meant to be a meaty restaurant, Jonathan Gold raved about the cabbage wedge? That Yasiel Puig hinted at buying a helicopter so he could arrive on time to Dodger practices and games? That puntarelle was popping at the farmer's market? That, after eighteen years in development, a blimp meant to detect cruise missiles, drones, and other low-flying objects had cost tax payers $2.7 billion and failed to "perform as promised," according to a Pentagon analysis? A lot was happening that week in February.

The *Los Angeles Times* wrote 496 words about Shawna Lynn Jones.

Shawna is the firefighter who warranted an article because she died on the line—while thousands of other female inmate firefighters work in anonymity. This is her story, but it's also the story of women who weren't celebrated or even acknowledged, a story about women who survived the system that killed Shawna.

⸺

California is on fire; it always was and it always will be. As Stephen J. Pyne wrote in 2016 in the prologue to *California: A Fire Survey*,

> California burns, and frequently conflagrates. The coastal sage and shrublands burn. The mountain-encrusting chaparral burns. The montane woodlands burn. The conifer-clad Sierra Nevada burns. The patchy forests of isolated Sierra basins; the oak savannas on hillsides turning golden in summer, the seasonal wetlands and tules; the rain-shadowed deserts, after watering by El Niño cloudburst; the thick forests of the rumpled coast range; the steppe grasslands of Modoc lava fields; sequoia, exotic brome, chamise, sugar pine—all burn according to local rhythms of wetting and drying. The roll call of combustible plants and places goes on and on . . . not only do fires burn everywhere, but they can persist for weeks and can, from time to time, erupt into massive bursts or savage outbursts.

If you live in California or are lucky enough to be from there, fire is a constant backdrop. It defines the evolving surface of the state, leaving forests naked and mountain ranges blackened, communities decimated and vineyards and orchards scorched. Extreme fires used to be once-a-decade events. I remember the 1991 fire in the Oakland Hills. Growing up we had a Christmas card of family friends on our fridge, posed in front of what used to be their house. Just the fence remained. I was born in Oakland, and it was shocking to see homes in the Bay Area leveled, the ground blackened. Now, fires in California are year-round—or, as Pyne puts it, fire season "lasts 13 months." Fires burn hotter, faster, and longer than they ever did. And because of climate change, invasive plant species, invasive beetles, and massive housing developments in high-risk fire zones, those fires are more damaging to structures, species, and human lives. Fifteen of the twenty most destructive fires in state history have occurred since 2007. Today, California logs seventy-eight more annual "fire days" than it did fifty years ago. A 2018 state-commissioned report on climate change projected that under current emissions trends, the average burn area in California will increase 77 percent by the end of the century. California has always had a fire problem; now that problem is a constant crisis.

Among California's solutions is a near invisible incarcerated workforce that has been laboring on the front lines since 1946. Depending on the year, inmate firefighters make up as much as 30 percent of California's wildland fire crews. CDCR works with the California Department of Forestry and Fire Protection (CAL FIRE) and the Los Angeles County Fire Department (L.A. County Fire) to operate thirty-five fire camps located in twenty-six counties. All the camps are minimum-security facilities and are staffed with correctional officers. When Shawna started the program, around 3,100 inmates worked at the conservation camps—2,150 were fire-line qualified, the rest supported the camps by working in the laundry room, as landscapers, in the office doing paperwork, as water treatment plant operators, or in the kitchen. In an average year, CDCR claims, the forestry program provides about 3 million hours of service to fires and other emergencies, and 7 million hours to community service projects, saving California taxpayers about $100 million a year. Other states, including Arizona, Kentucky, Oregon, Nevada, West Virginia, Wyoming, and Georgia, also use prisoners to fight fires, but none of them relies as heavily on its inmate population as California does.

In 2016, there were three all-female camps: one at Rainbow, between San Diego and Los Angeles, also known as Conservation Camp #2; one at Malibu, or Conservation Camp #13; and one at Puerta la Cruz, also known as Port, just east of Temecula, called Conservation Camp #14. The camps are located in high-risk fire zones so that the crews can be dispatched locally. The girls who fight fire are the ones who hike; those who have other jobs don't hike.

When I decided to write about Shawna's life and death, and the incarcerated women who fight fires, CDCR agreed to let me visit all three female camps and the California Institution for Women (CIW) in Chino, where there is a separate forestry wing for female inmates to train. According to CDCR, to qualify for the forestry program the women have to be minimum custody and are ineligible if they were convicted of sexual offenses or arson, or have a history of escape using force or violence. They said I could interview the crews at camp and women in training and talk with correctional officers, foremen, and captains about how the camps work. CDCR's only condition was that I didn't ask any incarcerated women about Shawna's death. It had only been a few months, the communications director told me, and CDCR didn't want to create any mental health issues by triggering memories of what some of the girls had seen firsthand. They were just trying to protect the crews, he said. They had gone through a lot. I agreed to those terms, a little bit shocked that CDCR was willing to let a reporter in at all.

In June 2016, I drove to Malibu 13. I passed through Calabasas, a suburban outpost in the western San Fernando Valley made up of gated communities, and Hidden Hills. (These two fire-prone neighborhoods are home to Drake, every Kardashian in the world, Kanye West, Will Smith and Jada Pinkett-Smith, Britney Spears, Katie Holmes—the list goes on. Some employ their own private firefighting brigades.) I skirted the northern edge of Topanga, and drove through the mountains. I passed signs for wineries and summer camps and horse farms. It was a part of California that felt unpopulated, just miles away from the urban sprawl of Los Angeles, the city I grew up in. It felt as if the land could still be claimed and tilled by a homesteader. Malibu 13 is surrounded by and responsible for protecting rich communities. Malibu's typical home sells for around $3 million; to the east, Calabasas's typical home sells for $1.2 million; to the south, Topanga's typical home sells for $1.4 million; and to the west, well, the west is all ocean.

The camp is carved into rugged mountains, shaded by oak trees, and looks more like a spiritual retreat than a state prison. The only sign it is a state prison is one crudely painted piece of wood, placed at the entrance, that announces rules and warnings in stenciled letters. (In all likelihood, it was painted by inmates who lived at the camp and hammered together in the woodshop.) It reads, "Notice to the Public: You are entering Fire Camp 13. A facility of the Calif. Dept. of Corrections. It is unlawful to bring alcohol, drugs, weapons, tear gas or explosives to the grounds. Cameras are prohibited. WARNING, entering this facility acknowledges consent to search your person, property and vehicle." Instead of fences, the buildings are sunk within a circle of shrubbery. The road is about twenty feet above the camp so that you can be on public property, look down, and see incarcerated women wandering around, occasionally glancing at the road.

Bill Sessa, the information officer for CDCR whom I'd been emailing with for a few months, had written me the day before, "You should have a great time tomorrow at the camp." He and I mostly talked about the fire camp programs, but because he lived in Sacramento and I had gone to UC Davis, we also talked about the weather in Yolo County—the heat, the rains, the flatness of the Central Valley. Sessa told me he was a former journalist. His email continued, "John, the camp commander, is a second-generation officer to work in the camp program. His dad was a correctional officer in the camp program before retiring. John is passionate about [camp] and will tell you so, but only if you know to ask. (He's a bit timid around reporters.) It's a side of the camp program that often gets overlooked—the dedication that the officers have to the program. Many of them wait for an opening, as John did, and then vow that they will not take an assignment back in a typical prison again." What went unsaid was that correctional officers prefer camps for the same reasons prisoners do: they're small, outdoors, and removed from some of the dysfunction and failures of the typical carceral system. Sessa went on, "Needless to say, they believe in the rehabilitative value of the program and get a lot of job satisfaction out of it and, of course, there is a synergy between their support for the program and the success of the inmates."

I asked how that success is defined, what the recidivism

rates are for camp as compared with non-camp prisons, and the answer was surprising—they don't keep track of the data. So, while CDCR is very proud of its forestry program, there's no way to show whether or not it's effective.

As I approached the main office of Malibu 13 at about seven a.m., I saw women in their oranges walking from barracks to a main building. Some with orange shirts already tucked into their pants; others wearing white tees, orange shirts tied around their waists. Some noticed me. Most didn't care. I checked in and met Bri first, dressed head-to-toe in orange, a slight brunette with blue eyes, who greeted me and explained that she clerked for the fire department, acting as the captain's assistant. Though she wanted to be on a crew. The way she talked, it almost seemed as if she were a spokesperson for the program or an inspirational speaker. She was instantly likable, open, and humbled by her past and present.

In 2011, she'd been charged with residential burglary, even though she was waiting outside the actual robbery. She was addicted to meth; a single mother of a four-year-old; as she put it, "a young woman who fell in with the wrong people." She took a plea deal and was sentenced to thirty-two months. "This is not my comfort zone," she told me while I waited for Camp Commander John Scott. "It's not easy, but it's a sense of accomplishment. They offer AA here once a week, and to go through this with other addicts, and go through this together with people you trust, it's the best scenario for a hard situation. We're in a little bubble here; I do worry about going back to the real world." Bri was earnest: "Camp is what you make of it," and "It's a challenge every day," and "It's ninety-nine percent mental," and "People can open their eyes and see beauty here. It's healing." But those words were more than talking points. She had evolved in camp. She told me she had chosen camp over the CDCR program CCTRP. "This program is what changed me," she said. I believed her; I also believed there was more.

While I was in the office, a couple of correctional officers talked about a woman who had tried to escape a week earlier. She just walked away. She'd have to go back to CIW, they said, go through a "rules violation" process, and she'd potentially face additional time. "She's no longer qualified for a community-based program," one of the officers told me. While I waited for Camp Commander Scott, a representative from CDCR's communications department explained the camp's setup. Malibu 13 has five low-slung open barrack dorms. There are usually twenty beds per dorm, 10 to 14 women assigned to each crew. At capacity, the camp can house 105 women, making up five crews. She showed me the inside of a barrack with the cubbies separating each bed. She showed me the craft area and the common room. She took me to the dining hall where the crews ate together. And she showed me a memorial—five tree stumps and a rain stick with a carved message: "Like the wind, felt but not seen, my sweet Shawna may you R.I.P." Next to it was an oak tree planted in memoriam by crew 13-3.

That day, Malibu 13 housed sixty-three women—camps were facing low numbers after a realignment in 2011, which sent felons with nonviolent crime convictions to county jails instead of state prisons. In the fall of 2014, as the state's courts were taking up the issue of overcrowded state prisons by order of the Supreme Court, the office of California's Attorney General, then led by Kamala Harris, argued against shrinking the number of inmates. Doing so, it claimed, "would severely impact fire camp participation, a dangerous outcome while California is in the middle of a difficult fire season and severe drought." Two years later, Proposition 57 passed, allowing felons serving sentences for nonviolent crimes to seek early parole. As a consequence, fewer inmates opted to become firefighters, and the fire camps' populations declined.

When John Scott emerged, he explained standard procedure on the CDCR side—correctional officers work three shifts at Malibu: the 6:00 a.m. to 2:00 p.m. watch, the 2:00 p.m. to 10:00 p.m. watch, and the overnight 10:00 p.m. to 6:00 a.m. watch. There is a mandatory count each shift and two random double-backs, when a CO walks around, checking off each inmate to make sure she's accounted for. "They live together, work together, eat together—they have to be on the line together. It's team building," he told me. He then showed me a printout of wages: inmate firefighters could make a maximum of $2.56 a day in camp and $1 an hour when they're fighting fires. There is no additional payment for being on call, and crews are on call for twenty-four hours at a time. Both he and Sessa mentioned that CDCR had tried to secure more money to pay the incarcerated firefighters, but each year when budgets were finalized, there were no wage increases. By 2019, the daily wage increased to a maximum of $5, but the hourly wage, when crews are actually on the fire line, remained the same.

Every morning after chow time, around 7:30 or 8:00 a.m., the crews stand in hookline formation. They step, one by one, on a thick painted yellow line with the words "STOMP AND ID." Each crew member stops at the line, stomps her left boot, and shouts her last name before formally crossing from CDCR custody into that of the L.A. County Fire Department. After the women cross that line, the half-dozen fire captains who work and sleep on the L.A. County side of the facility take charge from CDCR.

On the day I was there watching the crossover, my presence delayed the crews' physical training. They waited by their buggies for the L.A. County Fire press officer to arrive. While I waited, I noticed a communal board with a dedicated plaque and several articles about Shawna's death. Some people had written notes to her. There was a pamphlet detailing the "Shawna Lynn Jones Fund"—the Malibu community had raised $4,000 for her funeral and for Diana. While I stood by the communal board, Nichelle approached me. She told me she was in crew 13-3 and had seen Shawna die, and that she wanted to talk about it. "It happened very fast. We went to put in a trench and it was very steep," she said. "It just came down and crushed her. We scattered, we were crying, we were trying to help." Nichelle said what most people said about Shawna— she was funny, she was nice, she united the crew: "If something was bad or sad, she would turn it into a joke." Nichelle told me she was in prison because she pleaded to a carjacking charge. While she was at CIW she gave birth to her third child. From what I had read about CIW, this meant that although California does not allow inmates to be shackled during childbirth (some states still require shackling before, during, and after childbirth), her infant was likely taken away twenty-four hours later. Now, Nichelle's whole family visits Malibu from Carson, "And I can run around with my four-year-old and barbecue. It's nice not to wake up to bars every morning, but the state is exploiting us—everything we're doing is hands-on. Show us appreciation at least with the pay—we're giving our minds, our bodies, and souls to the state." Nichelle called over another woman from 13-3, Carla. She spoke quietly, but clearly. She also wanted to talk with me about Shawna's death. "It feels like it was yesterday. We were just standing there, she was so funny, never complained, she did above and beyond." Carla went on to give me a brief description of what happened, how quickly it happened, how scared they all were. She told me about the chaos. Then, the L.A. County Fire press officer arrived, and they had to go back to their buggy, the red fire trucks, and pretend like they hadn't approached me. Once he arrived, they officially had to start their day—PT, a morning hike with gear, then to work.

Four crews lined up in their oranges, doing stretches, then body weight–bearing exercises—burpees, squats, push-ups, crunches, jumping jacks. Next, the women went on a timed run through a hiking trail. If the run was completed one second after the time goal, the individual was written up. After several write-ups, a captain could send an inmate back to CIW, back to general population. There was a rhythm within the fire camp. The inmates worked hard; the captains rewarded them with the opportunity to work harder. What every foreman and captain knew was that female crews cut line tighter than men. Several told me that the women may be slower, "But the earth is bare when they're done. The female crews are just more thorough than men." They were more exacting, more measured, more careful with each section of land. When they cut, they left nothing behind.

One woman named Whitney completed the morning's full-gear timed hike a full fifteen minutes before anyone else, announcing her name as she crossed the finish line. The fire captains noted her time. They'd heard about her even before she arrived at camp. She was the ultramarathoner. The one who already knew the Malibu hills trails, because she competed in those races, and won. Fire captains don't often express admiration, but when it came to Whitney, they acknowledged she was a beast. One foreman, a former marine, would train on weekends, and Whitney was the only one who could keep pace; and sometimes she pushed him. "Being here helps me process what happened. I choose to stay here, it's more than fighting fires and saving the community. It's for us too." For Whitney, the program was actually rehabilitative. If she wanted to, she could have participated in CDCR's CCTRP program also, earning minimum wage. "But if I can save lives rather than what I did, which was the opposite, that really helps," Whitney said.

Whitney told me she'd been a supply planning analyst for Patagonia, and went to prison for gross vehicular manslaughter. She had killed someone while driving drunk. The scene of her accident was just forty miles north along the coast. She remembered flashes from the night but not details. She remembered drinking after work; it was a Friday. She left her road bike, the only vehicle she owned, at the Patagonia offices, and drove with a coworker to the bar. At 1:15 a.m., when she got behind the wheel of her friend's Subaru Forester XT, she didn't know she had a .19 blood alcohol level. She didn't know that a 0.2 percent blood alcohol level is, typically, when an individual can lose consciousness. She didn't know when she crossed San Marcos Street going southbound on Seaward Avenue that she was speeding, that she lost control, that she hit the curb and guardrail. She remembered the sound, the smack of metal popping into asphalt like a small bomb. Everything went black. The car rolled.

She didn't know that, as the car careened down the tree-lined street, Matthew Alvarado, fifty-three, was walking north to his father's house from Surf Liquor after his shift ended. She didn't know she hit him. She didn't know she killed him. She knew witnesses must have called 911, because a fire engine, a ladder truck, a battalion chief, and an ambulance showed up within minutes. She had crashed into a Southern Edison power line, which fell, crossing lanes of traffic and causing power outages. Whitney was in a state of shock; her coworker's arm was bleeding. It was severe enough that she pulled off her shirt and wrapped it tightly around his arm. They sat on the curb, waiting for the police, watching the red lights flash at the scene. An officer walked up to Whitney, sitting in her sports bra, and pointed to the scrum of EMTs surrounding Alvarado. "Do you see that man over there, he's probably not going to make it," the officer said.

Whitney was still under the influence. The words hovered. Seeped under skin. She felt guilt and shame. Guilty that she was not physically injured. She took the breathalyzer and a field sobriety test. "I felt too guilty not to."

After the tests, Whitney was handcuffed and taken to the hospital. She had a couple of bruises and scratches, and she resented the fact that she wasn't hurt more. It made her feel worse. She stayed in the hospital, handcuffed to a gurney until a doctor okayed her release.

She was taken to a holding cell, where she overheard the arresting officers talk about her bail. She heard them throw around numbers like five hundred thousand and one million. They were gossiping about what the judge would decide. She felt helpless, alone, wretched. She was visibly disturbed enough that the officers placed her in a Special Holding Unit (SHU), a version of solitary. "I tried as hard as I could to sleep. I just wanted to not be awake. Every time I woke up on that mattress-less slab, I was terrified." She couldn't stay asleep, she couldn't eat. The officers told her she had to eat if she wanted to make a phone call. They wouldn't let her out of SHU unless she showed some sign of wanting to live. She stomached what she could. And finally called her parents in Massachusetts. They had gotten calls from her before, and calls from her friends—about blacking out in college; about landing in the hospital after drinking too much. This time was obviously different. It was the worst possible outcome. Someone had died.

She apologized, crying. She couldn't imagine what her parents thought. They said, We're here. We're here for you. This was an awful mistake. They were worried she might hurt herself. She'd been depressed before.

On July 25, 2014, several days after the accident, Whitney pled not guilty to gross vehicular manslaughter and a special allegation of causing injury to more than one person. The judge set a $500,000 bail, which he then lowered to $100,000. Why not admit what was clear to everyone? She pled not guilty because her parents, who had flown in from Massachusetts, begged her to fight the charge, hoping it might mean a shorter sentence, a strategy that just about any defense attorney would recommend to any defendant.

Whitney knew how it looked. Before that night, she was a twenty-seven-year-old ultramarathoner who happened to work for Patagonia. If Mattel made an outdoor adventure doll, it would have looked like her. Just eight months before the accident, Whitney finished second overall and first for women in the 50K Santa Barbara Red Rock Trail Run, clocking in with a four-hour-and-twenty-minute time. Even after the accident, Whitney raced twice more—first in November, almost cracking the four-hour mark for the 50K in the same

Santa Barbara trail run, and then a 50K through the Santa Monica Mountains in Malibu. She finished first for women in both races.

Before her sentencing hearing on July 27, 2015, Whitney hugged her family. She was sentenced to four years in state prison, serving 50 percent. She'd be eligible for parole after two years. Whitney heard the judge's decision and knew that, at the very least, this phase was done. She would be serving time.

Matthew Alvarado's family was at every court appearance. Before Whitney was sentenced, one of his cousins came over and sat down next to her.

"We know you're sorry," she told her.

Whitney didn't feel like she deserved empathy.

"They just want you to say you're sorry," his cousin said.

"Sorry isn't even enough. It will never be enough," Whitney told her. That was the only direct communication she ever had with the Alvarado family.

Whitney was escorted from the defense table to a plexiglass holding cell. Her parents and brother were allowed to approach to say goodbye. From behind the glass, Whitney hugged the air toward her family. Her brother couldn't look up; they'd both be in tears.

The bailiff gathered her personal belongings—jewelry, a terra-cotta necklace from her mom that held the scent of essential oils, bracelets from friends. He waited while she tried to remove a permanent toe ring from her junior year abroad in Spain. It was stuck around her second toe so tightly, she needed soap to wrench it off. After they bagged up her personals, Whitney boarded a transport to Ventura County jail, handcuffed and shackled.

At Malibu, Whitney had only two complaints: a dislocated shoulder and a subpar weight room back at camp. As she finished the morning's hike, it was radioed in that a runner had quit halfway. A foreman went to pick her up in a Gator. "She cursed at the captain yesterday. You can tell, she doesn't have the heart for it," the foreman Matt Stiffler said. Then he mentioned that the two-week training at CIW was never enough to prepare the inmates. Firefighters "go through six months of training and probation and these inmates haven't seen fire or been near fire when they get here." That's a whole new experience, he explained, and "some of them don't understand the heat, and the impulse is to run."

The hikes every morning forced crews to traverse trails named Agony or Commando or Blue Ribbon or Pink Ribbon or Scoliosis or the Y. Some have official names like Break Down Twisted Face, which inspired the crew's nickname, Brokedown Twisted Bitch. Once fire season really started, crews would complete three hikes a week on top of morning runs. Every hike is militaristic; there is no laughter, no pausing. If there is laughter or if anyone takes a break, a foreman might call a halt and demand twenty-five push-ups. The hikes are not recreation, they are not fun. Every step calls to blisters, hardens calluses, and blackens toenails. The hikes are preparation for those times when breathing feels like a luxury, when the wind is so hot it burns, when fire is closing in from all angles.

After their morning run, I followed two crews in red buggies to the assignment for the day—clearing brush from a fire road. We drove along the Pacific Coast Highway, past bleached-blond moms running with strollers, surf camps, wet suits drying on concrete walls, and the breaking waves of an endless Pacific Ocean. We turned left, inland to the top of the Cameron Nature Preserve, a hundred-acre canyon once owned by the director James Cameron, who donated it to the City of Los Angeles. The fire road at the top of the mountain looked out over dry vegetation, what was rumored to be the compound of the NBA basketball player Reggie Miller, and ocean waves. After stopping, the crew was instructed to tool up and carve out six feet of vegetation on either side of the fire road. This type of preventative measure would make the road a containment line even before there was a fire. It widens the area of bare soil, so that if one part of the canyon catches fire, it won't jump the line. That's the logic anyway. As fires change, and their movement becomes less and less predictable, tactics like this one, which once worked, can be useless. If there's fuel, fires jump six lanes of freeway to find it. Fires don't care about preemptive measures. But this is the work, this is what CAL FIRE has done for decades, so crews continue to do it. Crew 13-4 hacked away at sumac and sagebrush. A woman with a chain saw cut through foliage; another raked it, lifted the brush, and tossed it down the canyon; then a second pair came through with sharp hoes and pulled up the roots. This went on, fast and furious, until the area was scraped down to mineral earth. One woman sang Remy Ma and Fat Joe's "All the Way Up." She told me it was the crew's hiking song. Then she tossed what looked like a tree hundreds of feet down the ravine. The crews, lined up and working, looked like chain gangs without the chains.

When the captain called "Tools down," the crews took a break for water. They drank from CamelBaks and ate snacks from their lunch coolers. The work was exhausting and the heat generated was enough to make them sweat through the several layers they were wearing. "The physical expectation is high and we're all breaking down. Right now, ibuprofen is my best friend," Sonya told me. "I can say, coming from the streets, when you're with your crew, that's your family. We may not like each other, but we're taking care of each other. Those disputes get left behind real quick." Then she added, "But the pay is ridiculous." The seasonal salary for equivalent work by a USFS wildland firefighter is $40,000; after restitution, Sonya would make significantly less, closer to $1,000 a year, depending on how many fires she worked. Even if she worked in California Conservation Corps (CCC), the natural resource work program, she'd make minimum wage. "There are some days we are worn down to the core. And this isn't that different from slave conditions. We need to get paid more for what we do."

When I asked her what it was like to fight fire, she said, "You have to be aware of everything. Every sound, the wind, the brush, you have to keep your head on a swivel."

———

There had been a lot of red flags in Sonya's marriage. She should've picked up on them, she thought. Sonya lived by the principle that, no matter what, two parents were supposed to raise the kids. A nuclear family was the best family, the only way to be a family. In 2010, Sonya's husband worked sporadically, losing jobs more often than keeping them. For three years, their family bounced in and out of homeless shelters. To make sure their three kids were safe, they'd alternate shifts overnight, keeping watch. Economic instability led to marital stress. There were drugs. There was abuse. She couldn't figure out how to extract herself, and she was stubborn. Sonya didn't want to be seen as a failure. She didn't want her kids to grow up in a split family like she had.

On the night of her arrest, she and her husband had been snorting cocaine and smoking weed. They were living in a trailer park, and a neighbor heard the sound of spanking. The neighbor called the cops, and the cops forcibly entered their home. The police listed torture as a charge along with twelve other counts, including assault with a deadly weapon (non-firearm) and willful child cruelty. Sonya did not remember most of the night. "I was just at a dark place at the time in my life," Sonya said. She had either blacked out or blacked it out later. She didn't want to relive it.

Bail was set for both her and her husband at $1 million. Based on the advice of her defense attorney, Sonya pleaded to lesser charges. Among those charges, she ended up with two counts of child endangerment and one count of child abuse. She told the court what she had told police officers that night, that she did not abuse her children. But, because she didn't remove her children from a dangerous situation, she was held responsible. Despite being a victim of domestic abuse, she was sentenced to eight years and four months. As part of her plea, she also earned one strike. Her husband was arrested, and all three of her children were taken and processed into the foster care system. Her oldest stayed in several group homes until she was folded into a foster family in Palm Springs; her two youngest were placed in a home together. One of the conditions of Sonya's plea was that she would have no visitation rights while she was serving her time, both in prison and on parole.

Her kids couldn't visit and she wasn't allowed to contact them—no phone calls, no letters. "You can't sit there and move forward if you're constantly looking backwards. I tried to see it for what it was—own my shit—and move on," Sonya said. Sonya had not given up custody of her children. She told her kids' foster parents that she would never let them be adopted. They could be legal guardians, and Sonya was grateful for that, but, eventually, she wanted to be a family again. She was never not their mom. They were never not a family. She just needed to serve her years, get out, get on parole, get off parole. Only then could she legally see her kids.

That process required appearing in court over and over again. Sonya continually had to prove she was making progress so that she could maintain custody. Every month or so she had to appear before a judge in Riverside. Every time a hearing was called, she was removed from Malibu, transported to CIW, then driven to Riverside, where she was housed until she could appear in court. In the two years she spent at Malibu, Sonya had to appear in court at least a dozen times to report on her progress, on her programs. "I know that jail in Riverside like the back of my hand. It's four blocks from my mom's house. I got shifted a lot. Then I would be transferred to another jail, which is in Indio, because I caught my case in Desert Hot Springs. I was housed in Banning and Indio and RPDC. I don't play well with others sometimes, but it's okay. I never got in trouble for what I stood up for." The appearances in Riverside broke the rhythm of camp. Sonya couldn't train in jail. Every time she had to go to court to prove herself, she'd push pause in her firefighting, pause in her training. She had to appear, but she also had to be ready to fight fire. This is one of the many complications of a labor force that is also fighting in court for freedom and negotiating for a return to life on the outside.

Sonya tried to put her head down and work. She worked through all her issues. At first, the physical labor was all she had—cutting and grinding. Every time she thought about how she had no visitation rights with her three children, she tore apart the earth. She worked until she was bone tired every day. And some days, the captain would send her back to the CDCR side.

"You're dehydrated, Sonya," he'd say. "You have to take a break."

Then, he asked her what was really going on. She told him about her kids. She didn't know exactly where they were moment to moment, who they were with. She tried to have a clear, level head. But the walls were closing in on her, even at Malibu where there were no walls. Sometimes her crew boss would tell her to take a break. "Why don't you take a vacation? Why don't you go back to CIW?"

"If I go to CIW, I'm going to sit in that room and I'm going to friggin' dwell on it." She wanted to stay at Malibu, she wanted to work through her anger and anxiety and frustration and fear. She could train, she could cut line.

Part of camp was working the programs. When substance counselors came through, she'd sign up. She'd go to Narcotics Anonymous, Alcoholics Anonymous, any meetings that could help. It wasn't easy to stay sober. In spite of CDCR rules, there are no prisons that are drug and alcohol free, even fire camps. Especially fire camps. Everyone knew, even the foreman, that it was easier to get drugs into camp than into prison. They'd get dropped in bushes on the perimeter, and girls would distribute, sometimes smuggling them back into CIW.

"Once you're in that bullshit, you're always going to be in that bullshit, unless you want to change," Sonya said. "You know what I mean? Like, if you want to stop doing dope, you're going to stop doing dope. But if you ain't done doing dope, you will continue doing dope. Most of the time, they weren't done. They weren't ready. But it was scary for everyone. Do you want to be under the influence of something that alters your mind, doing the work that we do?"

Whenever it was clear drugs were coursing through camp, a team from Investigative Services Unit (ISU), a division of CDCR, would begin showing up more often. "I guess they were drop scheming"—when drugs would be dropped in the surrounding bushes—"cause like when that shit would go on, you know who's getting high and you can tell who's high just by how they are acting. All CDC is, is a highly paid state baby-sitter. You know what I'm saying? They know your routine; they know your habits. So, if you're going to sit here and try to think that you're going to get one over on them, go ahead. Be my guest," Sonya said. ISU routinely tested Sonya. They'd show up two, maybe three times a month, to randomly drug test the women. But it never felt particularly random. They'd regularly ask Sonya to pee in a cup. "Every time they would fucking do a random test, I'd have to go and I'm like, are you serious? Like you already know I'm clean."

The girls who tested positive were cycled back into the system. County bodies went back to County. Prison bodies went back to CIW. Even if they'd been kicked out for drugs, sex, failing to meet the physical standards of the fire side, even if this was their second or third time in prison, women could qualify for camp again. They'd have to do the training again, and tell a sergeant and a lieutenant what had changed. How it was going to be different this time. Carla had been in camp twice. A lot of girls had.

Sonya told me that when she signed up for camp, she thought she knew a little something about fire. Her ex-husband had been a wildland firefighter for CCC—a government agency that paid young Californians ages eighteen to twenty-five minimum wage to build backcountry trails, maintain national parks, and respond to emergencies including fires, floods, oil spills, earthquakes, and agricultural emergencies. CCC was modeled after Roosevelt's work relief program, which gave millions of people jobs planting trees during the Great Depression, and in 1976 Governor Brown reinstated it with the tagline "Hard work, low pay, miserable conditions, and more!" Sonya remembered a look on her ex's face, something like satisfaction, after he'd been cutting fire line. She had helped him study and train. "I thought, Okay, if he can do it, I can do it." She had never hiked a mountain. She was scared of heights. But staying at CIW without a program would be worse than any mountaintop.

She arrived at Malibu 13 in May 2016, just three months after Shawna died. She was assigned to crew 13-1. She started at the back of the line, as everyone does, with a tool, scraping dirt, leaving nothing that could burn. Sonya saw the memorial for Shawna on the CDCR side of camp and the one on the fire side, and remembered the talk the captains gave at CIW the day Shawna died. She remembered that they said Shawna loved what she did and died doing it. Crew 13-3 still talked about Shawna; they still talked about that day. Carla didn't want another bucker; she didn't want someone to replace Shawna. Her death was a haunting.

PART II

"THE GIRLS IN ORANGES HIKING THE MOUNTAIN"

4.

THE TRAP: LANCASTER, ANTELOPE VALLEY

The sun in the high desert was blinding. I was on my way to the Trap, the bar Diana managed, and where she agreed to meet me for the first time. But I was lost. Google sent me north to Antelope Valley, east of the Angeles National Forest. The route was made up of long stretches of two-lane roads named with numbers or letters, the way Antelope Valley had been planned, with aspirations of expanding housing developments into hundreds of grids along alphabetically organized blocks. "Two miles on Avenue P, 6 miles on 240th Street E, 13 miles on Avenue J E, 1 mile on 110th Street E," and so on. I was east of any development—the acres flying past my window were flattened land, green from farming or brown expanses pockmarked by desert brush, stretching to a forever horizon line.

It felt like I was nowhere. No signs for gas. No town centers. No other cars. I pulled over to check that I was on the correct road, or a road at all, and got stuck in a sandy shoulder. I panicked, spinning my wheels, digging a bigger hole. I was at the western edge of the Mojave Desert and had no reception.

The Antelope Valley, where Palmdale and Lancaster are located, is flanked by the San Andreas Fault and the San Gabriel Mountains. I couldn't imagine the people who had been here before. This road was once used as a trade route for coastal tribes to inland territories in New Mexico and Arizona. Before the Spanish built missions and polluted the land with cows, the area was populated by the Serrano into the San Gabriel foothills, the Kitanemuk of the Tehachapi Pass region, farther east the Kawaiisu, whose territory covered the Fremont Valley into the southern Sierra Nevada, and the Tataviam, who ranged from the far western San Gabriel Mountains into Tejon Pass. The landscape likely looked different then. There were droves of antelope, described by a Spanish missionary: "As soon as they saw us, [they] fled like the wind, looking like a cloud skimming along the earth." Once the Spanish arrived and the Anglo expansion took hold in the nineteenth century, most of the indigenous population was murdered, enslaved, imprisoned, or infected with fatal diseases brought by Europeans. Joshua trees dominated the landscape, with bunch grasses growing between stands. It was in the mid-1800s that the yucca was renamed Joshua by Mormon settlers, who felt the tree (which is not really a tree) was like the Biblical figure, guiding them westward with its outstretched limbs. Mormons also brought dozens of enslaved people to California, to San Bernardino, relying on their labor to establish their settlement. The land east of me had been homesteaded by several Black families who came from Whittier and Long Beach to buy property, and later established Lanfair Valley, until the great drought of the 1920s drove them out. I was right in the pathway of the real *Chinatown* controversy, where the aqueduct built from Los Angeles to Owens Valley exploded after five hundred pounds of dynamite was strapped to the conduit. I was in dry land where water wars had been waged for more than a century. Now it looked desolate. After a few people passed, and some time, I waved down two cars to help push my car out of the sand.

———

The lettering for the Trap's sign looked cherry-picked from a 1970s junk heap. The parking lot, on the fringes of Lancaster, was dusty. Inside, the bar was dark, to keep it cool. It wasn't entirely empty, but was empty enough for me to notice the space was big and meant to be occupied by a raucous crowd. It had that day-after bar smell, when bleach dominates. There was a pool table and high-top tables, a stage in the back with three-foot-long speakers hanging from the ceiling for bands and karaoke nights, stray Christmas lights hanging from the ceiling, a TV, and all the free signs from liquor and beer salesmen a bar could want. Management wasn't partial to one label—Stella Artois, Modelo, Corona, Miller, Bud, Bud Light, and High Life were all represented. The walls were chock-full; decorations and framed photos of regulars adorned the back of the bar; a plastic chicken was lodged next to the register. I recognized the place from photos on Shawna's Facebook page. This bar is where she spent most of her last few years as a free person.

It had been three and half months since Shawna died. Diana was nervous; she was sitting on a wide stool at a tall table. She had a drink and a photo album.

"I was freaking out about the interview and I started drinking," Diana told me, apologizing.

I apologized back. I didn't want to make someone whose oldest daughter was just killed anxious. The next thing she told me was that she was angry with the Department of Corrections—"Shawna was in their care." She praised CAL FIRE, L.A. County Fire, Bailey, and the department's Chaplain Jake—they had all been there for Diana in those first couple of months. They called to check in on her. They told her all the ways Shawna was a firefighter. But CDCR refused to give her any more details than what was reported in the news. Shawna was dead; it was an accident; there was nothing to be done.

Diana opened a photo album. The first picture was of Shawna, age nine, dressed up for career day as a K-9 officer. In the photo, Shawna wore navy sweats and aviator shades with a gold star cut from construction paper pinned to her chest. She had a death grip on a plastic baton and a leash tethered to the neck of a stuffed Goofy doll. She stood on a brownish green lawn in front of a chain-link fence. Diana flipped through the book and showed me pictures of Shawna learning to ride a bike, learning jujitsu, at a petting zoo, wearing various hats. She liked hats because her dad liked hats. "She was tomboyish," Diana said. "I never saw her in a skirt or dresses or high heels or nothing." She showed me a picture of Shawna giving her a massage. "We were just two peas in a pod. She was more like my best friend in a way." She explained that she never wanted Shawna to be like her. She wanted Shawna to be independent, tough, strong. "I was a runaway at thirteen. I always winded up getting with guys that just weren't nice to me. I built this child to never go through that."

Diana's voice was raspy and Californian; she had a Valley Girl accent, like mine. She cared a lot about how she looked—her makeup was perfect and her naturally straight hair curled ever so slightly to frame her face. It seems cliché, but there was an open, childlike quality to Diana. She was so willing to share. To share her daughter, her grief, herself. She told me that when Shawna was in junior high and she had her first boyfriend, Shawna came home one night after someone had seen her boyfriend with another girl. Shawna wrote a note, folded it into a ninja star, and in class the next day, flicked it at the back of the boy's head. The note read, "We're done." Diana was so proud of this anecdote, this girl she raised to not give a shit about boys. This girl who was the opposite of her. Diana showed me Shawna in Halloween costumes, dressed as a pumpkin, a Pokémon character. She showed me a picture of Shawna's dad, Roger Jones, in one of his many stays at Wayside, a detention center in Castaic.

"We used to think she was going to come out to be a tour guide for Wayside."

Wayside was the nickname for Peter J. Pitchess Detention Center. (Pitchess was the sheriff of L.A. County from 1958 to 1982 and is largely responsible for turning the department into the nation's largest sheriff's department.) The jail started out in 1938 as a minimum security "Honor Ranch," a precursor to the fire camps, where inmates raised vegetables and worked on the camp's dairy and hog farms. Today, the detention center off the 5 freeway is Los Angeles County's largest jail complex, housing roughly eight thousand people, and is its oldest operating facility. While Roger was at Wayside, Diana and Shawna stayed with his parents—Glen, a World War II vet, and Yoko. They met during World War II, in Japan. Every six months or so, Glen would sneak off to the jail to pick up the just-released Roger, and Roger would quietly slip back into the house, back into the lives of Diana and Shawna. For most of Diana's six-year relationship with Roger, he was in and out of Wayside for drug-related charges. By the time Shawna was five, Roger's prison sentences had grown longer, and he and Diana separated. Diana told me she was "still partying" and that when she gave birth to her second child, Daniel, there were signs of meth in her blood tests. A couple who lived nearby offered to raise him, and did. Daniel and Shawna knew each other but didn't grow up together.

A few years later, Diana married Bobby. Shawna was nine when Diana gave birth to Ashley. Diana's husband offered stability, in that he had a house. It was small, but Bobby promised they would move to a proper house soon, in the kind of neighborhood where everything was laid out like perfectly proportioned Monopoly pieces, decorated in bright colors and contrasting trim. They did end up moving—to one of the nice modular home communities within walking distance of the Trap. It was idyllic. The curbs were rounded so that kids on bikes could slope up and down and around the neighborhood.

Diana told me she wasn't living with Bobby right now. They split up after Shawna died. "I don't think I would ever go back to him. I'm so mad. He's carrying a lot of guilt in his heart right now. And I told him I'm very sorry for that but I can't carry it for you." At the time, I didn't ask why Bobby felt guilty. I didn't ask why Diana was mad at him for a death that happened so far away, one that was seemingly unrelated to her marriage.

The way Diana spoke was skittish, a little nonlinear, and some of her stories were hard to follow. She was still grieving, still trying to find words to describe who her daughter was.

She spilled grief in incommunicable ways. But one thing was clear—she was a woman who could not catch a break. Ear marked for tragedy from birth, Diana told me that when she was five, her brother found her floating facedown in a pool. By the time an ambulance pulled up, Diana was pronounced dead. Diana doesn't know how, no one's ever been clear on the exact mechanics of how her life returned, how her eyes went from glassy and dilated to alert, how her breath went from still to wheezing, how her body went from limp to shaking. She just knows that she was gone from this world because that's what she was told. She was gone, but then, Diana survived.

She'd survived a lot. When she spoke, I could hear an urgency in her voice. She needed people to pay attention. Maybe that was because her dad used to tell her that her mom left when she was six because her mom didn't love her anymore. Maybe it was because she coupled young, after Roger approached her at a party and commented on how they had matching hair, feathered and long, like the bands that played on Sunset in the early eighties. Maybe it was because, the first time she felt true love, in the primal sense, was when Shawna was born, on December 8, 1993. In those first few months, she told me, she'd whisper to Shawna, "I'm alive because of you. Because I used to not care if I lived or died. But now I do."

Diana was nervous enough about meeting with me that she had asked a friend, Jason, to stop by the bar to make sure everything was going okay. Jason had just gotten out of Wayside after serving nine months for driving with a suspended license. He had a lot to say about his time there. "They treat you like the scum of society . . . when they send you to jail, all they do is sit there and ship you around, ship you back and forth from Wayside and back, Wayside and back . . . If you ask me, the United States is all gangland. You know what I mean? They want to say Christopher Columbus discovered it, you know, bullshit. What would happen if I went and got in a car right now and drove down the street and got pulled over and told the guy, 'I didn't steal it, I discovered it.' This whole nation was built on thieves, you know what I mean? They're just robbing, taking, and doing what they want, you know what I mean? Wild, wild west . . ." When Jason talked, Diana went silent, nodding every so often. By this point we were sitting in the Trap's outdoor patio, which was set up like an old gold-mining Wild West town—the back was called Trap Town. The themed decorations continued—wood facades of a casino, a drunk tank, a badge to indicate a sheriff of Trap Town, and a long bar in back, a place to rest your old saddle. The lawlessness of California's past seemed ever present here.

When Lancaster was first laid out as a suburb in the 1950s, forests of Joshua trees were replaced with a paved grid and planned communities. The new town—a desert respite from Los Angeles—was painted various shades of pink and blush and sunset. The idea of populating the Antelope Valley was optimistic. Intersections marked hundreds of streets, numbers crossed with letters, with the intention of infinite expansion. Tracts of desert, divided into ten-block chunks, remain empty today. Drive far enough east from the downtown district in Lancaster, almost to 198th Street and Avenue G, and you'll find the *Kill Bill* church where Quentin Tarantino filmed Uma Thurman taking some very bloody revenge; drive farther southeast and you'll end up in Joshua Tree National Park. Drive west and you hit the pride of California, a poppy reserve established by Governor Ronald Reagan in 1972 to preserve the state flower, the color of fire, which nearly met its demise from land clearing and invasive European annuals.

Through the sixties and seventies, Lancaster was designed to be a quiet exurb with a ninety-minute commute on the serpentine Antelope Highway to downtown L.A. Up until the 1970s, the Antelope Valley's population was predominantly white. According to the 2010 U.S. Census, 20.5 percent of Lancaster's residents were Black; 38 percent were of Latino origin. In Palmdale, Black Americans represented 14.8 percent of the population, whereas more than half of Palmdale's residents were of Latino origin. Between 1980 and 2010, because of a housing boom, and then bust, and then boom, the population increased eightfold, in spite of *USA Today*'s observation that the area was "the foreclosure capital of California."

In 1992, the year before Shawna was born, the housing market in Lancaster was so depressed that Warner Bros. leased an entire planned community for $25,000. The housing community was dubbed "The Legends," because each Spanish Revival house was named for an American legend like Babe Ruth or Marilyn Monroe, but the houses had all been abandoned and left unfinished. Why did Warner Bros. lease a decrepit housing development? For the final sequence of *Lethal Weapon 3*, when the director, Richard Donner, filmed Mel Gibson setting twelve of the empty buildings on fire while he drove through the tract housing in a truck spewing gasoline. Not too far from there, the year Shawna was born, the state opened its first men's prison in Los Angeles County: Los Angeles County State Prison.

Jason continued, "Because of how our society is corrupt,

just ass-backwards, other people, because of their status or because they're this or they're that, they don't have to face the system. The thing is, I'm poor and Black."

Jason told me that one of his last conversations with Shawna was when they were both in custody. He was working the hospital at CDC when five women were being led down the hall. "We're not allowed to see any females, right? You know what I mean? So, immediately they say, 'Face the wall.' I'm just trying to go home, cause I'm a short-timer. I'm not trying to get in trouble or nothin'. And I hear, 'Oh my god, Jason!' And I look, and I fuckin' see Shawna, you know? She's like the third person back, and she's like, 'Jesus, oh my god, I made it, I love you.' And I was like, 'You're going to fire camp?' And she was like, 'Yeah.' And I was like, 'Good luck,' you know what I mean? That was the last time I seen Shawna, she was ecstatic." Jason told me he felt guilty because before Shawna turned herself in, he told her that she should just do her time and get it over with, that there were programs, like fire camp, that would make time pass quickly. "I mean, fire camp, compared to jail, was like being free. You get good meals. Hot meals. You know what I mean? They treat you good. You're out roaming around, you know what I mean? There's no cages in there, no fucking bars."

On Diana's right arm was a half-finished tattoo of Shawna. The left half of Shawna's face was in skeletal form, bone dead; the right half, alive. Her left cheek was curlicued in red Day of the Dead marks; circles and shading around her eye socket made it look like her left eye was staring back from Mars; her left cheekbone was visible; the flesh of her nose was missing and her lips were stitched shut. Feathers in the formation of a wing replaced where her hair might have been. On the right side of her face, where she was depicted still in flesh form, her eyes were defined in the way she used to paint them, winged to perfection. The symbol for Camp 13, buried in flames, merged into her hair. She wore a helmet, and over the helmet cursive words cascaded down in broadly drawn flourishes: "Heaven was needing my hero." The tattoo would be anchored by the silhouette of firefighters saluting Shawna's face and the American flag. Diana told me it wasn't done. She was going back for more ink to finish it the next day.

Tattoos are permanent only because tattoo guns repeatedly shoot ink through the body's outer layer of skin into the nerves of the dermis, forming a wound. Cells fight tattoo ink for the duration of the life of the tattoo's owner. This memorial was a wound; Shawna would always be under Diana's skin.

5.

LYNWOOD, THE LARGEST WOMEN'S JAIL FACILITY IN THE UNITED STATES

Before Malibu, before Port, before Rainbow, women prisoners who want to be firefighters must travel through the California carceral system. First, county jail, where they await trial or sentencing; then, processing at Central California Women's Facility (CCWF), also known as Chowchilla; finally, they enter into training in the forestry wing of the California Institution for Women (CIW). By the time Shawna was transferred from Antelope Valley to Lynwood, L.A. County's jail, and processed, in 2015, Lynwood had yet to receive an audit required by the Prison Rape Elimination Act (PREA), passed by congress in 2003. The walls were moldy; the plumbing was rotted; cameras meant to protect inmates were blocked by laundry bins and extra-large cardboard boxes filled with dry foods. To be processed, Shawna and dozens of other women were lined up in a bus bay. Correctional officers processed up to sixty women at a time. The women were led into a room, past a metal grate that rolled up from the sidewalk, toward a mechanical door that opened to the reception center. To the left was a cinder-block wall; to the right was a partial wall covered by wood panels; overhead was a "roof" that was actually a chain-link fence covered by a blue tarp. This was the area where inmates were strip-searched.

Standard operating procedure at the time: Shawna was told not to speak unless instructed to; Shawna could not look in any direction except forward; Shawna was taken, fully clothed, in a straight line and told to stand with her left shoulder against the cinder-block wall; she was told to face the wall and stand shoulder to shoulder; she was told to hold all her personal belongings in her hands behind her back; her belongings were searched for contraband and placed on the floor; she was told to strip to her underpants and bra and hold her clothes behind her back; deputies searched for contraband and put her clothes on the floor; she was told to lift the back of her hair; she was told to turn around and run her fingers through the band of her underpants and under her bra; deputies told the bigger girls to lift stomach folds and large breasts; they checked for contraband there; Shawna was told to roll her tongue; her mouth was inspected for contraband; she was told to face the wall again.

The deputies instructed the women in the loading dock to raise their hands if they were menstruating. They were told to take out their tampons and put them on the floor. Then, the women were instructed to lower their underpants to their knees, to bend over, to look between their legs, to use their hands to first spread their butt cheeks, cough, then spread their labia, cough. If you were menstruating, you might bleed on your legs and on the floor, which had been bled on before. Shawna stood barefoot and naked in a bus bay with a jerry-rigged roof, on a floor covered with bodily fluids, oil spots, bird droppings, and insects.

Lynwood, formally known as the Century Regional Detention Facility, is the largest women's jail in the country and serves all of L.A. County. If you can't make bail, you go to Lynwood. If you're sentenced to County time, you go to Lynwood. If you're fighting charges or awaiting arraignment or just have bad luck, you go to Lynwood. Located just north of Compton, a mile and a half away from the mosaic masterpiece of the Watts Towers, and due south of downtown Los Angeles, the jail is surrounded by factories, lumberyards, and the Imperial Highway.

In 2007, when Paris Hilton violated her probation for driving while intoxicated, she was sentenced to serve forty-five days in Lynwood. She arrived, reportedly spent a few days there, and, after complaints of psychological distress, Sheriff Lee Baca approved an ankle bracelet and ordered Hilton to remain in her 2,700-square-foot Hollywood Hills home for forty days. "This makes a mockery of due process, and you're dealing with a spoiled brat, acting out to get her way instead of serving her time," a Los Angeles County supervisor told reporters. "She should pay the consequences for her actions and what's happened—she's now going home to her estate." A judge overturned Baca's decision, and Hilton finished her sentence at Lynwood, serving a total of twenty-three days in jail, in a private cell apart from the general population.

From those who had to serve time at Lynwood, the reviews are less than stellar. Lynwood received one star on Yelp. Among the comments published between 2015 and 2020:

- "They had 2 pregnant women and a few others (me included) waiting for a bed till 5am. They didint care what we had to say. The guards was rude af. . . . just cause someone gets in trouble really don't make you a better person!!! The food was crap. At least you can find some sort of solidarity with other inmates."

- "0 stars if there was a option. You guys should be ashamed of leaving a woman on the floor throwing up blood. Literally dying. Good luck on not seeing a law suit coming your way pretty soon."

- "When I first saw the 1 star rating, I just knew I had to give this place a try. So I came for the fine dining and stayed for the shit show. The cuisine was to die for. Literally . . . And the 'trustees' dropped off the meals in pre-used paper bags thrown violently through your cell doggie door. Now that's room service with attitude . . . However, the place is centrally located in L.A., convenient for all. However, please note that there is no valet service. No laundry service."

- "FYI to all the females try to stay clear of getting sent their their are many stories about this place that isn't right their was a incident with this lady who wasn't all their but was calm and 12 cops beat the shit out of her and threw her in a chair.its like is that how you treat people and if you knoe a person has problems beating them don't solve what they were born with."

- "While staying in this jail we were treated horribly by correction officers the facility is not up to code nor the food . . . they feed you watery meat with pieces of noodles that's expired . . . theirs mold in every cell all around the vents.their rude inconsiderate if ur pain won't offer u any meds. THEY KEEP YOU IN A LOCKED CELL FOR 23 HOURS A DAY WITH BABY MICE RUNNING THROUGH THE FACILITY . . . THEY

WATCH PPL FIGHT AND DON'T BREAK IT UP
BC THEY DON'T WANNA DO PAPERWORK
HORRIBLE HORRIBLE HORRIBLE FACILITY
NEED TO SEND AN INSPECTOR IN THERE."

Most of the women in Lynwood wear royal blue pants, one-size-fits-all, and electric yellow tops. Some wear mint green head to toe. Those with mental health issues—approximately one-third of the inmate population—wear all blue. Everyone is given a colored wristband so correctional officers can quickly differentiate one's status. One color indicates low-level crime, another indicates awaiting arraignment, another indicates medical needs. Each cell holds four bunks and has a slit for a window, just a few inches wide, allowing in the only daylight inmates see apart from thirty minutes to an hour a day in the yard. Lynwood is composed of two towers, with sleeping "pods" on the perimeter and a center area with chairs and tables. But if the facility is on lockdown, if a cop is in a bad mood, if there is too much noise, yard time is taken away.

In a promotional video the sheriff's department displays a culinary institute where women are stirring magic into industrial-size mixing bowls. When Carla was at Lynwood, she volunteered for kitchen duty, where she and other inmates made food for correctional officers. The deputies ate well, she told me—barbecue chicken, homemade pizza, chimichangas. *Good food.* Signing up for kitchen duty meant access to one police meal a week. Everyone else, on the other hand, might get goopy, gelatinous, chunky soup. Carla said what they served tasted like a combination of dog food, cat food, water, and some red rubber erasers. On Fridays, the kitchen served hot dogs, which were the closest thing to edible because they're salty and already pulverized. But that's only one meal, once a week. Basic nutrition was a struggle. When the glop wasn't served, there might be peanut-butter-and-jelly or bologna sandwiches, maybe a boiled egg or carton of milk, and Carla'd eat that. She tried to fill up on whatever she could. If you worked kitchen, you knew rats were everywhere, because the bread was covered in rat shit.

In June 2015, Shawna was transferred to Lynwood with 238 days' credit on a three-year sentence. She was a County body. Shawna was strip-searched, given her blues, and assigned a cell. Shawna didn't know Unique Moore. They didn't overlap at Lynwood. But, upon arrival, Shawna heard the rumors. In 2015, everyone at Lynwood knew what had happened to Moore the year before. Anyone who had been jailed and near unit 3400, a thirty-cell section of Lynwood, remembered; they'd heard her cellmate's screams. Eight months before Shawna was processed, Moore started coughing and struggled to yell that she couldn't breathe. Moore had told officers at intake that she had debilitating asthma, but they confiscated her inhaler, claiming she'd get it when she needed it. She told the guards and medics, repeatedly, that without her inhaler she would die.

On November 8, 2014, Moore felt flush; her body temperature was high; her cellmate fanned her to try to calm her down; her chest hurt; she wheezed; she coughed; her breath released in short bursts. Moore needed her inhaler. Her cellmate pressed an emergency call button and shouted for help from a guard. No one came. Her cellmate shouted again for help. She screamed louder this time. Inmates in neighboring cells screamed too. They screamed loud enough to wake up sleeping inmates, who also screamed. Screams were often ignored at Lynwood. Twenty minutes passed, according to witnesses, but no deputies arrived. Moore, according to her cellmate, collapsed to the floor of her cell, unconscious.

Eventually, guards appeared. Eventually, a deputy went to medical to retrieve her inhaler. But by then, Moore was unresponsive.

At 6:30 a.m., paramedics were called; they found Moore in full cardiac arrest. She was given CPR, plus four doses of epinephrine, and intubated to maintain an open airway so she could receive oxygen. She was transported to St. Francis Medical Center. At 7:41 a.m., Unique Moore was declared dead.

When Moore was arrested, she was on skid row, east of downtown L.A., trying to buy drugs. She was supposed to be completing a series of mandatory drug rehabilitation classes. She carried a diagnosis of bipolar disorder and schizophrenia, and had tried to silence voices in her head since the age of seven by self-medicating. At first with pot; later with PCP, cocaine, and meth. According to CDCR, almost a third of California's inmates have experienced serious mental health issues. People with mental health conditions make up 64 percent of the jail population nationwide, according to the federal Bureau of Justice Statistics. As the World Health Organization puts it, "Prisons are bad for mental health: There are factors in many prisons that have negative effects on mental health, including: overcrowding, various forms of violence, enforced solitude or conversely, lack of privacy, lack of meaningful activity, isolation from social networks, insecurity about future prospects (work, relationships, etc.), and inadequate health services, especially mental health services, in prisons. The increased risk of suicide in prisons (often related to depression) is, unfortunately, one common manifestation of the cumulative effects of these factors."

Among the women I interviewed, safety was a chief concern. They described good cops, who tried to help, and bad ones. In 2017, after a decade of employment as a deputy, Giancarlo Scotti was arrested on suspicion of two counts of rape and two counts of oral copulation while he worked as a guard at Lynwood because two former Lynwood inmates filed criminal complaints against him. Within months, four more women came forward to accuse Scotti of assault, for a total of six women formerly housed at Lynwood who filed lawsuits against Los Angeles County. In one of those lawsuits, one inmate described being cornered in dark, unmonitored parts of Lynwood's yard, where Scotti asked to see her breasts. When she didn't reply, she said that Scotti shouted, "I said, show me your tits." He told her he would punish her if she didn't comply. He groped her breasts. A few days later, Scotti told her to stroke his penis. She didn't reply; he grabbed her hand. When she tried to resist, Scotti threatened to take away her school programming.

According to the first lawsuit, Scotti forced one woman to expose herself to him, then he exposed himself to her and demanded that she perform oral copulation. She said it "felt like she had no other choice but to comply with Scotti's forcible commands." Another plaintiff said Scotti sexually assaulted her in the jail's shower the day before he was arrested. The suit also alleged that inmates had previously informed jail staff of other accusations against Scotti, but the complaints were ignored. The women said they experienced retaliation after they complained. One woman, who was pregnant at the time she was sexually assaulted, was barred from drug and mental health counseling and denied the special meals she had been receiving because she was pregnant.

After Scotti was arrested, he posted $100,000 bail and was placed on administrative leave. The Association for Los Angeles Deputy Sheriffs issued a statement the day after Scotti's arrest: "We urge the public to withhold judgment until the facts of the case are proven," it said. "We too believe there should be zero tolerance for any law enforcement officer who is proven to have taken advantage of anyone who is in custody." Before Scotti's trial, the Los Angeles County Board of Supervisors settled with two of the women, agreeing to pay them a total of $3.9 million. Scotti pleaded "no contest to engaging in unlawful sexual activity with the six different women, while continuing to insist that any sexual interaction between Scotti and the various women had been 'consensual.'" In California there is no such thing as "consensual" sex between correctional officers and women who are incarcerated—it is illegal and considered sexual assault. He was sentenced to two years in prison. The Board of Supervisors ultimately paid more than $5 million in settlements related to accusations of sexual assault against Deputy Scotti. Scotti never had to register as a sexual offender, and the judge, at Scotti's request, said she would be recommending him for fire camp. At least eight women filed federal civil rights lawsuits against the county alleging sexual assaults by the former deputy, who oversaw the lives of roughly two thousand inmates on any given day.

———

In 2015, Shawna told her mom about the abusive guards, and about Unique Moore and her fatal asthma attack. For four months, every call was one made in desperation.

"I've got to get out of here," she told Diana in October

2015. "There was a girl who was screaming for help and the guards thought she was just another crier."

"They thought she was faking it?" Diana asked.

"She had asthma. She died, Mom. They just let her die. I have to get out of here."

Shawna remembered the forestry camps. All the women spoke of them as a prison Shangri-la—*lobster, shrimp, ocean breezes.* If you could do your time in forestry, it wasn't time at all.

6.

CALIFORNIA INSTITUTION FOR WOMEN, FIREFIGHTING TRAINING

All women who qualify for forestry must pass a written test, a psychological evaluation, and a physical test before moving on to a conservation camp and being placed on a crew. All training takes place in the forestry wing of CIW. From an aerial view, CIW looks like a sprawling spaceship *Enterprise*, something out of *Star Trek* or *Star Wars*. It looks like it landed splat in the middle of Chino, California, a bucolic suburban-feeling unincorporated town an hour east of downtown L.A. Out of the roughly ninety thousand people who live in Chino, counting those who are incarcerated, the majority are white. One of the top employers of the area is the California Institution for Men (CIM).

Chino is more than just a prison town—it's almost pretty. It's where Ryan, the troubled teen with an alcoholic mother, came from in the TV show *The O.C.*—the faraway place that fictional residents of ultra-bougie Newport Beach in Orange County (O.C.) couldn't even imagine. Ryan, the juvenile delinquent, *he's from Chino.* What they didn't know was that

Chino is an Inland Empire dream. It's where LaVar Ball brought his family to remake Chino Hills High basketball by introducing his sons Lonzo and LaMelo to the world. The median household income is $80,000. Just a few miles south of CIW is Prado, a 2,000-acre park, with a recreational center and a massive lake with fishing, a shooting range, archery, camping, horseback riding, and a golf course. East of Prado lies Chino Hills State Park, a 14,102-acre open-space wildlife habitat with dozens of hiking trails.

If you live nearby, you might see training crews from CIW hiking up a trail in their oranges, with a CAL FIRE captain just a few feet behind, shouting commands. Some are new trainees struggling with the steep hikes and heavy gear. Those who have been there a couple of weeks shout encouragement. "Get it! Get there!" And, "You can do it!" They are trained to stay close to one another, hiking up just a foot or two behind the crew member in front. When they move forward, a swamper or captain shouts "Bump it up!"

These orange-clad imprisoned women have earned their gate passes, the privilege of time outside. After the hikes and the lunch breaks at the top of the mountain, crews return to chain-link fences capped with razor wire surrounding the 120-acre grounds of CIW. They return to the armed correctional officers pacing the top of three watchtowers surveilling the dusty campus. They return to the forestry wing, adjacent to the two thousand or so other women housed at CIW.

Housing quarters are separated into general population and forestry; the former wear denim, the latter orange. Before earning the orange shirt and pants, forestry inmates wear burgundy sweats. Burgundy sweats indicate participation in the program, but on a probationary level. An inmate in burgundy is not yet part of the three-week training. She isn't eligible to go on hikes outside CIW, and she doesn't have her gate pass. Most of the girls wearing burgundy wish for their oranges. The women who wear orange feel a sense of pride in their achievement, but they are subject to the same prison regulations as general population. If there's a yard-down, when an alarm rings from the watchtower's loudspeaker, all the inmates stop and drop, motionless, until a fight is defused, a culprit is found, an escapee is stopped. Sometimes inmates lie facing the ground for minutes, sometimes hours. A yard-down can mean no visiting hours for the entire weekend.

If you're accepted into forestry, the rest of the day's routine is defined by meals, training, and programs. When I visited, the forestry wing was chaotic and noisy. I walked through the four hallways and saw about thirty sleeping areas per hallway. The cells were divided by half walls, some decorated with family pictures. Others just had posters of trees and sunsets and inspirational religious sayings. Women walked the open halls with small radios on their shoulders booming discordant layers of different songs. TVs were tuned in to soaps and local news.

The women I interviewed said the rules for entry into the forestry program were subject to "interpretation." Felonies deemed violent by the courts were not necessarily considered violent by correctional officers. Lilli, Selena's bucker in crew 13-3, was frustrated by the contradictions—how could a state rely so heavily on the labor of those it deemed violent and unworthy of societal participation? "I would do my time for a robbery because I know I did it, but the person who accused me said we had guns, and we didn't. He wouldn't show up to court to testify for a year." Cops had to arrest him in order to get him to show up in court. "He pled the fifth on everything, he knew he was lying," she said. She thought she couldn't work fire because of her crime and sentence, and yet she was endorsed for forestry.

"You know how they tell you that if you commit violent crimes, you can't go to fire camp. Right? So, if I *did* have a gun and I did a robbery, I think that's violent, right? And I was still endorsed to go there. It's not how people think it is. They do whatever they want to do. The state or whatever is getting money for us being there, working for them."

———

At CIW, Laurie, twenty-three, knew she wanted forestry, but wasn't sure they'd let her in. When asked about her crimes, she answered honestly. When she was thirteen, Laurie was charged with assault with a deadly weapon. That was the beginning. After some girls at her junior high posted taunts on Myspace about Laurie being a lesbian, she was upset; her dad drove her to the home of one of the girls, and told her to take care of it; Laurie kicked the girl in the face; the girl pressed charges; Laurie went to juvenile hall for a month and then was released on house arrest. At sixteen, Laurie was arrested after stealing a little black dress from Dillard's. After she spent two days in juvy, her parents bailed her out, after which Laurie, still in high school, moved into her boyfriend's place, where he offered her meth for the first time. She was not naïve about drugs; both her parents were addicts. It was normal for them to stay up all night, to fight all night. But she didn't care about high school. The year Laurie moved in with her boyfriend, Laurie's brother was arrested, charged with murder, and sentenced to life in prison. At twenty-one, Laurie was arrested for stealing perfume and a belt from the Walmart in Lancaster. After a checkout clerk called the cops, Laurie dropped the merchandise and ran. She was ultimately charged with penal code 211, strong arm robbery—robbery with physical force. On the advice of her public defender, Laurie took a plea deal.

Close to two decades before Laurie's sentencing, in 1994, Governor Pete Wilson signed into law a sentencing statute inspired by the 1993 kidnapping and murder of twelve-year-old Polly Klaas in Petaluma. It was known as "Three Strikes, You're Out" because of its provision requiring twenty-five-years-to-life prison sentences for those convicted of three felonies (or misdemeanors, reclassified as felonies, such as petty theft). Seventy-one percent of Californians voted for the initiative, and though it promised to reduce violent crime by putting repeat violent offenders behind bars for life, the Three Strikes law targeted mostly low-income individuals, many of whom suffered from addiction and mental health problems. The law wasn't particularly effective at reducing crime either. According to the Center on Juvenile and Criminal Justice, in the decades after the law was implemented, "The eight counties with the highest rates of strike imprisonment—more than twice the level of the eight counties with the lowest rates—had nearly identical trends in violent crime rates." Among the counties to employ the new law, Kern County and Los Angeles County had some of the highest rates of strike imprisonment. Laurie lived in Antelope Valley, which was under the jurisdiction of both counties. When Laurie pleaded out on advice from counsel, she took the strike, thinking it was just another arrest and not something that could lead to mandatory sentencing if she committed two more crimes that carried strikes. Laurie's addiction continued, and with it came more crimes.

The first time Laurie and Shawna met, it was at Sunday night Trap karaoke. They drank shots of vodka and vodka tonics—*no calories!* They had both been onstage. She introduced herself after singing the Red Hot Chili Peppers' "Under the Bridge." She'd seen Shawna before. Lancaster was small; the Trap crowd was smaller. You don't go to a bar like the Trap without running into the same people.

Shawna nodded at the back room. "You play?" She had her pool stick; it was her constant companion and she wanted to rack up. Laurie nodded. They took their clear, no-calorie drinks to the table with quarters, started talking, and, of course, they knew the same people. The reason Laurie showed up in the first place was that her boyfriend, the father of her newborn, had been seeing someone else at the same time. Shawna knew the other woman. Shawna was good friends with her.

By the end of the night, Shawna had talked through Laurie's meth habit, her drinking, her Antelope Valley spiral.

"You can do better," Shawna told Laurie. "He's not worth it, and he's not going to change."

"Break up with your boyfriend," Shawna said. "You need to leave him. You need to get far away from him. You need to go."

Laurie's next arrest resulted in a litany of charges—armed robbery, fraud, identity theft, commercial robbery, and probation violation. Because of her previous strikes, the prosecution's first offer at her sentencing hearing was thirty-three years. Some of the charges were bundled with three other codefendants. After a plea, her time was reduced to five and a half years at 80 percent. She told me that her public defender said, "After all the things you've done, it's about time you do some time."

And so she assumed she wouldn't qualify for forestry. How could she, considering her charges? She told the interviewing correctional officers that she didn't know to fight the first felony charge, and she was not involved in the violent aspect of the crime for which she was imprisoned. The officers who interviewed her felt like that answer was good enough, endorsed her for the program, and housed her in the forestry wing. She was 178 pounds and five foot six. In the year between March 2014 and March 2015, while she was at Lynwood fighting her case, she'd gained sixty-four pounds eating the bread and hot dogs. She knew she had to lose the County weight. Every day, she'd wake up for training. There was no running allowed, so she power walked across the entire prison to the track. Sometimes it would take ten minutes, other times it would take an hour, depending on how many yard-downs were called. She signed up for yoga. For aerobics. And finally, she was admitted to Personal Fitness Training (PFT), the official forestry workout program.

The forestry program is both eager for new recruits because it's underpopulated, and hard to get into because of the qualifying restrictions. Once a recruit is qualified, the training is rigorous, as rigorous as possible while still in prison. As with many jobs in the California Prison Industries, the physical training program is run by prisoners. The trainers are other incarcerated women, those who might never qualify for camp because of the length of their sentences or the nature of their crimes. On an average training day, the workout starts with two hundred push-ups, step-ups, lunges, box jumps, burpees, crunches, and planks. Dozens of bicep curls, shoulder presses, tricep dips. CDCR doesn't provide weights or equipment—the women use ad-hoc weights made of water bottles full of sand.

One trainer, Amy, who had served twelve years and was not eligible for camp, told me girls like Laurie or Shawna arrived out of shape. "We get a lot of women that have never exercised before. They're overweight so they're already dealing with setbacks," Amy said. "But size, we tell them, has nothing to do with anything. We've had big girls come in and they're very, very strong. They struggle a little bit but they just gain strength and we've had those skinny girls come in and can't do anything. Size does not matter."

Amy talked with me in the classroom where crews learned basic firefighting. It was where they watched videos of fires. She talked about the program like many of the women I interviewed in prison, positively but also in platitudes. There were obvious benefits to the work. "It's definitely a test of patience, maturity," Amy said. "You're bringing out the best of these girls when they're at their worst. That's true. Our training isn't easy by any means. And they absolutely just want to fart out, die, give up, and you just have to find—you know, help them pull out whatever it is to make them go that extra distance to finish and get to the end." The end goal isn't just physical stamina, it's "to change their viewpoint. And to get everybody to work as a team when a lot of people are used to being an individual. That's the biggest thing, to have each other's backs. Look out for each other because when you leave, that's what it's all about. You're not by yourself anymore. You're with a group."

I met Marquet at Rainbow, but it took her roughly a year of training other women at CIW before she could become a firefighter herself. She trained Shawna, she trained Laurie. Eventually, she went through PFT with Sonya. Every morning Marquet woke up in Miller, a unit across from forestry made up of general population, and she went to breakfast. Most mornings, they served sausages and slop; sometimes, on good days, pancakes or eggs. The sausages were greasy, served with biscuits so hard, Marquet had to soak them in water to eat them. The meals were nutritionally counterintuitive for anyone training for and hoping to pass an intensive physical exam, and then hoping to be integrated into California's wildland firefighting brigade. After breakfast, Marquet met the PFT girls in the gym, where they ran through drills for three hours. She ate lunch in her cell and then went to study for her GED. Next she returned to her cell for afternoon count, which is when Miller went on lockdown to make sure everyone was accounted for. Then she ate dinner—mystery meat patties and more slop and sometimes chicken, which she liked enough. After dinner, it was straight to church. It was like that every day—breakfast, PFT, lunch, school, lockdown, dinner, church. Repeat. She trained and she prayed and took classes and sang in the gospel choir and danced in praise performances every Sunday.

Marquet told me she had been saved in Chowchilla, the state prison where all women are processed in the Central Valley. Marquet loved church at CIW, mostly because living in Miller was the opposite: hell. It was chaos. Marquet could recognize her past in the faces surrounding her; most of the girls were on drugs. In Miller, as in Chowchilla and camp, if you wanted drugs, you could get drugs. "Everyone around you was walking dead," Marquet said. "Like drugs are real, really real. There are all kinds of drugs. You would think that there are more drugs on the street. No. There are more drugs in prison than there are on the streets. And you would wonder, Oh, how do you get drugs in prison? It is the easiest thing ever. I would say about 80 percent of the prison is on drugs." Marquet was newly sober and trying hard to stay clean. A couple of years earlier, she smoked meth while waiting on sentencing in jail. It haunted her. "You ain't got nothing but walls, it was horrible," Marquet said. "It was ridiculous, man, I couldn't sleep, I was hearing stuff, the walls were talking to me and ever since I ain't hit the drug scene."

She avoided getting high in CIW by sticking to the schedule—breakfast, PFT, lunch, school, lockdown, dinner, church. After being saved in Chowchilla, she thanked God every day that he took her from darkness. In fact, she felt like being in CIW was the best time she'd known. She felt so grounded in faith and love, she felt free. She adopted the cadence of a minister preaching, mimicking lessons. "There's a lot of people who aren't in prison who are in prison, and to not be in prison, in prison, is a beautiful thing. The whole time I was down my locker stayed full. And that's because of God, nobody put money on my books but I didn't go without, so that was a major thing. I believe that God blessed others to bless me. There was a time that I ran out of deodorant and as soon as I said, 'God, I ran out of deodorant,' someone comes up to me with, 'Oh, you need deodorant, I have an extra.' Like, that is crazy. It's small things like that. Like, it's just amazing." Forestry felt like another gift from God, a way to work and learn and teach.

Selena was at Chowchilla for only a few months before transferring to CIW. She wasn't trying to go to fire camp but they needed the bodies, she told me. Her crime was also considered violent—it involved a "shank," she said, assault with a knife. When she met with the officers evaluating whether or not she could qualify for camp, they asked what her participation in the crime was. Did she regret it? If she could do it again, would she go about everything differently? Selena was smart, she knew how to answer the questions and of course she would go about her business differently. She would not have gotten caught, she thought to herself. It didn't take very long for them to determine her eligible. Camps were having a hard time filling out the crews because low-level offenders who could were opting for alternative custody programs. Selena was in good shape and practically line ready. The irony that Selena was not allowed to work a minimum-wage job but could fight fires was not lost on her.

Selena spent three months at CIW, training. It took three months, instead of the usual three weeks, because she wasn't trying, at first. She didn't want to be there. "There's a lot of people coming in that didn't request camp. A lot of them don't want camp and you can see when they get here that they were able to qualify for camp on paper, but they come to us, and they're running fifteen-minute miles, and we've got to work with them from there," Jennica, another trainer, told me. "We show them no mercy when it comes to push-ups. We do burpees, we do squat thrusts, we do jumping ledges. I mean, we just use them. One day, we'll hit legs only and go extremely hard. Next day, the girls can't even walk, but we hit the track just to work out all the lactic acid from their legs. And then we'll hit the arms really hard the next day."

Once physically ready, they enter the classroom, and inmates receive their gate passes to become eligible for hikes in the mountains surrounding CIW. They bring canteens full of water and lunch—a bologna sandwich, trail mix, an orange, packets of mustard—tied up in an orange handkerchief. They spend the second week of training sweating through full-gear hikes carrying fifty-pound packs through Chino State Park. They work with hand tools, like chain saws, Pulaskis, axes, and McLeods, and learn how to clear three hundred feet of brush in under an hour. This is to prepare them to cut line, one of the most important skills they'll learn. That is because inmate crews are California's first line of on-the-ground offense—they make up anywhere from 50 to 80 percent of the total fire personnel. Women have to be ready to hike, to cut line, to work through hot, choked air. They have to be ready to show up last and mop up—sift through blackened soil in search of sparks.

During the boot camp, there is no live fire training. Inmate firefighting crews learn about flames by watching videos in the classroom portion of training. One captain at CIW who has seen girls come and go said some would do the training, adhere to the schedule, hurl themselves into the books, get to camp, get released, and then end up back in CIW on another crime, either parole violation or burglary charge or disorderly conduct: "These gals, they have to go straight into the flames. Either they succeed or they fail, and they come back to prison."

There's a sense that the trainers who are stuck in CIW wish they could be on fires, beyond the gates of prison. But being a trainer offers some gratification. Amy told me, "I think you get self-satisfaction from watching the news, when there's a lot of fires and you see the girls in oranges hiking the mountain. I feel like a proud mom when I see that because I know I had a hand in getting them up that mountain. So, it just makes me very proud of them, that they took it to that level where they've finished the program, and now they're at their ultimate goal."

When I visited CIW, I talked with a woman named Maddy, who was scheduled to be transferred within days. She had the fastest run time among her group, and said, "I haven't really accomplished anything in my life; now I've actually done something. I can build a résumé, and pursue a career in forestry." She was eager to get to camp and start. She wanted to work, to be able to do what they'd been training for. She felt well equipped, mentally, physically. But the anticipation of what might happen made her nervous, the thought of live flame. She didn't know what to expect. "On the fires, yeah, it's gonna be very, very intense. A lot of hard, strenuous work," Maddy said. "We've cut line and stuff like that. So, we know what to expect with that. But just the whole atmosphere of working around a fire. It's going to be different." She remembered their last hike in Chino Hills State Park, a guy rode by on a bike and said, "Thank you, guys." She felt like it was nice to be looked up to. "It's hard—I haven't gotten a lot of that in my life, I guess. So, for people to actually look at me like, as if I'm accomplishing things, which I am, that's a big deal. This is the first time I've ever been to a graduation that's for me."

One afternoon, sweaty from burpees, Laurie finished PFT. She was getting in better shape, hitting the track as often as she could, being worked by the trainers every morning to lose that County weight. She saw the new bodies from County lined up against the cinder block of the housing unit. Usually, the girls placed in forestry were from Chowchilla, but this group came in from Lynwood. She scanned the faces and tried not to look directly at anyone, you weren't supposed to look directly at anyone. Eye contact was confrontation. But she noticed Shawna.

"What the heck happened? What are you doing here? Why are you here? What is going on?" Laurie hadn't seen her in years but . . . there she was. Why was she at CIW? Laurie ran over and hugged Shawna. The last time she saw her, Shawna was just a kid running karaoke and hustling pool. She asked about her crime but quickly retracted, "Don't answer that, you don't have to answer that. You're not supposed to ask people what they did. It's just one of those things." Laurie had a quick, frenetic way of talking, spilling her words, one on top of another. She was so relieved to see a familiar face, and so mad that that face was Shawna's.

In April 2014, Shawna was caught sitting in a car next to her boyfriend and a large quantity of crystal methamphetamine and some weed. It was enough to be charged with a 11378, possession of meth for sale, and a 11359, a usable amount of pot. The boyfriend had a lengthy record and two strikes, and didn't want to be locked up for twenty-five to life after a third strike. He told Shawna he would bail her out, if she would take responsibility for the drugs. All she had to do was say they were hers. He'd post bail, he wouldn't have to go to prison, she'd be out of jail in two days tops. She agreed, and was convicted of marijuana possession and possession with attempt to distribute methamphetamine. The boyfriend kept his promise and paid the bond on Shawna's $30,000 bail before her arraignment. A month later, after she was assigned a public defender, Shawna waived her right to a jury trial, and was informed of the consequences of a guilty plea. The court accepted her plea of nolo contendere—meaning that she accepted the guilty plea without admitting guilt—and she was sentenced to three years' probation. Shawna paid $625 in court fees and preliminary probation fees.

Diana was furious, not just that Shawna was arrested, but that she shouldered the blame for some asshole. Diana assumed Shawna was smarter than that, smarter than her, that if there was one thing Shawna could take from Diana's life, it was what *not* to do.

After Shawna's arrest, Diana's husband, Bobby, resented Shawna's presence. He didn't want cops around; he didn't want probation officers showing up. He put padlocks on the cupboards, to stop her from eating his food. Bobby didn't like Shawna; Shawna didn't like him much either, but she didn't care. By the time she was twenty-one, most of her waking hours were spent at the Trap. She danced and she drank and she'd smoke a blunt or two in the patio. Much of her extended family was in a hard-rock band called Seconds to Centuries (SIIC) that played the back room. The Trap, formerly known as the Boobie Trap, was notorious. There were always Harleys in front, belonging to the handful of Mongols or Vagos who were regulars.

Shawna was trapped in Lancaster. "No one can get out of here, it's like we're all stuck," Rosa Garcia, Shawna's friend, told me. People would get traffic tickets and DUI's just for dirt biking in the desert. With her pool stick in a satchel, Shawna would skate across town on her longboard to every pool tournament. She'd show up to the ones at Snooky's, a stripper hole; American Legion; or the Britisher, a dive bar. The underbelly of her board was striated and stickered with slogans that read

"I heart crack whores" and "Keep Pushin'" in big bubble letters. She sold merchandise at her friends' shows, drank Faygo, bummed cigarettes, wrote poetry, smoked weed, and skateboarded, sometimes all night. In some pictures from SIIC shows, her leggings are ripped and her eyeliner is winged, and she's standing victoriously over a riotous crowd. She was always right there, center stage, in the mosh pits and knocking down all the guys. She'd be at shows, sticking her tongue out aggressively, flashing a middle finger at a friend's cell phone camera; she'd rage at shows until her belly was red and raw from being slapped.

When Diana spotted Shawna on Facebook posts with new friends, raising their right hands in Heil Hitler salutes, she'd think, *What's wrong with that girl, she's half Mexican and a quarter Japanese. What is she thinking?* Laurie thought it was just a phase. It might have been the place.

The Antelope Valley was where Wesley Swift started his Church of Jesus Christ Christian in the late fifties. And where, in 1965, he preached the superiority of the white race and antisemitism. "If we had our way, we would outlaw the communist party so quickly that every one of them in these United States would be in a concentration camp by tomorrow morning," he said. "We would not coddle them and we would not let a bunch of Jewish attorneys to start talking about the civil rights of a bunch of people who desire to destroy the nation." In the same sermon, he spoke of twin imagined crimes, the prospect of an invasion of privacy by the government and a Black American rapist roaming the streets:

> Your phone lines are tapped. Not too long ago we had a
> rape condition in Antelope Valley, this was an assault and

rape. The department has not found the Negro who was moving through and moving out across the desert. But there are lots of sportsmen living out there who would know every route that he had to cross. We went to the phone and suggested that he gather up a few men, and help find the man. And instantly, officers cut in on the line and said—'Don't you move. You stay right on the line, for we are watching you and you are not to go after this Negro.' The rapist and murderer was to get away.

———

Within a year of her methamphetamine arrest, Shawna was back in trouble. She was among the 1.2 million women under the supervision of the U.S. criminal justice system. Four months after her plea, a bench warrant in the amount of $100,000 was issued, and her probation was revoked. She had violated the terms of the court at least four times—stealing puppy food from Walmart for her pit bull, Charlie Barkin' Jones, stealing groceries, selling marijuana, missing court dates. By the end of 2014, Shawna admitted violating probation and the court added a stipulation to her probation: *stay away from all Walmart stores*. Eventually, Bobby kicked Shawna out of his bucolic candy-colored home. She couch surfed, staying with friends. In solidarity, Diana left Bobby. Shawna and Diana couch surfed together, homeless together. Shawna found an apartment and gave her mom $500 for a deposit. When Diana asked where the cash was from, Shawna showed her mom pictures of a wedding ceremony. She'd gotten married to a Sri Lankan chef looking for citizenship.

By May 2015, more trouble. Shawna's ex-boyfriend had left

a gun in Bobby's trailer, where she had previously been staying. When her stepdad saw it, he reported her to the courts. A warrant was issued for her arrest. Friends who had served time in prison, Trap regulars, told her, *Just get it over with*. Do the time and emerge with a clean slate. Start over. They told her to plead out, take the years. It would be easier to go to prison than continue to live in fear of arrest. Tired and without options, Shawna decided to turn herself in. On June 2, 2015, she wrote a post on Facebook: "I can only handle so much bad stuff at one time, and I have reached my quota for the year so it can stop now. I want some good stuff to happen soon." The Trap hosted a party. Rosa Garcia got the dollar-taco guy to bring his truck to the parking lot. They ordered a million tacos. They all knew that she'd have to suffer through some kind of version of food. They wanted her to remember what real food tasted like. A friend made her a personalized T-shirt with her nickname, "Baby Hooker," scrawled on it. Everyone signed it, and by the next day she was ready.

Before Shawna left for Lancaster City Hall to turn herself in, she went back to the Trap for one last hug. She wanted to be enveloped in her mom's body before giving herself over to the state. As she crossed the threshold from bright desert sun into dank dark bar, Shawna locked eyes with her stepdad. Their shoulders brushed. Shawna slammed her skateboard against the doorway, shattering her deck. She hugged her mom, who was crying. Their bodies merged, mother and child. They rocked on the sticky floor. Then, Shawna left and walked toward the Michael D. Antonovich Antelope Valley Courthouse to turn herself in.

The four-story courthouse, built in 2003 for $109 million, looked like a sandstone suburban mall surrounded by

Joshua trees. The lobby of the 380,000-square-foot building was decorated with photos, faded from the high desert sun, of athletes and politicians shaking hands with Antonovich. Big smiles from the likes of George W. Bush, Ronald Reagan, Kobe Bryant, and Bob Hope shone bright next to a ninety-four-foot mural of what Antelope Valley is most well-known for—its hills of fluorescent orange poppies. At the courthouse opening, the *Los Angeles Times* reported, the Lancaster vice mayor, Henry Hearns, said, "It's simply beautiful. I think even the people who are going in there who are being judged will appreciate having a place like this. Now, if you're going to go to jail, at least you can go from a decent place of judgment."

Shawna likely did not feel that way. The convenient and expansive parking lot did not help when Shawna was standing before a judge. The mural of poppies did not help when she admitted to the court that she had failed to comply with her probation conditions. The shiny new courthouse did not help Shawna when she was sentenced to three years in county jail, and taken into custody.

By the time Shawna arrived at CIW, she had that County belly on her, so Laurie took her on as a training buddy. They both needed to lose weight. They both wanted to get to Malibu. It was near the beach, and closer to home than the other camps. *Steak, lobster, no fences.*

When I talked with Whitney, she also told me she had wanted to go to Malibu. She knew she'd have the fastest time. After her trial, she was transferred from Ventura County to

Chowchilla, where she spent three months. She worked in the counseling office, hoping to get to forestry faster, since that office administered the endorsements. One CO consistently spilled his coffee on the floor so she'd have to get on all fours to clean. "He was a total scumbag. Me and the other girl in the office avoided him at all costs. I felt so demeaned. I wanted to throw cleaner in his face. But I would have put myself in a worse place if I said anything. I would have lost my job in the counselors' office, and then I wouldn't have been endorsed for months. In there, you pick your battles, which means you pick no battles." She got to CIW in October 2015, and quickly got her forestry oranges. She was the perfect candidate for the program, and was already so trained up, she could probably complete the test twice in half the allotted time. All the CAL FIRE captains were impressed with her hike times, her strength, agility, speed, and endurance. In every spare moment, she was working out. Running on the track, yoga, meditation, anything she could do to stay in shape and stay focused. It didn't change her day-to-day reality: "Six months was enough time in the regular prison system, six days is fucking enough."

7.

THE CONSERVATION CAMPS: PUERTA LA CRUZ #14 AND RAINBOW #2

A year after my visit to Malibu 13, I drove past "the Napa of Southern California," Temecula, an area marketed in the 1990s and 2000s as an upscale retreat, replete with manicured golf courses, wine tastings, balloon rides, a quaint main street. It seemed like it had been built yesterday. A sprawl of gated communities crowded the town center. Behind the gates sat four-thousand- and five-thousand-square-foot houses with turrets, faux backyard grottoes, and six-car garages. Incorporated in 1989, Temecula grew rapidly—between 2000 and 2020, the population doubled to roughly 110,000 people. It also happened to be built in what CAL FIRE deemed a "very severe hazard zone" for wildfire. Like Napa in the north, the area was frequently on fire.

On my way to camp, I passed the Pechango Resort Casino and the Palomar mountain range in north San Diego County. The mountains, like most parts of California, are earthquake prone. They're relatively young, pockmarked by jagged rocks jutting out and up at odd angles. The south side of the six-thousand-foot-high peaks was blanketed in purple sand verbena, white dune evening primroses, and more orange poppies. In some years, drought years, the mountain flowers are sparse. But when heavy rains drench the area, as they did the year I visited, in 2017, thick patches of orange and magenta and purple blossoms emerge adjacent to lime green grasses. The colors blurred into a quilt of neon petals. The superbloom. At the time, it was the pride of California, and Instagram. But heavy rains and growth worried fire experts. When the last drought ended with heavy rains, in 2010, the following fire season was even more extreme than the previous one. Rain caused more grass to grow in places it ordinarily didn't, and when summer temperatures topped one hundred degrees, as they routinely do in Temecula, that grass dried out and became kindling.

At Port, about an hour southeast from Rainbow, I met the camp commander Keith Radey, who was very clear about the nature of the work inmates do: "They're doing the basic firefighting, the grunt work. They hike into the fire, and then they cut a line around that fire to try to get it under control. They'll make a control line and then, once the fire is basically under control, they can work from that perimeter to go in and extinguish it. Yeah, you got planes that do drops and you got helicopters that do drops and all that, you might even see engines out on fire too"—those are manned by professional firefighters, he explained. "But basically, the hand crews are the ones in the trenches, and they're mostly made up of inmate crews." He said the only reason female camps were established in the 1980s was that CDCR was forced to offer the same opportunities to female inmates that they did to males. They deserved a shot at doing time in a place with better food and no fences and the chance to earn two-for-one credits to shorten sentences. He showed me the grounds. Port was massive compared to Malibu. Radey explained that the space had been used in 2013 as a command center for a fire that ultimately consumed fifty thousand acres. "They set up a full-on base camp right over here in this field. They had helitack operations, their own communications trailer with a satellite. We had a thousand people out here managing this fire." The inmates at Port fed the free world crews and captains, and were dispatched alongside them.

The field Radey pointed out was made up of short green grass. Technically, the state had been in a drought for six years. "As this grass dries out, that's what they call flash fuels. They actually will spread fire to the larger vegetation such as trees and what have you. So, grass fires are actually probably the most dangerous fires, because the fire will move so quickly." He echoed what I'd been hearing from fire experts for years—the heavy rains of 2016–2017 would make the following fire season catastrophic. While the drought might've been a typical drought, in all likelihood, it was an extreme weather event intensified by climate change. This long period of no rain, with a short winter of intense rain, could, in fact, be part of a megadrought. The last time the west experienced sustained arid conditions over multiple decades was a twenty-eight-year dry spell that ended in the year 1603. The difference with this megadrought is that researchers believe it's caused by humans. Global warming has driven temperatures in the west up by 2.2 degrees Fahrenheit, increasing the risk for wildfires.

Radey also pointed to a small terror that makes every fire expert and captain shudder: the bark beetle. Smaller than a grain of rice, nearly invisible, this invasive species, originally from Central America, has been moving north as the weather warms each year. The bark beetles attack trees until nothing is left but dead carcasses, which become more fuel for fire to spread faster and burn hotter. "It's like these last few years of drought combined with all these dead trees from bark beetles, and all that makes for a bad fire season. So, I'm thinking we're going to be busy this year." He described the responsibilities of the crews during fire season—they respond to small local calls or any out-of-counties from the Mexican border all the way to California's border with Oregon.

He showed me the bunks where kitchen staff sleep, where the clerks sleep, and the baseball fields. He said they used to play softball against Rainbow and even made trophies, but that hadn't happened in a while. "In the summer time when it's nice out, we'll let them make bonfires. You can sit out here and visit, talk, we'd have a couple of inmates that would play guitars." Then we talked about the birds at camp. They had peacocks once, but it was the woodpeckers that Radey was focused on. "Destructive little guys. They'll peck holes in the building and stuff them full of acorns. Our telephones go out, we'll call AT&T, 'Oh, yeah, well, the woodpeckers have been busy.' They'll open it up and acorns will be spilling out."

During fires, Port crews provide food services from mobile kitchen units sent to base camp operations throughout the state. "They'll feed them like, rib-eye steaks, baked potato, vegetable, with a roll. They have a full-on salad bar. We have a beverage station, any kind of drink they want. Coffee, tea, milk, soda, juices, water—if you've ever been on a film production, like a movie set, it's real similar to that. These inmates eat as well as anyone working this fire—it's very physically demanding. These meals are like four or five thousand calorie meals. Cause they're going to burn it off, you know? It's easy to spend anywhere from sixty to a hundred thousand dollars a day just on food. And if it's not up to speed, the chiefs that are managing the fire, they'll address it."

Inmates from Port installed ziplines for the San Diego Zoo and cleared brush for the tiger attraction, cleaned water reservoirs, did brush abatement in state parks, maintained hiking trails. "The training they get here from CAL FIRE, if you were a civilian on the street, you'd be paying a chunk of change to get this kind of training. That's what makes these inmates so valuable when they parole, they've already got all the basic training." At the time, the state wouldn't employ parolees or ex-felons. In his seven years at camp, Radey said, about seventy-five to a hundred women had expressed interest in working in fire after release. But they'd have to retake courses and wait until they were off parole—sometimes up to ten years. The camp provided more than just training for fire, he said. "Some of these girls, especially the young ones, they don't have a work ethic, most of them never even had a job, never had any job skills, so this is all new to them. You know, working as a team is something new, so they're getting all these different skills and with the expectation that you work as a team, you work, you get paid, and so when they leave out of here, a lot of them—because we'll parole them directly from this camp, we'll put them in a vehicle and we'll take them to the Amtrak station, we'll take them to the Greyhound station, and they'll tell us, 'Hey, you know what, this program is the best thing that ever happened to me. It got my life turned around.' So even if they're not following through with the fire service, we're actually building up their self-confidence and their self-esteem to be able to, you know, once they parole and hit the streets, they'll be able to get a job in whatever field they choose to go to and they understand work ethic now, they understand what it is to be productive, they understand what it is to get rewarded for your labor."

Radey walked me back to the CAL FIRE side of camp, to the saw shed where sawyers work on their chain saws—sharpening the blade, switching out the blade, doing basic maintenance to make sure equipment is ready for the next fire call. The press officer from CDCR said that they asked all the women in camp if they wanted to speak with me, but it seemed more like CDCR had hand-selected representatives of the program who excelled. The women were open but hesitant, as if they were self-censoring. They couldn't talk to me freely, because a correctional officer was always present. I was a visitor looking in, and the crews were paraded around.

Radey introduced me to Alisha, a swamper, the highest position on crew. On fires and during work hours, the swamper communicates between the captain and foremen and the women on her crew, and leads them into battle. Sometimes, as they're dispatched, she sits in the front seat of the fire buggy. We stood in the saw shed, where she was cleaning and arranging tools. She had long brown hair and was about five foot four; she was stronger than I've ever been in my life, or ever will be. She seemed cautious. Her crew had just gotten back from an hour-long hike near Bautista Canyon that included two pushes in elevation. The day before, her crew had been called out to the Palomar Divide to help contain a controlled burn that the Forest Service had started. "They lost it," she said. "But it was only three acres—by the time we got up there, there were no flames." She seemed disappointed. "We just put in a line to make sure that the fire didn't jump again."

Alisha told me about her crime—she was arrested and charged with residential burglary. She was twenty-three, on meth, and had been addicted to meth since she was fifteen or sixteen. "I come from a good family," she said, apologetically. "I'm the black sheep of my family." Her dad was a retired cop, and her mom worked in medical coding. As a kid, family vacations were spent in Sequoia National Forest. "I just kind of rebelled." She told me about how the forestry program changed her life and attitude. How the work helped her focus on planning for the future: "I've already been doing S-190 classes"—introduction to wildland behavior—"I'll take any classes they offer here, and I'm working on my résumé so when I do leave, I have a plan. A set plan, and I'm not just going out thinking, 'What am I doing?' I really want to try for the Forest Service and get a job on an engine."

She knew that she couldn't apply for a job through CAL FIRE or municipal agencies, because they require EMT licenses, which you couldn't get if you were an ex-felon or on parole. She wanted a plan for her daughter. "Everybody can carry what we learn here to the street. Just the responsibility, and being able to multitask. Everything that we do here, even if you're not going to actually do this when you get out, you can carry this on to the rest of your life."

After Alisha's arrest, her parents became legal guardians of her daughter, Kayleigh. They lived in Long Beach and would visit Alisha at Port once a month or once every two months. When Alisha was in Chowchilla and CIW, she wouldn't let her parents bring Kayleigh for visits—it was too grim. Alisha couldn't stand the idea of her daughter seeing her in those places. At Port, she could bring out the rainsticks made from yucca or plaques painted in hobby craft and give them to

Kayleigh. Alisha's dad would pick up Mexican food from Az-
tek Tacos on his way. They'd eat at the picnic benches. Alisha could show Kayleigh the birds and the mountains that she
protected. They'd walk the grounds of Port looking for peacocks and wild turkeys.

Alisha told me about her first fire, going into Napa Valley as residents were evacuating. The town was burned over;
cars were blackened. She wondered why they, as a crew, were
racing in as residents were racing out to save themselves. She
understood it intellectually, this was the job she signed up
for, but practically, she could feel the heat, the terror coursing
through a community. She cut line for ten hours, almost until
dawn. The first few hours she was hotlining, cutting roots and
trees and stumps as they burned. She told me the heavy labor
and the danger create a bond among the crew members, that
you have no choice but to work together.

She also talked about more practical things, skills beyond
fighting fire that she learned, like truck maintenance, roofing,
operating a chain saw, working a weed whip. "I've dropped
trees," she said casually. She has also poured concrete, changed
oil, done demolition, and painted structures. The crews were
always at work. And when she wasn't at work, Alisha worked
out or read or was just so exhausted, she passed out. "Everything happens for a reason, and I really feel that this is what
I needed," she said. "Now I can be a mother to my child, and
be there. I'm ready to go home to her. It kills me that I've been
away from her for so long, because I got locked up right before
her second birthday, so I was only out for her first birthday
and she's turning six this year."

Before I left, Radey showed me a few other parts of camp—
the cosmetology department, where haircuts, makeup, and

blowouts happened. This was where cosmetologists who also happened to be firefighters trained and received licenses. He took me and my correctional officer minder toward the dining hall, where the inmate kitchen staff was preparing for dinner. There was a morning cook and an evening cook, and each cook had prep staff; inmates cleaned up, some were dishwashers and scullery workers. About seven women worked the dining room. Radey would poll the inmates to ask what meals they craved and set a menu—"There's like five weeks of menus and we'll just rotate them through. If there's a dish that the inmates want to try and it fits our criteria, like they want to go a little healthier instead of just meat and potatoes so they're hitting me up, like, 'Hey, yo, like, could you do, like, a salad thing tonight for dinner?' We'll do a chef's salad, it's like a salad bar and they get, like, a grilled cheese sandwich, tomato soup but they get a full-on salad too with all the little things that go on that you would see at a salad bar—cherry tomatoes, mushrooms, bell peppers, grated cheese, bacon bits, all that kind of stuff." He showed me the industrial-size mixer, the size of a small human, used for baking cookies, cakes, pies, cinnamon rolls, pizza dough, bread. There was a deep fryer, a burger grill, a prep station for chopping. The food was clearly better, but crews were served in the same manner as in prison—every inmate lined up in front of steamers to receive four ounces of meat, a scoop of starch, a scoop of vegetable. Exactly the same plate, same quantity.

Radey asked the afternoon cook what she was making and if she could serve us a plate. We sat around a stainless-steel table on stainless-steel seats where crews would ordinarily be eating in hookline order. I was served several pork chops and steamed vegetables, which the COs dug into. The chef was proud of her work—and it tasted good—but I felt guilty. I was eating inmate labor.

———

The next camp I visited is located just south of Temecula. Rainbow is spread out, and dustier than Malibu. It houses one hundred at full capacity. On my tour of the grounds, I saw a dirt softball field and busted speed bag for boxing. Like Malibu, Rainbow also had a cabin that could be rented out for overnight visits. Again, the COs asked if anyone would be willing to sit with me and talk, and about a dozen women offered.

Marquet, the same Marquet who had found sobriety in County and religion in Chowchilla, was the first woman who entered the room. She was so shy, she seemed to be hoping that the correctional officer monitoring our interview would help her share her story. She'd look over to her for approval, guidance, a way to navigate talking to me. She spoke softly but confidently. "I came here because I wanted to better myself. I've never really accomplished anything. I always had jobs, but I only had them for a week. So, I came here and decided that I needed something to work on me. It helps me with people—how to deal with people, how to handle situations." Marquet arrived at Rainbow with her 10s and 18s already memorized and a kind of authority and assuredness. She described a life prior to prison riddled with abuse, drug use, and homelessness. When she talked of fire, she took on the command of a captain. Her eyes widened and she recited details of procedure and proper conduct. Here, at Rainbow, she was a firefighter.

"You always have to be aware of where your fire is, because

if that fire comes back at you, it either can kill you, or you can survive—regardless, you have to know. You need to know where your escape route and your safety zone is, and if you can actually get to that safety zone where you can deploy your shelter. If you can't deploy your shelter and your fire is coming toward you, there's a possibility you could die." She rattled off all the scenarios in which she would need her 10s and 18s: "While you're fighting that fire and cutting that line you need to have it in the back of your mind, 'Look up. Look around. Keep your ears open. Communicate.'" Lessons she had already learned at Chowchilla and CIW—watch your surroundings, communicate—but applied in different ways. Now, she was inside a prison and deployed to fires. She explained the rules she'd learned at CIW. She explained that she had been one of the trainers until she herself could qualify for camp.

She gave me a supercut of what she went through to get to this point. Marquet wanted love and stability. She wanted someone to take her in and count her among those who mattered. Counting all of her half siblings and stepsiblings, which she did, she was one of fourteen children, and the fifth youngest. When Marquet was two, her mother was sentenced to Chowchilla and then CIW; her father was in and out of jail. Marquet was from Southeast San Diego—her whole family was there. She said "Southeast" with pride, but in 1992, the same year her mother was incarcerated, a San Diego councilmember made a big flashy show of saying "Southeast" was a "disrespectful nickname." In a dramatic attempt to distance the communities from the violence and crime being reported in the press, he buried a coffin filled with drug and gang paraphernalia.

If Marquet could have chosen where to live, it would have been with her aunt Sue and her sisters and brothers from her mom's side of the family in Southeast. Instead, her thirty-eight-year-old sister, Olivia, on her dad's side, took her in. Olivia became her foster mom, and her husband, Robert, signed on as her foster dad. Caregivers receive roughly $800 a month from San Diego County to cover food, clothing, and rent for taking in foster children. California has the largest number of children entering the system each year. Black kids are historically and currently overrepresented in foster care, making up 23 percent of foster children while being only 13 percent of the population. There are endless studies about the foster-care- and group-home-to-prison pipeline. But, for Marquet, there weren't a lot of options when, at age two, both of her parents were incarcerated.

With Olivia, Marquet had her own bedroom and food. The facade of home existed, but Marquet never felt folded into a family. If Marquet misbehaved, she was left at home in her bedroom by herself with no food. Much of the time, she was tasked with taking care of her sister's youngest son, Joseph, a baby with physical disabilities who eventually needed a wheelchair for mobility. Marquet resented him, and she resented Olivia for saddling her with adult responsibilities.

There were other problems with living at Olivia's. Marquet didn't get along with her brothers, her nephews, or anyone in the house she technically lived in. So she avoided the house. By the time she was ten, Marquet had been sneaking out of her sister's house regularly, running away to her aunt Sue's place. She'd hop the trolley, then the bus, and then walk three miles uphill. If a bus driver asked why she was alone, why she wasn't in school, why she was carrying a backpack full of belongings, she'd make up a story or start crying and just say she was trying to get home. She'd tell herself, or the bus driver, "All I need to do is get to the Meadowbrook stop."

It wasn't even technically a stop, she just knew to get off at the Meadowbrook apartments, then she'd be at her aunt Sue's house. If she could make it to her aunt's house, she could make it through the day. Once there, she would try to be as quiet as possible. She didn't want her aunt to call her sister, triggering her return. She'd sneak in the window and plead with her cousins, "Let me stay here. All I want to do is live here." There, she had warmth, the siblings she liked and got along with, the ones who felt more like kin. Marquet saw her own face alongside hundreds of framed family photos in the back wood-paneled room. It felt like home. Sometimes she would sit in that room in the overstuffed easy chair, looking at her relatives—old, young, dead, and just born. She was willing to do anything to not stay at her sister's place. Olivia always told Sue that Marquet was doing great, that she had everything she needed and was happy. Olivia pointed to Marquet's room, to her new clothes, to the family she was surrounded by. To the fact that Olivia was her legal guardian, and Sue couldn't do much. Sue wondered why Marquet kept running away.

After every escape, Olivia would show up at Sue's to collect Marquet. One afternoon, Marquet got out of school early and asked Olivia if she could go to the mall with a friend. She felt certain the answer would be yes, or she wouldn't have asked in the first place. Marquet had done her chores, and she'd watched Joseph the previous few days. But the answer was no. Olivia wanted to go out and she needed Marquet to watch Joseph again. Instead, Marquet ran. She met up with her boyfriend at the time, they wandered the mall, then the park. She figured if she was going to disobey Olivia, she might as well be out past curfew.

They ate a pretzel and wandered around until well after dusk. At the park, she noticed a figure moving toward them.

It was Robert, her foster dad. He started chasing Marquet. She booked it in the opposite direction, but he ran faster. He snatched her, grabbing her hair and dragging her to the gate. She panicked. Her scalp tightened in pain. Her skin scraped against the concrete of the park. It ripped open, droplets of blood staining the ground. She had a lighter in her pocket.

"Let me go before I burn you," she said.

He grabbed the lighter and set her hair on fire. She felt the heat travel toward her face. The sight of flames and the smell of singed hair propelled Marquet to fight back, to hit and kick and scream until several bystanders ran over and intervened. They yelled. One helped Marquet put out the flames, another called the cops. Robert was arrested, and ended up in County for one month. Whatever stake Olivia had as Marquet's foster mom vanished. She wasn't willing to sacrifice her marriage or her real family for a sister who barely counted as a sister.

After that, Marquet unraveled. She had nowhere to go. Her aunt Sue couldn't take her in. Between the ages of fourteen and sixteen she was placed in multiple foster homes and group homes. She lived in Hillcrest House and was kicked out; then Oceanside for two months before being kicked out ("I don't even remember why, I think I was just being bad"); she went back to living in Hillcrest; went to a group home in Mira Mesa and was kicked out; went to juvenile hall, programmed out; then finally she lived in Woodman, another group home. During this time, she was enrolled in El Camino High School, but because of repeated fights with other students and truancy, she was kicked out. Then, at eighteen, Marquet aged out of the foster care system.

Some members of Marquet's sprawling family held her up as much as they could. She'd see cousins and siblings and parental figures. They'd hang out, there were relationships, but no one claimed her as their own. She watched her mom cycle with drugs, demanding Marquet's presence at times, and kicking her out of the house at others. Her behavior was erratic at best, abusive at worst. Marquet and her mom were two of a kind: stubborn, bullheaded, opinionated.

Marquet gave birth to her first son, Bernard, in 2009. Just twenty-six hours later, Bernard's dad "Left with his other baby mama and never came back." For a while Marquet and Bernard stayed with her ex's parents. Marquet moved on to her next relationship. "Be careful what you ask God for, because I said, Look, please don't give me someone who cheats, and I got a woman beater. That relationship right there, that's when I started doing drugs."

The first time Joe hit Marquet was when she told him she was pregnant with her second child. He didn't grow up with a mom; he didn't want a son. He didn't even want Bernard around. "He wasn't physically abusive to Bernard, like he didn't hit him or nothing, but he would do or say stuff to him. He tied Bernard to a dog once and made the dog run. I asked him why he did that," Marquet said. "And Joe just started laughing." Marquet had the baby and named him Unique.

After she gave birth, Joe told Marquet she was fat. She believed him. Joe did drugs. Marquet thought those drugs would help her lose weight, help her win back Joe's affection. She thought, *I can always kick meth, how hard can it be. I can just take a little, I can lose this waist, these hips, that ass scarred with stretch marks, and he'll stop calling me fat.* The drug wasn't so much a shot of ecstasy as it was a gift of time, time for Marquet to feel free and good. Marquet let go and felt adrenaline and power and like her life was straight. She felt smarter and focused and more diligent. She felt like a better mom, a better person, someone whom other people wanted to be around. She felt welcome and whole.

Marquet walked down the block. She didn't know the street. She didn't know the time. She broke into a stranger's house. She described the night to me: "I was just under the influence on meth and felt like doing something. When you're under that drug, you really just go with the flow. You feel like you're invincible. Can't no one stop you—you're just the king or the queen of the world. I got under the influence and started walking down the street, saw a house with the window open and decided to go in. Through the window." The woman inside the house called 911. With two strikes already, Marquet knew she would be sentenced to a mandatory minimum sentence if she was caught. So she ran. The police took down a description of Marquet—young, maybe early twentics, Black woman with a slight gap in her teeth. Enough information, when processed through the system, for police to narrow their search. Just a day after Marquet's living room visit, she applied to work in Urban Corps, a paid job that offered training, support services, and a second chance for Marquet to earn a high school diploma. Part of the application process included submitting a California state driver's license and a Social Security card. She was chopping trees down as part of her landscaping program, working to beautify the city, when the police arrested her. She was charged with first-degree burglary and taken to San Diego County jail, the same jail where Joe had been taken just months before.

Marquet became a number, another person within the Black community targeted by the War on Drugs, a strategy that was older than she was. In 1971, President Richard Nixon had infamously declared an invented "War on Drugs," a campaign that framed certain Americans who were thriving and rising in opposition to his worldview. In a 1994 interview with the journalist Dan Baum, President Nixon's domestic policy chief and co-conspirator in the Watergate scandal, John Ehrlichman, explained the War on Drugs campaign:

> You want to know what this was really all about? . . . The Nixon campaign in 1968, and the Nixon White House after that, had two enemies: the antiwar left and black people. You understand what I'm saying? We knew we couldn't make it illegal to be either against the war or black, but by getting the public to associate the hippies with marijuana and blacks with heroin, and then criminalizing both heavily, we could disrupt those communities. We could arrest their leaders, raid their homes, break up their meetings, and vilify them night after night on the evening news. Did we know we were lying about the drugs? Of course, we did.

Nixon initiated the War on Drugs, but nearly every politician since has continued waging it in one form or another. The number of Americans arrested for drug possession has tripled since 1980, reaching 1.5 million arrests per year in 2015. Black Americans are nearly six times more likely to be incarcerated for drug-related offenses than their white counterparts, despite equal substance use rates. In 1986, President Ronald Reagan signed the Anti-Drug Abuse Act, a bill written by a Democrat-controlled House. The law included specific funding to build new prisons and to create drug education and treatment programs. However, it also established mandatory minimum sentences, including sentences on crack cocaine use that disproportionately affected Black Americans. Just eight years later, President Bill Clinton passed the Violent Crime Control and Law Enforcement Act, which increased drug treatment programs but also introduced the Three Strikes law. That same year, thirteen states, including California, adopted Three Strikes–type laws. By passing these bills, Congress reduced the discretion of sentencing judges, requiring imprisonment for many offenses because of mandatory minimums and Three Strikes laws. Between 1980 and 2019, the number of women incarcerated in the United States increased more than 750 percent. This increase is directly linked to the War on Drugs and harsher sentencing.

- The number of women incarcerated rose from a total of 26,378 to 222,455.
- While there are still more men in prison than women, since 1980 the incarceration rate has been twice as high for women.
- During the 1980s, the number of women in state prisons whose most serious offense was a drug crime grew tenfold.
- According to the Vera Institute of Justice, "between 1980 and 2009, the arrest rate for drug possession or use tripled for women—while the arrest rate for men doubled."
- The population of American women inmates has been among the fastest growing of all incarcerated populations— over half of all women in U.S. prisons are mothers, most of

them primary caretakers of their children, and there are a quarter million children with single mothers in jail.

- An estimated nine thousand women are pregnant when they arrive at prison or jail each year. Often, those mothers are separated from their newborns within twenty-four hours of birth.
- The United States incarcerates 133 out of every 100,000 women, the highest incarceration rate for women in the world. While only 4 percent of the world's women live in this country, the United States accounts for over 30 percent of the world's incarcerated women.

Overall, the U.S. incarceration rate is falling, but the rate at which women are being imprisoned remains at an all-time high.

At Rainbow, Marquet didn't have visitors. Her kids, Bernard and Unique, were under the care of her younger sister. Her sister worked, and they couldn't make the drive up from San Diego. Marquet sent her earnings to the family and tithed. She went to prayer meetings after dinner every Sunday, Monday, Tuesday, and Thursday. The ministries would visit camp, and speak the Word in the training room beyond the administrative offices. When I met her, Marquet had just added the weekly Friday prayer meeting, Moms in Prayer, to her schedule. Each woman would sit in a circle and say a prayer for her children and the caretaker looking after them. Marquet prayed for a lot. She wanted "Him to bring someone in their path to bring them to a church—not just any church, a church where they can grow in Him, a church of Him. Cause a lot of churches say they're of Him, and they're really not, so I would want a church that is based on Him. Praying for them to do good in school—to not be on the streets, cause a lot of kids look toward the streets when they don't have compassion at home. To break generation curses, for them to do good in school with their grades. To get into sports. To let them know that I love them, cause a lot of kids—when you come here, they don't understand, they don't know what's going on—all they know is they don't have a parent there. They don't have their father—both their fathers left a long time ago, I was the only one there. So now they don't have me, it's like, 'Why isn't my mommy here?' You know? And so, like, so I pray for their hearts to be softened and compassionate."

Marquet worked on her drug addiction by attending Narcotics Anonymous and Alcoholics Anonymous meetings. She thought about meth, but didn't miss it. "I felt free but it don't last long," Marquet said. "After that first time, it's like you're chasing that freeness again. You're constantly chasing that freeness but you never find it. On fires it was just me and the fire, I was alive, I was accomplishing something. It takes all your fear away, it was an escape route. It became my new drug. Everybody is addicted to something, it's in our human nature. It's just what you do with that addiction."

On her first fire, the Pala Fire, Marquet told me she was nervous. It was close, just south of camp in Temecula. Her captain and foremen and swamper didn't say much. Even the dragspoon, the woman on crew responsible for inspecting line and administering first aid, didn't relay any information. They didn't explain the circumstances of the fire until they arrived. She knew she'd start like everyone else, at the back of the line. She hoisted her McLeod and piled into the buggy first, ready to exit last. She'd carried a McLeod at CIW, and used it to clear brush, but never in live fire. She'd clean up behind the dozen crew members ahead of her, tugging and scraping the roots from the soil to prevent further burns. Her captain explained that the Pala Fire had started at one residence earlier in the week and spread through forty-five acres before it was contained by CAL FIRE and San Diego County Fire. But containment does not mean the fire is controlled, particularly when it occurs during a heat wave and high winds. When they arrived, embers were being blown off still-smoldering brush and hot spots began skipping through the landscape. The Pala Fire wasn't out, and now its flames threatened seventy to one hundred structures. Homeowners on the east side of Pala Temecula Road evacuated to a high school in Temecula. Marquet's crew and Alisha's crew, among other crews, were there to protect those homes and the vineyards that supplied grapes for the wineries of Temecula.

Marquet had never felt anything like fire before. She wanted to run. "It's hot, you have all this gear on. And you have to hike through. Just when you feel like you can't go no more you keep going. It helps you to work as a sister crew, cause you have other people on your crew and you learn how to work with them, you know—cause, really all you have is each other on that, when you're on a fire. If someone goes over that cliff, you have to help that person get off that cliff. If someone passes out you have to bring them down the cliff." This was the kind of camaraderie and responsibility that Marquet had never trusted or been entrusted with. "Your feet are hot and tired and they have a pulse of their own. You feel like you can't breathe, but you're breathing. Your face feels like it's about to melt off, but it's there. It's just—you have to be aware of everything. You have to be—you have to be able to listen. If you cannot take instructions from either your swamper or your dragspoon or your captain, you're not going to survive. You have to be able to receive it and to be able to get it." Receiving instruction had never been Marquet's strength. But now, her life depended on it. "Say there is a widowmaker up ahead and someone is telling you there's a widowmaker up ahead—which is a tree that's broken, that's about to fall—say someone's trying to tell you but you're so irritated, that's another thing, you have to be humble. So, you're so irritated, you're so hot that you're not trying to hear them—you're just like, 'Whatever, I don't care.' You got to be able to know to listen. Because if that widowmaker falls on your head, you're gone." Shawna's death was in the back of her mind every time she went on a fire. "You have to be humble, you have to be patient, you have to be open ears— you have to be willing to receive instructions." Most of what we talked about at Rainbow fell into two categories: detailed descriptions of fire or her feelings of faith. They both seemed to be religious experiences.

She could see that what she was doing helped. On a fire in Nevada County, kids held signs that said, "Thank you for saving my house, thank you for saving my dog." Most women I interviewed recalled signs of thanks. People wrote cards. Brought out snacks and cake. It felt good to save someone's house. "Some people, they look down on us because we're inmates, you know, and sometimes you want to say, 'Well, I'm the one that saved your house!' But you don't. You just be like, 'Well, that's them. That's their problem.' But there's a lot, a lot, a lot of people that actually are thankful and are happy—even little kids that got tears in their eyes."

In Marquet's first winter at camp, just months before I met her, California was inundated with rain and snow, generated by the El Niño weather system. Between October and January, downtown L.A. had recorded more than thirteen inches of rain—216 percent more than the norm. Since official record keeping began, more than 140 years ago, the past 5 years had been the driest ever in downtown L.A. Now, the state was drenched. Climate experts pointed to the extremes of our changing environment—five years of dry heat and parched land shifted into a season in which the Sierra mountaintops were white with snowpack. For five years, hundreds of thousands of acres had gone unplanted; Central Valley water tables plunged. With the rains, farmers in the Central Valley celebrated what seemed to be the end of the drought. They could count on more than drinking water; they could plant again and cultivate trees. But extreme rains and El Niño winters can be as destructive as fire seasons. And inmate crews are responsible for responding to catastrophic flooding in addition to fire. The years of loose, parched soil created perfect conditions for mudslides and unhealthy riverbanks. Roots that held earth in place had been so dry and ravaged by previous fire seasons, and by the infestation of bark beetles, that heavy rains, despite providing welcome relief from drought, were not welcomed by all.

In late January 2017, a storm dumped nearly eight inches of rain over the course of four days in the San Diego area. Thunder shook the mountains and valleys and beaches. Cars were submerged; trees uprooted. The beaches were under high wind warnings and waves peaked at sixteen feet, bringing strong rip currents and coastal flooding. As flash floods hit the inland communities nearby, Governor Jerry Brown issued a state of emergency for San Diego. While people hunkered down in their homes, inmates were put to work as first responders. Rainbow camp crews assembled sandbags and hauled them to low-lying, vulnerable neighborhoods. Marquet's crew dispatched to a different assignment. The Monday after the series of storms began, during the rain's waning hours, they drove to the Rainbow River in Rainbow, a small town in northern San Diego County. The town had known fire—in October 2007, the Rice Fire was one of the thirty wildfires fueled by Santa Ana winds that burned almost one million acres, from Santa Barbara County to the U.S.-Mexico border. In the two small valley towns of Rainbow and neighboring Fallbrook, almost ten thousand acres burned, leaving 248 structures destroyed. Crews from Rainbow and Port helped then. And now, ten years later, when the town was drowning, inmate crews returned.

Marquet wasn't told much—just to follow Search and Rescue Swift Water teams and stick close behind them. She could see the men wade through the raging river, still swollen and higher than the community had ever seen it before. She could see them hack away at fallen trees and debris blocking forward progress. She could hear the cadaver dogs barking. Everyone who was out, including the sheriff's crew, was looking for a five-year-old boy and a seventy-three-year-old man, whose car had careened off the road and into the river. Marquet tried to focus on what their assignment was—follow Search and Rescue. Be a second set of eyes. Hack away at all the growth that had fallen in the heavy rains. By the time Marquet was out at Rainbow River, bucking for her saw, the old man's body had been found. But the sheriff's department, Search and Rescue, cadaver dogs, and now CAL FIRE inmate crews were all looking for the boy, hoping he might still be alive. The river was eighty feet wide and sixteen to eighteen feet deep. Marquet and her sawyer marched in the shallows behind Search and Rescue, continuing to hack away as they tried to uncover areas they might not have seen. "I was praying he was still alive. I was really praying he was still alive."

At one point, when the Search and Rescue crew moved ahead, Marquet's captain told them to stay behind, to work that part of the riverbank a little bit longer. Marquet had been in camp for nine months, had worked her way up from rake to bucking for a saw. She was training to be a saw, and her captain said it would be a good time to practice, a good place to get in some cuts. He showed her one spot to work. She cut, her sawyer bucked, and they cleaned out the area. They moved to another area, same thing. Marquet cut through the debris while her bucker cleaned out the wood and cleared the soil. The captain watched, then motioned for Marquet to move on to another spot. As her bucker was clearing the debris, Marquet saw the body. The little boy was partially buried under six feet of leaves and dirt and muck. "I believe that God played a part in that, you know—from me not cutting and my cap telling me to stop and move over there—cause it would have hurt me even more to find out that I had cut a body up." The inmate crews were rushed back to the bus while the captains finished the body removal. The CAL FIRE division chief Nick Schuler called it "a needle in a haystack to find this boy." Marquet sat in the buggy, shaken. "Our minds were crazy with just that little piece." He was the same age as Marquet's eldest son.

PART III

THE GOLDEN STATE OF INCARCERATION

8.

INMATE LABOR: SAN QUENTIN TO THE PACIFIC COAST HIGHWAY

n 1850, when California was admitted to the Union as a free state, California's constitution proclaimed, "Neither slavery nor involuntary servitude, unless for punishment of a crime, shall ever be tolerated." Yet state archives show that slavery was practiced openly. In 1850, the federal Fugitive Slave Act required government officials and ordinary white citizens in all states and territories to actively assist slaveholders in recapturing enslaved people who had escaped from slaveholding jurisdictions. In California, enslaved people worked mining claims, on farmlands, in settlements. If they tried to escape, they were imprisoned or routinely returned to their "owners."

If you google "who was the first female firefighter?" an 1818 illustration of Molly Williams pops up. Most capsule descriptions include that she was enslaved, owned by a wealthy businessman in New York, and "as good a fire laddie as many of the boys." In an illustration, she's tilted at a forty-five-degree angle, wearing just a dress and a scarf in the snow as she singlehandedly pulls a pumper that holds water to douse flames. As she strains, white men in overcoats and top hats run away from the fire and don't help her pull the massive machine on wheels. There's a children's book about her heroics, and articles and Wiki entries that celebrate her performance as a firefighter. *She was the first! She was enslaved! She was a very good baker! She was brave when men were not!* None of them go into much detail about her life.

George W. Sheldon wrote in the 1882 oral history *The Story of the Volunteer Fire Department of the City of New York*, "One of the most famous 'volunteers' of the earlier days was an old negro woman named Molly, a slave of John Aymar (the father of William Aymar), Mr. Aymar, by-the-way, was the last of the old Knickerbockers—a long-tailed coat, knee-breeches, silver shoe-buckles, and the inevitable queue. One of his sons was Benjamin Aymar, the founder of the eminent mercantile house of Aymar & Company. Well, Molly was his slave, and a very distinguished volunteer of No. 11 Engine." Sheldon identifies Molly as a "slave," but at the time of the fire, it's more likely she wasn't—her husband, Peter, had bought their freedom thirty-five years earlier. Benjamin Aymar, a wealthy businessman who ran clipper ships trading brandy, port, mahogany, and coffee from New York to California, had originally owned Molly and Peter, then sold the Williams family to Wesley Chapel, the first incarnation of the John Street United Methodist Church in Manhattan's Financial District, in 1783 for forty pounds sterling. They lived in the basement of the church as indentured servants. Peter served as the sexton in charge of buildings, maintenance, and grave digging; Molly cooked and cleaned. They had a son, Peter Jr., and eventually bought their freedom.

Molly continued to work for Aymar as a servant. She cleaned Aymar's house at 42 Greenwich Street, cooked, and tended to his eight children. Aymar was a volunteer in the city's fledgling firefighting corps—a prestigious position he agreed to out of self-interest, one that many wealthy merchants took part in to protect private property and business assets. The firefighting corps wasn't associated with a governing body, but fires broke out frequently, and those most affected were those with the most property. One out-of-control spark could wipe out all of Aymar's merchandise in the warehouses along Lower Manhattan's docks. When Aymar went to work at Oceanus Engine Co. 11, near what is now Zuccotti Park, he'd bring Molly. She'd cook meals and clean the station. And when outbreaks of flu, yellow fever, and cholera erupted, she'd care for the crew, sometimes replacing the crew altogether. According to Sheldon:

> She used to be called "Volunteer No. 11." I can see her now, with her nice calico dress and check apron, a clean bandana handkerchief neatly folded over her breast, and another wound about her head and rising up like a baby pyramid. Once, during a blinding snow-storm in 1818, there was a fire in William Street, and it was hard work to draw the engine; but among the few who had hold of the drag-rope was Molly, pulling away for dear life. This may have been the only time that she took hold of the rope, but afterward, when asked what engine she belonged to, she always replied, "I belongs to ole 'Leven; I allers run wid dat ole bull-gine." You could not look at Molly without being impressed by her really honest face—it was a beaming light-house of good-nature.

She's identified as a volunteer while serving a former master. Who's to say how much of her service was offered in good nature or out of fear or out of necessity; certainly not those who wrote her history. In fact, one detail not mentioned in the oral history but found on her gravestone was that she died three years after the fire, at the age of seventy-four. She pulled that ole bull-engine at the age of seventy-one. It's a fair guess that she didn't do this out of goodwill alone.

Like most women, Molly was defined by the men around her. Her husband was a successful businessman (after being a sexton at the church, he opened a tobacco shop), her son a priest and an abolitionist, her employer and former owner a wealthy scion of New York. (Aymar is buried in Green-Wood Cemetery. There's more of a record of his funeral than of Molly's life.) When I reached out to the New York City Fire Museum to see if it had any more archival records of Molly or Aymar, the email I received simply said, "It's a frequently asked question and unfortunately there is not." Benjamin Aymar lived to be eighty-four, dying in 1876, roughly fourteen years after the Emancipation Proclamation and eleven years after the Thirteenth Amendment was ratified on December 6, 1865.

The same divides that led the United States to the Civil War existed in California, also along a north–south axis. In 1859, the California legislature, which was intensely proslavery, passed the Pico Act, calling on Congress to divide the state into two. Though it was signed by Governor John B. Weller, and overwhelmingly approved by voters in Southern California, the federal government did not split the state because of the Civil

War. Northerners supported the Union effort, while white Angelenos who had migrated from the south supported secessionists. Approximately 250 Southern Californians enlisted in the Confederate Army. In 1861, the Los Angeles Mounted Rifles became the only militia company from a free state to fight for the Confederates. During Reconstruction, California was the only free state to reject the Fourteenth Amendment; it also rejected the Fifteenth Amendment, which guaranteed crucial civil rights for Black citizens—equal protection under the law and the right to vote. Remnants of L.A.'s Confederate proclivities lingered for more than a century in a cluster of thirty-seven graves in the Hollywood Forever Cemetery, where plaques and a granite rock memorialized the service of the men who had fought for the Confederacy. It was not until 2017 that the markers were removed.

Bryan Stevenson, the author of *Just Mercy* and founder of the Equal Justice Initiative, has written at length about the through line from slavery to mass incarceration. "We are living at a time of horrific injustice and inequality in our criminal justice system," he told me, "where we are tolerating racial bias and discrimination and police violence." During the course of our interview—and more than anything, it was a course—Stevenson said California was not excepted from racial oppression and violence: "California didn't permit interracial marriage in the 1940s, just like Alabama and Mississippi."

Despite a long history of propaganda arguing that California was and is a liberal bastion, the state was founded on principles of white supremacy. The Golden State governed by the noted progressive Jerry Brown was also where Reagan twice got his political start. Early on, the California frontier was promoted in pamphlets to individuals living east of the

Mississippi as an unending pot of gold with free land—160 acres was available to any household head, according to President Lincoln's Homestead Act of 1862. Lincoln described the law as an effort "to elevate the condition of men, to lift artificial burdens from all shoulders and to give everyone an unfettered start and a fair chance in the race of life." In reality, when approximately 10.5 million acres of California, nearly 10 percent of the state, were given away to frontier people, most claims went to white settlers and corporations. The expansion not only displaced and robbed Native Californians of their land. In practice, the Homestead Act rarely benefited Black Americans in California. Lanfair Valley, in the Mojave Desert, is one of the only recorded Black communities in California established with homesteaded land.

In the 1880s, not too far from where Malibu 13 is now, John Ballard, a man formerly enslaved, left central Los Angeles to become the first Black American to settle in the hills above Malibu. By the mid-1880s, he and his family had claimed 320 acres through the Homestead Act. In the time he lived in the hills, Ballard's house was burned down at least twice by racist ranch owners in Malibu before he finally moved. He left a sign on the charred ruins that read, "This is the work of the devil." After Ballard moved, the area was referred to with a racial slur into the 1960s, when his homestead became officially known by the state of California as "Negrohead Mountain." It wasn't until 2009 that the Los Angeles County Board of Supervisors voted to change the name to Ballard Mountain.

Farther south, Jesus Santa Maria was able to stake a homesteading claim in the Santa Monica Mountains only because the notorious Mexican bandito Tiburcio Vásquez (said to be one of the inspirations for Zorro) agreed to share

Topanga Canyon with him. Homesteaders used fire to tame the land, but occasionally out-of-control blazes destroyed what they'd built. By the late 1800s, a rural infrastructure had been created. If water was found up a mountain, the path with the fewest granite boulders became the route to reaching it, though sometimes that meant a roadway of whiplash turns. In the early 1900s, Francisco Trujillo, one of the three original homesteaders in Topanga Canyon, along with inmate road crews, built the community's first mountain pass from the Pacific to the San Fernando Valley, what is now Topanga Canyon Boulevard. Today, inmate crews, specifically the women of Malibu Camp 13, maintain the fire roads and mop up fires in the area. When I was reporting on a story in 2019, I ran into crew 13-3 just hours after a small fire had been knocked down. A spark from a resident's Weedwacker had lit up three acres of hillside in Tuna Canyon. It had been three years since I first met 13-3, and the crew was entirely different. They eyed me, probably wondering how I knew their foreman and what we were talking about. A year later, 13-3 was called to another assignment—containing the fires from the helicopter crash that killed nine people, including Kobe and Gianna Bryant.

The evolution of California's prisons and its use of prison labor has mirrored the nation's. The '49ers arrived seeking gold, and within the year California's population grew from twenty thousand non-Native people to a hundred thousand. In 1850, California entered the Union, but the territory had no basic mechanisms for either governance or a prison system. Prospectors from Oregon, northern Mexico, and the Great Plains continued to migrate to Northern California, while Bostonians and New Yorkers boarded clippers to fulfill the

United States' claim to Manifest Destiny. With the newcomers and newfound wealth came crime.

Once the state was seen as a valuable and necessary asset to the United States, the Anglo takeover of California was supported by laws that enabled the use of inmate labor to build California's infrastructure. Between 1848 and 1880, Los Angeles underwent a transformation from a small diverse town to an Anglo-dominated city. To build the city, to lay the roads, to dredge the wetlands, and to irrigate the fields, landowners relied on an inmate workforce. In 1850, California passed a law, written and signed by California's first elected governor, Peter Burnett, called the Act for the Government and Protection of Indians, which allowed white people to buy Indigenous children as "apprentices." According to the historian Jim Rawls, "Any white person under this law could declare Native Californians who were simply strolling about, who were not gainfully employed, to be vagrants, and take that charge before a justice of the peace, and a justice of the peace would then have those Native Californians seized and sold at public auction." For four months, the uncompensated labor of the seized Native Americans would belong to the person who brought the charges of vagrancy.

The California legislature followed states like Kentucky, where convict leasing had long been in use. In developing a convict leasing system, a private company or individual would provide security and "care" to convicts in exchange for the right to sell their labor. In 1851, as part of a private convict leasing arrangement run by James Estell, a corrupt businessman, thirty inmates imprisoned on the *Waban*, a 268-ton ship docked in San Francisco harbor, began working on the construction of California's first official state prison, San

Quentin. The prisoners on the *Waban* were from six county jails—they came from San Diego, Los Angeles, Santa Barbara, Monterey, San Jose, and San Francisco. Deputies were paid a dollar a mile for escort services, which added a profit motive in jailing people for their labor. On the *Waban*, the men's crimes ranged from gruesome murders to being drunk in public. The *Waban*, a ship meant to house 50, eventually held 150 convicts, most of whom slept on deck.

Fate being cruel, convicts collected the rocks and quarried the bricks that they used to build the dungeon cells that would eventually house them. The iron doors that sealed off the cells included a slit known as a "Judas hole." Inside the vermin-laced cells, men slept on straw matting next to night buckets for waste. Floggings were a standard form of punishment, as were "shower baths," in which naked prisoners were tied to ladders and sprayed with a pressurized stream of cold water.

In 1855, after a series of scandals (drunkenness, escapes, bookkeeping discrepancies), California took control of the prison from Estell, then proceeded to spend half a million dollars in eleven months running San Quentin—half the state's budget. A few years later, the governor contracted with the scandal-plagued Estell once again, this time paying him $10,000 a month to run San Quentin. In 1860, the state controller reported that the total cost of keeping state convicts for the previous eight years was $1.5 million. This became a key factor in motivating the state to contract out prison labor. California authorities assumed the goods manufactured by prisoners would cover the cost of running the prisons, but in 1894, after heavy lobbying from labor rights organizations that did not want to compete with prison-made products, the state agreed to limit prison work to hard labor. In San Quentin, that meant sewing jute sacks in mills; in Folsom, that meant breaking rocks.

By 1865, the constitution legally abolished slavery except in one instance—imprisoned people. The Thirteenth Amendment read, "Neither slavery nor involuntary servitude, except as punishment for crime whereof the party shall have been duly convicted, shall exist within the United States, or any place subject to their jurisdiction." In the excellent *City of Inmates*, Kelly Lytle Hernández wrote about how settler colonial theory—Manifest Destiny on steroids—fueled carceral practices at the time. Humans, especially Native Californians and Mexicans, were exploited early in Anglo California's history, she wrote. "Held every Monday morning at the Los Angeles County Jail, the auction of Natives was a spectacle on the streets of Los Angeles. As one city resident recalled, the local Marshal would begin arresting Natives on drunk and vagrancy charges at sunset on Saturday evening. In the morning, the jailer tied the incarcerated Natives to a wood beam in front of the jail, allowing white employers to inspect and bid on them as convict laborers." Between the 1880s and 1910s, authorities in Los Angeles expanded the city's carceral capacity, targeting poor white men, who were considered "tramps" and "hobos," for migrating, working seasonal jobs, and living beyond the nuclear family ideal propagated at the time. By the turn of the twentieth century, the American West was the epicenter of incarceration in the United States.

Prisoners in the early 1900s laid streets, broke rocks, and made furniture. Much of their work, especially road building, allowed for the center of Los Angeles to expand westward and provided access to inhospitable mountain regions. By 1902, convict labor was tasked with cutting and filling Sunset

Boulevard, a twenty-two-mile stretch of road that wound its way from downtown to the Pacific Ocean and became the northern border of Los Angeles at the time. Most of the significant infrastructure of early California was built by inmate crews.

In 1894, Dr. John L. D. Roberts, a doctor who lived in Monterey, was called to a shipwreck off the coast of San Simeon. It took him three and half hours to get there in his horse and buggy. Very little of California's coastline was developed or accessible, so he had to take an inland route. The length of time it took his horse and buggy to arrive at the scene of the accident convinced Roberts of the need for a road to San Simeon. The only problem was that the shoreline was jagged with rocks and prone to landslides. His vision for a coastal road was to be the first of three sections of what would become Highway 1, or the Pacific Coast Highway, or PCH.

Without inmate labor, the PCH would not exist. Skilled tasks were supposed to be performed by free men, but few would travel to the rocky, mountainous coast to blast through granite and lay concrete for Roberts's road. According to the California Motoring Authority pamphlet published in February 1916, "Convict labor on state highways is one way of solving California's tremendous mountain road problem, which has been beyond the state's resources since the 'early days of gold.' The convict takes work from no man, but builds roads that otherwise could not be built."

In 1928, prisoners from San Quentin were assigned to "Honor Camps," one of the earliest forms of inmate road crews and the predecessors to inmate fire camps. They worked a hundred-mile northern stretch of California between Carmel and San Simeon, leveling the edge of the coastline to lay a ribbon of road that would eventually connect Northern California to Southern. At first, there was no compensation for the laborers, but road building was a preferable alternative to the jute mills of San Quentin. (In 1911, one inmate reported that "the air [in the mill] is charged with fine particles of dust, fatal to the weak-lunged." Two years later, there were twenty cases of tuberculosis among San Quentin inmates, which were attributed to the mills.) The roadwork was so dangerous, it required special incentives. Eventually, legislators passed a bill granting wages and early release if prisoners agreed to go to the Honor Camps. The pay for work on the PCH was $2.10 per day (equivalent to less than $30 in 2014). Meals, clothing, transportation, medical and dental care, camp management, tools—even their own guards' salaries—were deducted. Of that $2.10, each man was allowed to pocket a maximum of 75 cents, "provided he could save that much." From the beginning of the road camps in 1915 until 1936, convicts built more than five hundred miles of roads—including highways connecting rural parts of the state to urban areas, stimulating tourism and travel to and from the cities, and providing a way for the timber industry to transport logs.

The inmates lived in temporary forestry camps of the Civilian Conservation Corps, a public work-relief program created during the Depression. During World War II, when California turned its prisons into factories for the military industry, inmates replaced professional firefighters on the fire line. (The first all-female forest firefighting crew was formed in 1942, but women had been fighting fires in California since 1915, when wives of Forest Service rangers helped battle a fire in the Mendocino National Forest.) In 1946, as part of Governor Earl Warren's Prisoner Rehabilitation Act, the state opened

Camp Rainbow. Under the joint supervision of the state's Division of Forestry and the California Department of Corrections, Rainbow housed inmates to clear fire lines and act as a backup firefighting brigade while CAL FIRE's workforce was depleted due to the war. The inmate crews built roads, harvested crops, and repaired infrastructure. By 1958, when 979 inmates were working on the crews, the Department of Corrections officially changed the name of the program to "conservation camps," because the "name designation honor camps was somewhat idealistic rather than a practical title."

The conservation camp setup was so cost-effective and addressed issues of overcrowding so well that in his 1959 inaugural address, Governor Edmund G. Brown promised to double the size of the Conservation Camp program. The conservation camps seemed to address his twin concerns of overcrowding and idleness. Within a year the camps' population rose to more than 1,750. In the decades since, the population has doubled again, to roughly 4,000 prisoners serving as inmate firefighters. Since the coronavirus pandemic, those numbers have dropped significantly, to just under 2,000. Eight camps closed in 2020, including the first camp, Rainbow, which had become an all-female fire camp in 1983.

9.

CARLA: CHOWCHILLA TO CHILDBIRTH

hadn't seen Carla since my visit to Malibu 13, when she told me about Shawna's death. Carla's baby was beautiful. When I met her, she was tiny, just a few weeks old. Carla's boyfriend's aunt had flown in from Mexico to help take care of her, and was holding her. Carla had been out for two years, and her life looked very different from the last time I saw her. She looked different too. In spite of having just given birth, Carla had carefully applied makeup—penciled-in brows, a subtle shade of brown lipstick, and long lashes. Her nails were hot pink and a tattoo of Hello Kitty poked out of the neckline of a striped top. I almost didn't recognize her. That was the point of the orange outfits. That was the point of prison. No makeup, no deviation, no recognition of the individual. You were called an inmate, a body, you were given a number, and once you were on the inside, that's how you were treated. But each woman I talked with—post-release, her entire appearance had changed. It was the difference between seeing a sick person and a healthy one.

Carla and her boyfriend, Miguel, lived in Little Rock, near

Palmdale, with Miguel's family, about ten miles south of Diana and the Trap. The main house was dark, in order to keep the rooms cool. Carla was out back in a smaller house with the AC on. Carla told me she was from Granada Hills and had paroled there in January 2017, about two years earlier. When she first got out, she felt like she was still in prison, still tethered to camp schedule. Carla would wake up at five, make her bed, tighten the corners, tuck in her shirt, drink coffee—she never drank coffee before camp. She'd do chores, tie some towels to a stick, and mop the floor. One morning, her mom caught her. "What are you doing?"

"Mopping."

"We have a mop."

Carla hadn't realized she was doing anything out of the ordinary, tying towels to a busted stick. That's how she mopped the barracks in Malibu. It's how everyone mopped, as far as she knew. She had been incarcerated for only three years, but she was nineteen when her sentence started. More of her adult life had been spent in the system than out.

When Carla had arrived at CCWF in Chowchilla, she was ordered to be quiet. After she was taken into a cell, she was immediately ordered to strip naked. Cough and squat. Bend over. Same deal as Lynwood. They asked how much she weighed, her birth date, her Social Security number. They took her picture. They searched her personal effects, the few things she was allowed to bring from County. Administrators issued her a blue polka dot muumuu. Then they placed her in another cell. It was one o'clock in the afternoon. She sat there with the other women from her transport until midnight, when she was housed in receiving on A Yard.

Chowchilla is in the dead center of California, and it's also the center of the Central Valley, an area dominated by farm life and the cycles of growth that have been forever manipulated into a variant of the natural order that suits the California economy. Driving through, there are signs along the highways that read "Food Grows Where Water Flows," and "Stop the Congress Created Dust Bowl," and "No Water = No Farms." The most striking display in the Central Valley occurs every February, when white petals grace the almond trees, then blanket the dirt below. The blooms represent the beginning of the Valley's growing season each year. Almond trees are the first crop to bud, flower, and fruit. The rows of trees form a grid of acres upon acres of geometrically pruned to perfection trees. The endless sea of snowy blossoms attracts tourists and drivers, who pause to gawk at the surreal, unnatural, infinite beauty. The beauty belies a starker reality; it obscures the largest women's state prison in the country, CCWF, or, as it's known to guards and inmates alike, Chowchilla. CDCR even has an almond orchard of its own, tended by inmates.

Once Carla was allowed out of receiving, some of the other girls pointed out a two-story cinder-block building where women were held on death row. Originally, when Chowchilla opened in 1990, the top floor of building 270 held nine women in six-by-eleven-foot cells, while the bottom floor functioned as a secluded workout space. As Chowchilla's death row population grew, the private yard on the first floor was converted into more cells, which limited exercise to a narrow cement walkway, known as "the freeway." California has condemned more women to death than any other state; it leads the nation with twenty-six since 1973, almost half the total amount in the United States in 2020, and roughly double the number of condemned women in Texas and Alabama combined. One inmate on death row told the *Los Angeles Times*, "What kind of life is this? Waking up every morning to a cement wall is an unbearable future. I sometimes think the gas chamber is better than staring at these walls for the rest of my life. I'm not afraid to die. If they want to murder me, let them murder me. My life is ruined anyway."

The prison was built to hold 2,004 female inmates, but currently houses 2,795 prisoners, at 140 percent capacity, in fourteen dormitory buildings and two traditional cellblock buildings. Roughly half of those women are incarcerated because of drug crimes or thefts related to addiction. The housing quarters are divided into four yards identified by the letters A through D. For her first two months at Chowchilla, Carla was on A Yard, where they check mental health and do an overall evaluation to determine if special programs, including camp, are an option. The administrators decide if inmates are stable, if they're nonviolent, if they're likely to try to escape, if the inmate can contribute in a specific way, if the inmate is a danger to others or a danger to herself. If the inmate carries a life sentence, she won't qualify for programs or work. There are coveted programs such as forestry, training service dogs, or hospice, but most incarcerated laborers in California—95 percent—get assigned to prison maintenance jobs, like laundry, kitchen prep, or janitorial duties.

Carla didn't want her family to have to drive up from Granada Hills to Chowchilla for visits. She didn't want them to go through the razor wire gates, then imagine her behind fences, and she didn't want them to have to pass through metal detectors. Carla was still being processed, still in orange rather than blues, which meant she was only allowed no-contact visits. The first time her mom and grandmother drove up, her grandma had on slip-on flats decorated with a small chain. When they attempted to enter the visiting area, a correctional officer said the chains violated the prison's dress code. There are so many rules for entry, the atmosphere intentionally daunting, the rules arbitrarily enforced. It was easy for first-timers to feel over-whelmed by the restrictions. Carla's mom and grandmother drove into town to buy new shoes, then went back to Chow-chilla. Again, the correctional officer stopped the two women. Carla's grandma's new, open-toed shoes were *also* against the rules. The women gave up and drove five hours home.

The next day they tried again—again they drove five hours, up the 5, up Interstate 99, through the Central Valley, passing the almond orchards, vineyards, and industrial citrus farms. By the time Carla's mother and grandma had passed security with-out being turned away, their visit was reduced to an hour. "My grandma just looked at me and started crying for the first ten minutes," Carla said. "Because you're behind the glass, you're in orange. All the other people in visiting are hugging their fam-ily and they're in blues and they look a little bit more normal. And she was crying because your visit is behind the glass and it's really dark in there. It's like you're in, like, a dark place, like when you're going to adopt a puppy, and you see the puppy just in that cage?" Carla's grandmother couldn't hold her hand or hug her. Carla kept saying, *I'm okay*. She was eating okay, the food was better than at Lynwood, she told her grandma. She didn't want her grandma to worry. "The hardest part of doing time was knowing my grandma was crying before visiting or after a visit. You're supposed to be doing the time but they're doing the time with you. Prison wasn't hard because of the fighting, it was the same shit I was doing on the outside, just with a bunch of old ladies. I could handle that. It was knowing how much my family suffered because of what I did."

———

Once Carla crossed over, from A Yard to D Yard, women were already training for camp. Repeat offenders were lifting and pounding through burpees and crunches on A Yard. They all told her, *Anything to get a head start on passing the final physical. Camp is the way to go. You get better visits. Better food. Everything is better in camp.* The same lines Shawna heard in County. While getting a yard assignment meant she could finally have contact visits, it also meant she was housed in a cell with lifers. She thought of her public defender, how when they met, she had asked Carla for a statement. Carla refused. She could have told her, yes, there was a physical altercation, yes, there were bruises and scrapes. But not what this girl said in the police report. An ambulance? No. A knife? No. Carla didn't think it would matter. She asked her public defender, *Why bother?* What was the point, she was going to do time regardless.

Carla had heard a lot of things about how to handle yourself once you were inside. It wasn't that different from when she was a kid, proving that she was tough, that she would fight, that she wouldn't run. She could deal with the new rules: that lifers would take your food, insist you wear a hairnet, make you take your shoes off in the cell, bully you. Fights were inevitable— they were encouraged and manipulated by the guards.

After interviewing more than 130 Chowchilla prisoners in

2016, the Prison Law Office, a nonprofit public interest law firm that provides free legal services to adult and juvenile offenders, found that COs incubated an atmosphere of fear and violence. "They do this by setting up prisoners who complain," the Prison Law Office reported. "Officers facilitate violence by letting assailants into buildings or rooms to fight and commit violence. Staff also 'stir the pot' by spreading gossip to create jealousy among domestic relationships." One woman said that an officer paid prisoners to beat inmates up—that custody officers blackmail prisoners into physical violence by holding incriminating "dirt over them," or intimidating them, or retaliating in punitive ways.

The report detailed an inmate who recounted an incident on the yard in which a woman was assaulted by a prisoner wielding a lock hidden in a glove. An inmate said she'd "never seen people with so many black eyes." Another CCWF inmate said that being housed there "scares the life out of me." COs were physically brutal, either directly, as when one unloaded two cans of pepper spray into the eyes of an inmate, or by intentional negligence, such as allowing inmates five minutes to fight, "taking their sweet time" to break it up. Often, the guards were also emotionally abusive, calling inmates degrading names and racial slurs.

Also noted in the report was the fact that guards got away with quid pro quos all the time, sneaking in contraband in exchange for sexual favors, which in California is considered rape. In addition to quid pro quos, women were subject to assault and harassment. When one inmate was called to the "cop shop," the protected bubble in the center of the cellblocks, a guard asked her when she would be released, and told her, "I wouldn't mind fucking you for a week. I wouldn't mind trying it out. You have a nice personality." Another guard demanded that prisoners pull out their waistbands and lift up their shirts, then he would look up their shirts and down their pants, "inspecting" their clothes. Prisoners had to pass him in order to get to their programming areas and jobs. Some reported skipping their programs and meetings during his shift, and missing work. And if you missed work, you were fired from your job. If you missed your job or your programs, you got additional time.

One deputy harassed Carla. He called her over to the area where cops watched over the women through plexiglass.

He asked her, "What's your favorite food?"

"Why are you asking me about outside food?"

"I'll bring in whatever you want," he said.

Then the CO asked her to come in and close the door behind her. Carla couldn't walk away because she knew she would get in trouble—added time, no phone access, no visitors. She knew not to shut the door either.

He explained again that he could get anything for her from the outside.

"Come on, just close the door."

Carla knew what this meant.

"I could be your daughter's age," Carla said. "Like, I'm young. You know how old I am. You have my information in the system."

"Oh, I like it when you get mad," he said back.

"I wonder if you're why we have these rape meetings," Carla said.

Incarcerated women depend on correctional officers for basic needs—access to clean laundry, phone calls, tampons, time out of their cells. COs can write up inmates and extend a prison sentence. Between 2014 and 2018, CDCR fired at least six officers for sexual misconduct, but it's rare for guards to be disciplined or fired. In 2018, 337 staff-on-inmate incidents were reported in California prisons. Investigations substantiated just 3 of those allegations. In contrast, the Prison Law Office reported in 2016 that out of a random sample of eighty women, nearly all had said they experienced sexual abuse or harassment while incarcerated. In Chowchilla, there was rarely a time when inmates felt safe. Even in the cells, inmates were forced to change clothes in full view of the semifrosted window and encouraged to wear only a bra during count so that male guards could see the women naked.

After dinner, and after count, Carla would wander around the yard. It was like a swap meet at night. It reminded her of home, of the San Fernando swap meet she used to go to. Inmates made boxers out of sheets. They'd draw weed leaves or 2Pac's face on the boxers. Everything was for sale or barter. They could customize a shirt or a wallet or a pillowcase. Carla could get her face painted on a T-shirt; some women specialized in beach scenes. Pants were made into shorts, shirts sewn into tank tops, friendship bracelets knotted with personalized names. There were paintings for sale, barbers to cut hair, cosmetologists who trained at the prison, ready to do makeup. They had homemade tattoo guns, engineered from the motors of CD players and guitar string and batteries; they'd even give prison guards tattoos. And drugs. There were always drugs for sale or trade on the yard. Carla thought that a lot of the things for sale could be sold in the free world—there were a lot of talented artists on the yard. Some artists traded, others asked for money orders to buy drugs.

Sometimes, girls just sold their wares because they were cold and needed an extra set of thermals, which cost twenty bucks. Sometimes, girls used the money to buy hygiene—soap, shampoo, tampons, the things that cost extra in the canteen. Hygiene was expensive. The state never provided enough. (It provided hygiene only if you were deemed "indigent," which was defined as having five dollars or less in your canteen for thirty consecutive days; then CDCR would provide shampoo, toothpaste, four disposable razors, deodorant, floss, lotion, Vaseline, hair oil, two golf pencils, twenty stamped envelopes, and twenty sheets of writing paper.) "There's a lot of wasted talent," Carla said. "It's like, imagine, if they could do these projects out of scrap material, what can they actually do with the real material?"

Carla kept a composition notebook of all the fires she'd been on—the ones from when she was on a crew at Rainbow and Malibu. She wrote down the names of the fires, the dates, and if something funny happened. When a municipal crew's dog bit her on a fire in Sequoia, she wrote down a description of the dog. *Black Lab.* It was a seemingly inconsequential list of the dozens of fires she'd fought. Apart from the Mulholland Fire, they blurred together. The list was an indication of the passage of time. Carla still had a year or so left at Malibu after Shawna died. She tried to concentrate, she tried to work, but it was hard without Shawna.

A month before her release date, on January 26, 2017, Carla slept through count. Her rhythm was off because the whole camp had just returned from a stay at Port after black mold was found in the Malibu barracks. The crews were sleeping in temporary bungalows. She lost track of time. Carla was tired. She was tired of being a full-time firefighter and full-time prisoner. When Commander Scott wrote her up, he told her she could have attempted an escape. "But I didn't go anywhere, I just overslept," she told me. "I missed a count. Even when the CO came to wake me up, I was in bed; I didn't leave." The write-up meant an additional ninety days. She called her mom, who called an advocate in Sacramento, who got the additional days reversed. When I asked why she thought the extra days were added for a seemingly small infraction, Carla said camp was often strict, more punitive than Chowchilla. She thought it also might be a way to keep bodies in crews longer. The camps needed bodies to continue to operate and the state needed crews.

Once Carla left Malibu, she took whatever work she could find. Waitress shifts at night and weekends at Denny's; stocking shelves at a 99 Cent store; receptionist at a flooring company; collection coordinator at a U.S. Postage Meter Center, a company that arranged mass mailings. Sometimes during job interviews, she was asked on application forms if she was a felon. Most of the time she skipped the question. She needed the work. Her last two jobs came from postings on Craigslist. Carla liked working at the Postage Meter Center, which was mostly call center work with no public interaction.

In July 2017, a friend who had just gotten out of federal prison took Carla to a party in Antelope Valley. (He had been locked up on drug charges after trying to help out his mom after his dad was deported.) Carla liked the Joshuas that grew behind strip malls like lost earth plants that refused demolition. The only time she'd seen Joshuas was when some crews were taken from Malibu to a firefighter convention where they served breakfast and were restricted from talking to any free world crews or personnel. As they drove farther and farther toward the party, markets were replaced by sprawling acres. Behind some fences were dogs and horses and chickens kicking up small dust clouds. The roads were paved in spirit only. They didn't need to be, most people had trucks. At the party, Carla was introduced to Miguel. The party was at his place, a sprawling rancho. Apologizing, he explained that he had to feed the animals to help his parents out. He tossed some hay around. Carla noticed his strength, and was impressed that he helped his parents. Miguel dressed different, talked different from the guys Carla was used to. "He wasn't into gangs and he just seemed like an older person," even though they were the same age.

The party felt different to Carla too. Miguel paid attention to her and made sure she was having fun. At one point, a goat got loose and beelined toward her. She kept her cool for the sake of first impressions, but she was freaked out. She'd seen fire, but a charging goat was not something she was ready to contend with. Miguel grabbed the goat and put him back in the pen. They shot BB guns, got Jack in the Box, drank Coronas and Modelos, and chilled like she was twenty-three, which she was.

Carla moved to Miguel's ranch near Palmdale shortly after they met. She'd commute to her job at the U.S. Postage Meter Center in Valencia every day, waking up at 5:00 a.m. to drive forty-five miles west on the 14. Her work was located near a Southern California landmark for every kid—Magic Mountain. It was a long drive, and stressful. The 14 was prone to high winds, the worst of Los Angeles traffic, and cars hugging hairpin turns at maniacal speeds. Sometimes trucks overheated from the mountainous climb, sometimes they overturned. Toward the end of 2018, the business was in trouble and Carla was pregnant. On her commute, she'd pull over periodically with severe morning sickness. There weren't a lot of places to pull over, so sometimes she would just have to fight the nausea or barf in a brown paper bag while driving. Her boss told her that because she was a new hire, her hours and pay would be cut. Miguel told her to stop working. They'd be okay—she needed to concentrate on taking care of herself and her body.

Carla was released from parole in 2018, on the day of her baby shower. Before the baby and to celebrate freedom, Miguel and Carla went to Rosarito in Baja. They drove down, skirting the Angeles National Forest, through San Bernardino and Riverside, passing the mountains in Temecula, through Escondido and San Diego, all the lands that Carla had protected as a firefighter. She was paralyzed with fear and anxiety. She told Miguel she was scared. She told her PO the same thing. "Don't worry, you have your discharge card. You're fine." But Carla still felt like a criminal. She couldn't look at cops and feel secure. At the border, Carla was convinced the cops would pull them over, she'd go to jail, she'd be pregnant in jail, something terrible would happen. It kept circulating in her mind, over and over. The fear that she would get caught doing something wrong. She'd been imprinted with that fear of doing something wrong, that she'd be sent back to prison for a violation she didn't understand. Miguel asked her to stop thinking like that. But she couldn't. Prison is a trauma. Trauma changes the makeup of your brain. Trauma allows anxiety to override rational thinking.

A couple of months later, when Carla's water broke, her temperature was high. She kept drifting in and out of consciousness. The last thing Carla remembered hearing was the nurse saying that, if the fever got worse, they'd have to perform an emergency C-section. The nurse stopped telling Carla how high her fever was after it reached 113 degrees. Doctors tried to combat the infection with medications through an IV, but none worked. They gave her pills; the pills didn't work. She was so drugged that she told Miguel, "I don't think I'm going to be able to push her out. I'm so weak right now." Every time she woke up, she felt weak. She wasn't prepared for how physically taxing childbirth would be. But after twenty-two hours of labor, she held her baby, Rebecca.

It was so hard to hold her baby. She was so tired. Whenever Carla tried to put Rebecca to sleep, a nurse would come in to take her temperature or do a test or take blood. Carla couldn't rest. Then, when she finally got home, Carla, still exhausted, refused to let go of Rebecca—she didn't want anyone to think she couldn't take care of her baby. So she held on to her baby. They'd ask, Did you sleep, did you eat, did you shower? The first night, Carla cried. She loved Rebecca, but she didn't know what to do, and she thought she had to do whatever it was all on her own. In the first few days, Carla worried that she might suffocate Rebecca, that the blanket would be wrapped wrong, that Rebecca was hungry, that she needed a diaper change. She didn't let anyone else hold her. But Carla was so tired. Her head would droop, her eyes would shut for quick naps. Miguel told her, "No, dude, everybody gets help when they have their baby. Especially in the beginning."

"She's so small, she needs me."

"You're not the only person who's ever asked for help. You're not going to look weaker."

For the first two weeks, Carla treated motherhood like fire camp—she'd get a couple of hours of sleep and then devote everything she had to her baby. She lived with the tired. Eventually, Miguel and Carla's mom convinced her that help was an acceptable strategy too; that she couldn't do it on her own, and shouldn't. And that it was important for Rebecca to bond with the rest of her family. Carla's mom took off work to help. Miguel's dad fed Rebecca bottles, and beamed love. Carla got more sleep, felt closer to human. But even in the first few weeks of being a mom, and well after she was off parole, Carla would startle. Did I forget to call my PO and check in?

10.

SELENA: CRS CRAZY RIDERS TO FIRST SAW

When I talked to Selena, she told me about her first day in camp and her last. Her first day she was sent on a fire, and on her last day she was dropped off at a bus stop with $200. Selena had never been to Malibu before serving time and didn't really know how to get home. She found a pay phone, called a friend, and said, "Hey, I just paroled, can you come pick me up?" And she was back in MacArthur Park.

In 1926, the park was described as the place "where palms whisper in this island of quiet in the midst of roaring city traffic." There were still towering palms, grass slopes for picnics and birthday parties, and a lake that was once, in the 1800s, an alkaline-laced marshland populated by waterfowl. When downtown expanded south and west, the marsh was used as a dump for garbage and animal carcasses. In one of the many corruption scandals that plagued the founding of California, Mayor William Workman, who owned several lots in the neighborhood, decided that a dump would decrease the value of his land, so he lobbied to transform the area into one of

L.A.'s first public parks. He called it Westlake. In its heyday, on the cusp of the twentieth century, visitors rented rowboats or sailboats; thousands of people flocked to Sunday concerts held in the park's band shell; patrons strolled through cactus gardens; women carried parasols to shield their face from the sun beaming between palm trees; two streetcar lines led directly to the park; by 1898, a small pool held barking seals as an attraction. MacArthur Park became a vacation destination, surrounded by luxury hotels. It was known as the Champs-Élysées of Los Angeles. There were also canoes, gondolas, paddleboats, and a three-story boathouse; on Christmas the park floated Douglas firs along the surface of the lake; on the Fourth of July, the city staged mock warship battles on the lake.

During Selena's childhood, the area was different. In the 1990s and 2000s, the park was considered a war zone fueled by a drug trade that the FBI and LAPD deemed one of the worst in the country. The LAPD considered MacArthur Park to be a neighborhood riddled with prostitution, drugs, extortion, violence, and theft. If you weren't part of a gang, you paid for protection from gangs, and from police harassment. The LAPD had a long history of harassment in south Los Angeles. It had been broadcast during the Watts rebellion in 1965, and during the uprising after the Rodney King verdict in 1992. In 1999, when Selena was four, at least seventy LAPD officers from the local Rampart division were implicated in various types of misconduct, ranging from unjustified shootings to drug deals in the notorious Rampart scandal. Most of those officers were part of the LAPD's elite antigang unit CRASH (Community Resources Against Street Hoodlums).

After an investigation revealed that officers had brutalized people, stole drugs from evidence, sold those drugs, robbed banks, and harassed citizens, nearly a hundred convictions that had been secured by the CRASH unit were overturned. The Rampart scandal ended with the City of Los Angeles paying out roughly $125 million in civil damages. A 2001 report written by Erwin Chemerinsky, now dean of UC Berkeley's law school, stated that the LAPD minimized the magnitude of the Rampart scandal and failed to acknowledge the extent to which its internal culture allowed corruption to fester.

By the time William Bratton took over as LAPD chief in October 2002, a partnership with agents from the FBI; the Bureau of Alcohol, Tobacco and Firearms; the Drug Enforcement Administration; and Immigration and Customs Enforcement specifically targeted the leaders of drug organizations and gangs in the MacArthur Park neighborhood. As with most law enforcement operations that purport to target high-level criminals, the people affected were mostly the opposite—low-level, less violent criminals.

Selena was one of those people; she was well-known by local cops for dealing drugs, and by the LAPD's gang unit that patrolled MacArthur Park. They even had a name for her—La Loca, even though everyone in CRS Crazy Riders called her what she tagged, La Niña. It's likely that Selena was entered into the CalGang database early on (this is impossible to verify, since information recorded in CalGang is available only to law enforcement agencies). CalGang is an internet-linked software database created by California's Department of Justice and implemented by law enforcement agencies across the state. The database catalogs intelligence that officers have collected in interviews, and stores names and personal details of nearly ninety thousand people suspected of being active gang members. When CalGang was first implemented, it was lauded in *Government Technology* magazine in 1998 as "A New Tool in the War on Drugs." One officer said, "The biggest problem we have had is in underestimating how well it would work, how much it would help and how quickly local law enforcement would embrace the system. We went from 366 end-users on the first day to over 1,600 now, and growing every day. It helps solve cases."

One of CalGang's most glaring failings, however, was that it included people with no connection to gangs at all. When cops entered details such as tattoos, nicknames, cars, or what color sports jersey a person was wearing in routine traffic infractions, random people were designated as gang associates. In 2016, a state audit found that many so-called gang members in the database had been falsely and inaccurately ID'd as gang members—including a one-year-old child. By 2020, California Attorney General Xavier Becerra announced he had "revoked access to CalGang records generated by the Los Angeles Police Department (LAPD)." But for decades before that, the database targeted people in low-income neighborhoods when charged with a criminal offense, who were then additionally charged with gang enhancements, adding years to a prison sentence.

On July 17, 2015, Selena's first day at Malibu, 13-3 caught a fire. It was 10:00 p.m. when the call came in. She'd never seen live fire. She didn't know where she was. She'd never been to Malibu before. At least Lynwood was close to MacArthur Park.

She didn't know where the buggy was headed. The only thing she knew was that the fire was located near the Mountain High ski resort; that's what the captain told the swamper, who told the crew. In the fire buggy, they set out to the base camp, a two-hour drive toward the hills of the Angeles National Forest. The fire was the second major fire in the area that day. The first, the North Fire, started in Cajon Pass off Interstate 15 in San Bernardino County and spread over 3,500 acres within a few hours, charring structures and burning through twenty-two cars. After rains stopped its progress, it was contained at 4,250 acres.

Hours later, and just ten miles west of the North Fire, crew 13-3 arrived at the Pines Fire, the sixty-fifth fire in California in 2015. By 1:00 a.m., 90 girl scouts and 130 deaf or hearing-impaired children had been evacuated; as were people sleeping in tents in the campsites Apple Tree, Lion, Verdugo, and Peavin. A shelter was set up at a high school in Palmdale. Crews from the North Fire drove to the Pines Fire. Even though the fire was small—about two hundred acres—it had the potential to spread throughout the San Gabriel Mountains, climbing Mt. Baldy and any other peak it could. The forest was dry from hot July days and, in the moonlight, Selena could see trees that were parched from drought, backlit by orange flames along the entire hillside. It looked like a parody of a Sierra Club pamphlet. Instead of an orange sunset illuminating nature, the fire was torching everything in its path. It smelled like her neighborhood in summer, when families barbecued at the park. The orange ombre of flame distorted the shapes of trees, consuming the Aleppo pines and firs. One way or another, Selena was supposed to protect them, the whole network of trees.

"At CIW, they just worked us out and trained us to hike and maybe they trained us a little to cut line, but we weren't trained on fire until we actually got to fire camp," Selena said. "CIW is just the physical part. They train you to be in a physical state to do what you need to do at fire camp." The flames she saw were small, just three feet. The thing that alarmed her most about a real fire—more than the heat—was the sound of animals crying. Early the next morning, 13-3 cut line around the fire. She was last in line, scraping dirt.

Her captain yelled, "Selena, we don't scrape dirt! We scrape the fire, the grass, the grass on fire." Until this moment, nobody had told her how to cut line during an actual fire.

She said she was sorry, and continued to scrape. The crew in front of her cut brush before she got to it. She could hear the trees groaning and snapping. She kept hearing the sounds of the animals. Where did they go during fire? The captain moved her up to the middle of the line, so she could scrape brush and get a sense of working in embers rather than bare soil. Selena felt bad, like he thought she was being lazy. She didn't want to fuck up her first fire.

She worked the line. She sweat through her undershirt. She was drenched. From the heat of flames. From the digging. From the Nomex suit that protected her. From the hundred-plus-degree days that Southern California had been experiencing all July. She didn't know that every fire she'd go on, she'd end up drenched. She'd end up smelling nasty. She'd end up covered in dirt and soot. Though she was wearing her shroud, the flame-resistant face protector covering her mouth, the air was already so smoky, she felt like she was choking. She felt like her face was melting. Like her eyes were burning up, even though she was wearing safety goggles. Her muscles were aching from the repetitive motions of raking and hoeing hot earth. She knew not to stop. If you stopped, you'd get in trouble.

By 1:00 a.m., the fire was mostly contained, so the crew watched it burn within the containment line before picking a level spot in the dirt, higher than the line, where some girls went to sleep. Selena ate her first Meals Ready to Eat (MRE) that night. They were meant for emergencies, but she was starving and her captain allowed it. She'd done good work, he said. Selena didn't want to sleep. So she told jokes to anyone who would listen, corny jokes that could be found on the bottom of Cracker Jack boxes.

"What's one animal you can't play cards with? A cheetah."

Crew 13-3 got back by ten in the morning the next day. Exhausted, Selena fell asleep, and was allowed to, because it was a Saturday.

Two weeks after the Pines Fire, twenty-three large fires were burning across California, requiring eight thousand firefighters to work them. By July 31, Governor Jerry Brown had declared a state of emergency. Eventually Selena's body adjusted to the shock of working fire. She got used to the schedule, the expectations. She caught a fire in Yosemite that started in a Stanislaus National Forest canyon. Selena had never seen trees that big or rocks that protruded from the earth in such peculiar formations. It was also her first time that far north. "The trees were humongous." Over the next month and a half, Selena and her crew jumped from fire to fire as the flames spread. Her crew would do twenty-four-hour shifts—one day on, one day off, depending on the workday. They'd stay at the nearest fire camp, in one tent for the whole crew. "It was kind of cool. We'd get buffets the next day. It was nice to see guys"—the base camps were often male inmate fire camps—"but, hell no, we could not talk to the guys." The CO who traveled with them warned her many times, "Selena, stop looking at them." Selena had just turned twenty and was the youngest one on the crew and a little boy-crazy. She didn't see a lot of fire in Yosemite, just the grunt work, the containment line.

She didn't want to go back to Malibu; it was easier to be on a fire. She didn't interact with COs as much when she was on the line; she could go twenty-four hours without seeing one. Men were cooking and serving the food, and it tasted better. Every now and then, Selena would get a little word in with dudes, flirting, "Hey, how you doing, thanks for cooking my food." COs would chide Selena, but she would continue and look up at the male cooks and say, "I'll see you at dinner."

Six weeks away fighting fire meant more commissary money—enough for hygiene and snacks and whatever Selena needed. And when she returned to Malibu, she developed a side hustle. Selena collected lizards and traded them to other girls in exchange for twenty-five-cent noodles, off-brand ramen packages that she could eat after dinner. The girls kept the lizards as pets for an hour or two then let them loose, back to wilds of the Santa Monica Mountains.

11.

THE SAND FIRE AND
THE DETWILER FIRE

Fire camp wasn't all fire, all training, all the time. The women passed the hours, days, months, years in different ways— pool in the rec room, puzzles, meetings, prayer, meditation, yoga. Whitney asked one of the CDCR sergeants if they could start a vegetable garden between the cafeteria and the workout area. She planted beets, kale, carrots, peppers, squash, cucumbers, watermelon, cantaloupe, and some flowers to attract bees. Her garden also attracted gophers, who would steal the fruits and vegetables. After birds snatched sprouts, a couple of foremen donated gardening tools and netting to protect the plants.

Another benefit to being in camp was that the living quarters and rec areas weren't as thoroughly monitored as they were in prisons. Whitney could lose herself digging in the dirt; others made shovels and rainsticks out of yucca plants in the hobby craft area. Selena read *The Life of Pi*. And there were other extracurriculars. The showers weren't guarded; the areas behind the workout facilities were covered in brush. Those who were courting romance or "gay for the stay," as Whitney put it, could maximize their time with inter- and intracrew relationships. Some women were considered studs, others femme. They would hook up in the showers and enlist a third person to look out for COs.

Alisha, the swamper I met at Port, told me that having a girl-friend at Port was the only way she could get through her time there. "She was my first girlfriend. I don't know if it was out of companionship; we were together for a year. Now, she works for forestry in Sequoia, as a helitack. We met up in the streets when I got out but I was already dating my ex again, so it was kind of weird. She was one of my best friends that I had there. I knew that she was the one person that would always have my back." Alisha also told me about how there was a room in the back of the for-estry wing at CIW where guards would have sex with inmates. She said the guards would bring in cell phones or hygiene in exchange for sexual favors. "The guards at camp were flirtatious but it was worse at CIW," Alisha said. "At camp, sometimes we'd find used condoms, which you know, how does that hap-pen? And one time a guard said to us, 'If you let me watch you and your girlfriend, I won't tell on you guys.'"

Occasionally, women were busted. On Whitney's crew in Malibu, her lead saw got together with a woman nicknamed Little. "Penny and Little got rolled, because they got caught hooking up in our dorm. That was the same night they got drunk off hand sanitizer and alcohol squeezed from sanitation wipes." They both got sent back to CIW, then one was sent to Port and the other to Rainbow. On another night, Whitney saw a group of women getting drunk on hand sanitizer and told her swamper, "If we get a call, I am not bucking for Lynn. I don't think she should have a saw in her hands. They're loaded."

They didn't get a call, but Lynn suffered through the hikes and workouts the next day, hungover. By the end of her stay, Lynn was just tired. She'd done her time. She'd done her fires, and she didn't want to hold the saw anymore.

On one of Lynn's last fires, the Sand Fire in the Angeles National Forest, she just about gave up. Before they even got to the fire, Malibu crews heard foremen talking about red-flag conditions in the Santa Clarita area, about forty-five miles east of the coast, near Antelope Valley, Palmdale, and Lancaster—a particularly fire-prone area, although, in July 2016, everywhere in California was fire prone. It was the fifth year of the long drought. Temperatures were high, humidity was low, and winds were gusting through the mountains at speeds of up to twenty-five miles per hour. The Sand Fire started during an unrelenting heat wave that clocked temperatures of over 110 degrees. It ripped through the Santa Clarita Valley, burning chaparral stands and steep arroyos. The terrain was impossible to navigate, and because the area hadn't burned in sixty years, flames jumped fifty feet, climbing skyward. During the first weekend of fighting the blaze, the L.A. County Fire Department chief, Daryl L. Osby, pointed out the obvious in a press conference: "Five years ago, if we had a similar fire, we probably would have caught it at the ridge." Instead, because of dry soil and changing weather patterns, it was impossible to predict its direction.

Whitney and Lynn's crew was assigned to punch in a line near the wooded areas. They couldn't initiate containment because the fire was barreling toward them. "The fire behavior was all over the map, it, like, shifted and we had to pull out. The fires started coming our way." Stiffler and Brondyke, their foremen, told the crew they were seeing action that most free world firefighters never see. Flames towered far above them, smoke blackening the skies. The Sand Fire was different. When crew 13-5 pulled out of its initial task, it was reassigned to structure protection. "Lynn was really big into Skrillex," said Whitney. "So, we had Skrillex thumping in the buggy as we're hauling ass toward this black-smoke crazy fucking situation. And everybody else was driving the opposite direction." People's faces were stricken with panic. They were frantically evacuating their horses, their pets, packing anything they could save. Whitney saw a golf course, nice homes, a neighborhood that looked middle-class. The California dream. And then she saw the flames. Hundred-foot walls of flames. The front closed in on crews 13-5 and 13-2, the strike teams assigned to protect the neighborhood; 13-2 ran, nearly trampling 13-5.

Stiffler pulled his crew, 13-5, aside and told them, "We know our escape routes, we know what to do, and that is not it. We don't panic. We don't freak out." They went back to the buggy, back to another section of the containment line.

Lynn handed her saw to Whitney.

"I'm done," she said.

The Sand Fire burned almost forty thousand acres, required almost three thousand firefighters, and prompted the evacuation of ten thousand homes. But increased fires that burned longer and hotter were just one consequence of drought. Between 2010 and 2016, 102 million trees had died in California. In 2016 alone, 62 million trees died, an increase of 100 percent across the state from the previous year. Drier, weakened trees were more susceptible to disease and insect infestations. Citing the unprecedented tree die-off, Governor Jerry Brown declared a state of emergency and formed a Tree Mortality Task Force to help mobilize additional resources for the safe removal of dead and dying trees. The people who would remove those trees were federal wildland crews and inmate crews.

In July 2017, crew 13-3 arrived at base camp for the Detwiler Fire in Mariposa County. It had been reported on the afternoon of July 16, and within three hours the fire had spread to a thousand acres. By nightfall, it had nearly tripled, with zero containment. It had doubled again by the next morning. It was hot, dry, and windy, the beginning of what CAL FIRE had predicted would be a deadly season. Because of the rains, because of the tree die-off, because of the bark beetle. From camp, Lilli could see blackened hillsides, acres still smoldering, trees gnarled like witch's fingers, Half Dome and El Capitan shrouded in gray smoke.

Crew 13-3 had been cutting line for about ten days. Every night, women would find a spot where the burn was out. They'd level some dirt, scrape out the debris, then just lie down with a space blanket and sleep, using their backpacks as pillows. Their foreman did the same thing. If he was near the truck, he'd sleep in the truck. At this point, Lilli had worked her way up from bucking for Selena to dragspoon. Part of her job was to haul coolers of ice back and forth. On one trip, she heard a pop. Suddenly, she was in so much pain that her foreman told her to stop working and to relinquish her pack. She could barely move, and the pain from throwing out her back, then sleeping on the ground, then hiking through, was unbearable. She was lucky she had a foreman who told her to stop working. But the pain pulsated and reached every cell in her body, every thought in her brain. CDCR rarely talks about the deaths in the forestry program. The year after Shawna died, a man was crushed by a falling tree in Humboldt County; another inmate firefighter died two months later after accidentally cutting his leg and femoral artery with a chain saw. CDCR also almost never discloses injuries that occur. In November 2018, *Time* magazine reported that more than one thousand inmate firefighters required hospital care between June 2013 and August 2018.

"If I wouldn't have been in camp, my back would be okay, but nobody is gonna do anything about it. I have to live with it. It's just what you chose," Lilli told me after she was released. "I messed my back up and I didn't get treatment. They're not gonna replace my back."

12.

CDCR HEALTH CARE, A.K.A. "CRUEL AND UNUSUAL PUNISHMENT"

Once a week, COs from Malibu take inmates back to CIW on dental or health runs. The transport drives one route to Chino and a different one back, so that no one can intercept the vehicle. A return to CIW was always painful. When I was at CIW, a crew from Rainbow was there on a dental run. "I always up-talk the program. I want to recruit girls because it's a better way of life. We dread going back to CIW," one woman said to me. "You see it on the women's faces, on the staff's faces. It's just sad."

Carla told me she went to CIW regularly, because as second saw she "got oak a lot." The leaves were low to the ground or choking tree trunks in clusters of three, and sometimes blushed red. She could ID poison oak most of the time, but it didn't matter. If Carla was tasked with taking out shrubbery for a fire road, she had to cut through everything. Inmates worked rugged and overgrown terrain. That was the point: to take out the dry, flammable growth that blanketed the Santa Monica hills. On some hikes, Carla's skin grazed the leaves.

That meant at the end of a day, her forearms were marked in constellations of red, angry blisters. She got rashes all the time. She also got headaches from lack of sleep, backaches from carrying the saw, full body aches from hiking the trails. Aches that were exacerbated by morning physical training—the dropping down and popping up for burpees, the hundreds of crunches, the push-ups, squat jacks, and lunges.

When the pain was bad or she needed to see the dentist, Carla went back to CIW for medical checks. Correctional officers drove inmates in transport vans that were known as the dog vans because they were set up like kennel cages. Sitting in the back, Carla watched L.A. unfold with each freeway exchange, neighborhoods blurring together. They passed Paramount Ranch, then Malibu Canyon, Calabasas, Woodland Hills, Tarzana, Encino, Sherman Oaks, Studio City, Glendale, Eagle Rock, Pasadena, a Costco, Raging Waters water park, another Costco, Chino Hills, a golf course, and, finally, they arrived at CIW. A slow descent took them back to the Death Star sprawl of CIW, the prison that houses the second-largest population of female inmates in California. Carla remembered hearing COs talk during the drive. "They'd say things to us, 'You're lazy,' or 'You're never gonna do nothing,' or 'We're just overpaid babysitters.'"

Carla tried to ignore them. There were always other women in the back and they spoke among themselves, chattering about camp gossip, which COs were cruel, which ones might be lenient, which foremen pushed the hardest, which crew got away with the most. Carla liked Malibu better than Rainbow. She felt like one CO at Rainbow was punitive and harsh, especially toward Carla, when she didn't need to be. The women talked about her and what a bitch she was until they arrived at CIW. "Next thing you know, there she is walking at us furiously. She's like, 'If you have something to say, you could say it to my face.' And I just started laughing. I was like, Is this lady serious? Like what is the most that I can do without getting in trouble? I can't even call her a bitch to her face, I can't even tell her, You're so fucking mean all the time for no reason, because I'm going to get in trouble. She could write me up for that. I can lose time for that and stay extra time here because of that. 'Yeah, that's what I thought,' she said. She was trying to act so gangster."

Most inmates refer to the state prison system as "CDC," intentionally leaving out the *R*, for Rehabilitation, which was added by Governor Arnold Schwarzenegger in 2005. At the time, Schwarzenegger was attempting to rebrand the corrections and parole departments of California. He was hoping to start a new era of criminal justice reform after a report from the former governor George Deukmejian inspired the headline "California Corrections System Officially Declared Dysfunctional—Redemption Doubtful." In addition to the *R*, Schwarzenegger added $2 billion to the system's annual budget.

In reality, rehabilitation was hardly the foremost concern. Despite declining crime rates, two new prisons were scheduled to be built, and Schwarzenegger proudly announced them in his 2006 State of the State address. The additional budget wasn't used to rebuild the deteriorating women's forestry training center at CIW either; that work was done by inmates—in 2008, a CDCR carpentry apprenticeship training program demolished the facility used by female inmate firefighters. Fellow inmates replaced it with a new structure— they built the skeletal frame of the building, drywalled it, taped and textured the walls, painted, and installed the roof.

Schwarzenegger told inmates, "It has been a top priority of my administration to reform California's prison system by focusing on rehabilitation programs that will reduce recidivism and increase public safety. Both the carpenter training and firefighting programs give inmates skills to take their lives in new directions. These programs and the will of these women to improve their lives is what I want for as many inmates as possible, because it will make our communities safer and will save taxpayers billions of dollars in the long haul."

He was not wrong about how much the inmate firefighting program has saved taxpayers. In the thirteen years since his statement, CDCR estimates that the Conservation Camp program has saved the state at least $1.2 billion.

Many women told me they avoided medical and dental care in prison as much as possible. For good reason. CDCR has a long history of substandard care. In 2005, a federal court pronounced that CDCR's medical care of inmates violated the U.S. Constitution's prohibition of cruel and unusual punishment—a judge found that California's prisoners were subject to barbaric medical conditions in some prisons, resulting in as many as sixty-four preventable deaths of inmates a year and injury to many others. In response to a class action lawsuit filed in 2001 by the Prison Law Office, U.S. District Judge Thelton Henderson, citing conditions of "outright depravity," called for the California prison health care system to be placed under federal control and ordered a federal receiver to rectify the system. Judge Henderson said he was "driven in large measure by the stunning testimony that was uncontroverted that a prisoner in one of California's 32 prisons dies on average every 6 or 7 days as a result of malpractice, negligence, or some other deficiency in the State's medical care delivery system." The judge also noted that one witness for the state admitted, "The State hired anyone with a license and pulse and a pair of shoes." Another problem that court investigators found was that health-care staff were under the authority of security staff; guards were responsible for getting inmates to medical appointments, which often didn't happen.

In 2005, CDCR was providing health care to roughly 164,000 inmates at an annual cost of $1.1 billion. Two years later, in 2007, a state auditor's follow-up report still considered the CDCR a high-risk agency. In 2010, CDCR was relieved entirely of the responsibility of providing medical care to inmates. In a 2020 audit, inmates were accused by doctors of faking symptoms, and the Office of the Attorney General identified one prison where opioids were prescribed unnecessarily and substandard care was provided for diabetic patients. Today, California Correctional Health Care Services (CCHCS) provides care that includes medical, dental, and mental health services to California's prison inmate population at all thirty-five CDCR institutions statewide.

Even with an outside agency taking over medical care of California's incarcerated population, a 2013 project by the Center for Investigative Reporting (CIR) revealed that doctors under contract with the California prison system had sterilized nearly 150 incarcerated women without their permission or the required state approvals. Dr. James Heinrich, a contracted OB/GYN for CDCR, told CIR that the $147,460 the prison system paid doctors from 1997 to 2010 to perform sterilization procedures was minimal "compared to what you save in welfare paying for these unwanted children—as they procreated more."

In late 2015, just after Shawna transferred from Chino to Malibu, CIW was experiencing an epidemic of suicide and suicide attempts. According to CDCR, between 2013 and 2016, six women had killed themselves in the prison, and there had been seventy-three suicide attempts. The suicide rate at CIW was five times California's state average and four to five times the national state prison average for women.

The state senator Connie Leyva, whose district includes CIW, declared that she was going to call for "an audit" to "find out exactly what's going on" at CIW. By August 2017, the audit had found that the number of suicide attempts recorded at the two women's prisons in the study—CIW and Chowchilla—went from eighteen in 2012 to forty-nine in 2016. The audit documented a shortage of mental health staff, noting that almost one-third of the state's positions for psychiatrists were vacant. In addition, suicide prevention plans were inadequate: prison employees often missed required fifteen-minute check-ups on suicidal inmates and fabricated visits; prison staff failed to bring cut-down kits to three of fifteen hangings examined by auditors; and, on occasion, prison employees did not know how to relieve pressure on an inmate's throat during an attempted hanging. By the end of 2018, Governor Jerry Brown signed SB 960, legislation that required CDCR to submit an annual report cataloguing how the institution was dealing with its mental health crisis.

The next month, Dr. Michael Golding, the chief psychiatrist for California's prison system, leaked a 161-page report detailing mental health care failings observed within California's state prisons. The leaked report also included the fact that CDCR had been submitting cooked data to a judge in an attempt to regain independence after a 1990 class action lawsuit charged that the mental health practices within the prison system were inadequate. The conditions for the settlement of that lawsuit—thirty-one years ago—included court-ordered supervision of all mental health services within CDCR.

One observation in Golding's report concerned Inmate Patient X, a woman admitted to CIW on psychiatric medications and diagnosed psychotic. She refused to take her meds and, after two appointments with psychiatrists, was deemed in stable condition without her medication. Then, when her antipsychotics cycled out of her system, as they typically do, she experienced a psychotic episode. She was ordered to wear a strong gown, an article of clothing used to restrict movement, which she refused. She was isolated. The admitting psychologist did not consult the on-call psychiatrist because he assumed Inmate Patient X would refuse medication. Golding wrote that a psychologist with no medical training is not qualified to make this decision. For four hours, Inmate Patient X screamed every fifteen minutes as she lay face up on her back, pawing at her face. By the end of the fourth hour, she had used her left hand to gouge out her own left eye. Two correctional officers were called, and when she was asked to relinquish the eye, she swallowed it. Golding concluded, "The tragedy is that any competent psychiatric physician or general medical physician would have medicated the patient, and likely the patient's eye would still be in her head."

CDCR is responsible for the physical and mental health of all incarcerated firefighters who perform some of the most physically and mentally taxing jobs. Even professional firefighters in California suffer from the trauma of the job. In

2017, when California experienced some of the deadliest wild-fires in its history, more California firefighters died by suicide than in the line of duty.

⸺

All the women I spoke with could see the benefits of the fire-fighting program, but most bristled at the idea that they had volunteered. When an incarcerated individual is trying to avoid sexual assault, violence, trauma, mental and physical degradation, poor nutrition, solitary confinement, and retaliation, she might be looking for any alternative, she might even be willing to risk her life. The word "volunteer" is repeated on loop by COs and CDCR representatives. But "volunteer" is a relative term for the incarcerated.

PART IV

RELEASE

13.

ALISHA: ON TRIAL

The exterior of L.A. County's Superior Courthouse in Inglewood is industrial, mushroom, cement color, the same shade as Lynwood County Jail. Both buildings have imposing exteriors with slim recessed windows that look as if they barely let light in. Alisha's public defender, Conrad Barrington, bought her clothes to wear for trial. They were too small, so her dad, Eugene, got a second outfit—black slacks, a white shirt, and ballerina flats from Old Navy. Before each court appearance, Alisha would change from her County blues into civilian clothes. Giselle Chang, the district attorney prosecuting Alisha's case, was new to the office. She didn't offer a plea. Chang told Barrington, who told Alisha and her dad, that she was planning to take this case to trial with a jury. In 2013, only 2 percent of felony cases were settled by trial. Of the 2 percent of cases that were resolved by jury trials, 81 percent resulted in felony convictions, 4 percent resulted in misdemeanor convictions, and 14 percent resulted in acquittal, dismissal, or transfers.

On Thursday, October 17, 2019, the first day of jury

selection for Alisha's trial, Judge Vincent Okamoto, seventy-five, a former DA, a Vietnam War vet, and a two-time novelist who was born in an Arizona internment camp to Japanese immigrant parents, told the pool of jurors at midday, "I'm going to release you early to get a jump on the freeway, have you come back tomorrow at 1:30, at which time I'll introduce you to the attorneys, and the parties, and we'll begin jury selection . . . please drive carefully." Alisha changed from her court outfit back to her blues, then she was hand-cuffed and transported back to Lynwood. For the first two and a half days of Alisha's five-day trial, Chang and Barrington negotiated jury selection. Some prospective jurors were dismissed because they were related to cops, socialized with cops, or empathized with cops; others because they'd been robbed. One was dismissed because he didn't believe in California's Three Strikes sentencing laws and said that would influence whatever conclusion he came to about the crime. Some were sick; others claimed financial hardship. No one was dismissed who claimed a loss of income while serving on the jury.

Finally, on Monday afternoon, Judge Okamoto explained the proceedings to the jury. There would be opening statements, witnesses, evidence, facts, references to laws, objections sustained, objections overruled. He told the jury, "You must not be influenced by sentiment, passion, or prejudice, public opinion, or public feeling." After more detailed explanations regarding court procedure, Okamoto asked Chang if she wished to make an opening statement. She did.

"Exactly one year ago, October 21, 2018, it's about 1:45 in the afternoon, Mr. Lloyd Quiggle was at home in his residence on Thirty-Second Place in Manhattan Beach and his wife, Patricia Ziegler, was also home." Their house, a taupe,

Mediterranean-style, three-story 2,240-square-foot residence, was located a block and a half from the location where beach volleyball was invented. At the time, the house was worth more than $3 million, not as much as the oceanfront mansions a block away, along the Strand. Chang continued, "Mr. Quiggle went outside in the back of the house. And he noticed that a ladder had been moved and placed—leaned against the house, reaching the first level of scaffolding, and as he was walking back there, he heard the sound of glass breaking. So, he ran around to the front of the house and called out to his wife, Ms. Ziegler, to come out, and she came out of the front of the garage. And as they were coming around to the front of the house, they saw the defendant scrambling down the scaffolding in the front of the house, wearing a painters' outfit, carrying a crowbar. Mr. Quiggle shouted to her to stop, but she took off running. So, she started running and he started chasing her and he told his wife, 'Call the police.' So, he chased her up to Manhattan Avenue"—a block east where "she made a turn. They went back down toward the Strand. And at some point, the defendant stopped at a—behind a wall near the Strand. And Mr. Quiggle caught up with her. And she took off the painter's outfit, and he—Mr. Quiggle had his phone out, and he snapped a picture of the defendant." Chang went on to tell the jury that she would call Quiggle and Ziegler and the police officers who arrived on scene as witnesses. She said, "The jury selection process has been long and drawn out, but once the evidence starts, the trial will move very quickly. So, I ask that you pay close attention, listen to what the witnesses say, and at the end of this trial, I will come before you again and ask that you find the defendant guilty." Barrington made no opening statement.

When Quiggle took the stand and spoke, he first identified Alisha as the person he witnessed on the scaffolding outside his house. He then was presented with photographic evidence that supported the state's argument—a picture of the broken window at his residence, a picture of his residence, and the photo Quiggle took of Alisha. She was standing over the painter's coveralls described by Chang, wearing gloves, olive green skinny jeans, a white T-shirt, and black flats. Not the kind of shoes you would wear if you anticipated a foot chase. Her wavy brown hair hit the middle of her back and was pulled back in a half ponytail. From the angle it looks like Quiggle shot the photo from several feet above. "I noticed she was there on the patio taking off the white overalls," Quiggle said. "I readied my camera. My purpose was to try to get a picture of her. I wanted to help the authorities try to apprehend her, so I said, 'Hey,' or something. Snapped a picture." Quiggle had jumped the wall to chase Alisha, fracturing his foot. Chang asked Quiggle if the defendant ever said anything to him. "She said, 'Sorry, sir.'"

The state called Patricia Ziegler as its second witness. She confirmed her husband's testimony, adding that when she saw the figure jump from the scaffolding, she was surprised it was a woman. During cross-examination, Ziegler said that she had heard a noise from the side of her house, jumped up, and ran downstairs to see if her husband was okay. She saw Alisha; she saw Quiggle chase Alisha. Then, she went back in the house, locking the glass door behind her, and inspected the damage. Barrington asked Ziegler what she saw—a broken window on the third floor—and the next day she saw the cuts in the screens. Judge Okamoto dismissed the jury, as he had every day since the trial began: "Drive carefully, folks."

The next day, Chang called her last witness to testify—Jesse Garcia, the Manhattan Beach police officer who had arrived on scene when Ziegler called. Garcia identified the three pieces of evidence he found at the brick wall where Quiggle snapped the picture: the coveralls, a ventilator, and a crowbar. He also testified that after examining the house, "Based on seeing how the window was shattered, I formed an opinion that the window was shattered with a blunt object such as the crowbar found behind that little brick wall."

On cross-examination, Barrington asked the officer, "When you got the ventilator, the jumpsuit, and the crowbar and booked them into evidence, did you look for fingerprints on them?"

"No," Garcia said.

Then Barrington asked how involved Garcia was in the case after the initial day of the robbery.

Chang objected to the line of questioning; Okamoto overruled her objection.

"The only portion that I had in this investigation was to take the initial statements and collect the evidence found at the scene," Garcia said.

"Do you have any personal knowledge as to two other individuals who were arrested in connection with this case?" Barrington asked.

"Yes."

"Do you know who those individuals were?" Barrington asked.

"Not by name," Garcia answered.

"But you were aware that there were two other individuals that were arrested," Barrington said.

"Correct."

"Nothing further," Barrington said.

The People rested their case.

The first witness Barrington called was Alisha. She had never testified in court before and was nervous. She didn't trust Barrington. And she didn't trust the jury. She knew how the facts of the case looked; and she agreed with most of the prosecution's assertions. She was on the scaffolding; she broke the window; she was wearing the coveralls; she ran from Quiggle; she changed her clothing; and she evaded arrest. She also knew that the jury would hear about her two prior convictions. Before the trial had even begun, she asked if she might qualify for a mental health diversion. When she was fifteen, she had been admitted to a rehab facility where she was diagnosed with ADD and clinical depression. At the time her mom thought she exhibited symptoms of bipolar disorder, but because Alisha was also smoking meth and drinking, it was hard to identify the source of her mood swings.

"I thought her childhood was good—she was on swim team and water polo at Millikan High School. Maybe junior year she started doing drugs," Alisha's father, Eugene, told me. "I don't do drugs. My wife didn't do drugs." In fact, Eugene worked for the Los Angeles Police Department. He worried about Alisha and sent her to several rehab facilities; she went to AA meetings, NA meetings, group therapy, therapy with her parents. A psychiatrist prescribed meds, which she took, until she didn't. They made her feel lethargic and foggy, the opposite of how she felt when she went to Long Beach parties. About a year after Alisha graduated from high school, she enrolled in community college. Eugene bought her books, but she never went to class.

On the witness stand, Alisha spoke softly. Barrington asked the jury if they could hear her. Alisha described the night before the crime—October 20, 2018, almost a year after she'd been released from fire camp. She was homeless, crashing occasionally in motel rooms. A friend she met at Port, a woman on a different crew, introduced Alisha to two men. The foursome spent the night drinking and smoking meth. Barrington asked if this was something Alisha had done before.

"On and off for the last fifteen years," she said.

"And has that meth habit had an effect on your life?" Barrington asked.

"It led me to being incarcerated," Alisha said.

"Why were you in prison?" Barrington asked.

"In 2013, I was arrested for burglaries, six counts of burglary."

"Were you convicted of those counts?"

"Yes."

"Were those burglary offenses related to your meth addiction?"

"Yes."

"So, how were they related to your meth addiction?"

"I was young. I was a lot younger. And I didn't—I just was thinking about what I could do to support my habit at that time in my life."

"I assume you were not smoking meth while you were in prison?"

"No. I was sober. I paroled from fire camp. And I was in the process of getting a job with Santa Monica—as a firefighter after I paroled."

"After you got out of prison, were you using methamphetamine?"

"I slowly started going back, yes."

"As of October 21, 2018, you were obviously using meth. Were you using it regularly by that point?"

"Yes."

"So, you stayed the night with these two individuals, Louis and Joseph?"

"Yes."

"And were they still there in the morning?"

"Yes. Joseph had told me that it was Louis's birthday and they wanted to go party down by the beach."

"What were you planning to do down at the beach?"

"To go—to continue. We bought a bottle of alcohol. They had a bottle of alcohol, and so we were gonna go drink down by the beach."

"You were going to drink. Is that all?"

"Yes."

"And again, these are the two people that you had just met?"

"Yes."

The motel where they stayed was in Bellflower, just east of Compton, close to the Los Angeles River, an aqueduct that usually ran dry. That morning the foursome piled into Louis's white sedan and drove toward the beach. Louis stopped at Home Depot in Paramount, explaining that he needed to buy something for his mom. Alisha got out of the car and smoked a cigarette while she waited. Once Louis was done shopping, he placed the bag into the trunk of his car. Alisha couldn't see what was in it; she didn't really care. They were beach-bound and continuing the party.

In the back seat, she constructed a water bong out of two plastic bottles. They still had some meth to smoke and tequila to drink. Alisha took four or five shots of tequila and a couple of hits of meth on the way to Manhattan Beach, about a thirty-minute drive west, depending on traffic. Louis parked on a small street just a couple of blocks from the ocean. They continued to drink and smoke, then drove a few blocks to the house on Thirty-Second Place.

Alisha told the courtroom that Louis said, "I have an idea. I want to rob a house." He pointed to Quiggle and Ziegler's house.

Alisha laughed.

"I don't know why you're laughing," he said. He knew what Alisha had been arrested for—her friend from Port had told him.

"Bitch, don't play dumb with me. You've been smoking for free. It's time for you to go make some money," Louis said. Alisha said she wouldn't. She had an eight-year-old daughter; she had been arrested when her daughter was just one year old. She knew if she was caught attempting a robbery on parole, it would be her third strike. Alisha said Louis hit her, then took a crowbar and pinned her against the side of the car from the driver's seat, choking her.

"You're gonna do it," he said.

On the witness stand, Alisha told Barrington and the jury, "I was scared for my life." Alisha went on to describe how Louis retrieved the painter's suit, the crowbar, and the ventilation mask from the trunk. "He had me by the hair, I started putting on the painter's suit and then he pointed to me and said, 'Get in the house.'" She walked toward the scaffolding and noticed that there were people inside. She thought she saw lights on and heard voices, but she was afraid to return to the car. A diversion was the only thing she could think of. So, she scrambled up the scaffolding.

"The best line of thinking I had was to create a loud noise. I'm high. I'm under the influence. I just didn't know what to do. I just hit a big window to create a large noise so somebody would hear me," Alisha said.

"Okay. Now, you committed burglaries before, you told me?" Barrington asked.

"Yes."

"When you committed those burglaries, did you create loud noises?"

"No."

"Did you often commit burglaries in the middle of the day?"

"No."

"Would you commit burglaries on the spur of the moment just without any planning?"

"No."

"Would you commit burglaries without a partner that you trust?"

"No."

"Would you do it by yourself?"

"No."

"I assume, you wouldn't commit burglaries in the houses where there were people inside?"

"No."

Barrington's defense was that Alisha was such an accomplished burglar, this bungled attempt couldn't possibly have been her plan; that she was forced to do it. Alisha broke the window and jumped from the scaffolding, and when she saw Quiggle race around the corner of his house, she said "I'm sorry" and ran in the opposite direction from where Louis had parked. Barrington asked if she had a plan in mind. Alisha shook her head.

"To get away from him," she said.

"To get away from Mr. Quiggle?"

"To get away from Louis."

"Why didn't you ask Mr. Quiggle for help?"

"Because I just broke his window. I'm on parole. I have a crowbar in my hand and I'm in a painter's suit."

During cross-examination, Chang repeated the series of events but implied that Alisha went inside the Home Depot with Louis, was not threatened physically, and was responsible for cutting the screens. Alisha denied all three points.

Chang went on to say, "You pleaded to six counts, six different separate residential burglaries; is that right?"

"Yes."

"So, you were charged with—in the case where you were convicted back in 2013, you were charged, in fact, with nine different counts, and you pleaded to six counts of residential burglary; is that right?"

"Yes."

"And you said there was a codefendant in some of those counts. But isn't it also true that for one of the counts that you pleaded to, you were the only person charged?"

"I was unaware of the package deal that—what counts he pleaded to too, but he was present."

"And then besides for the residential burglaries that you already talked about, on direct examination, back in 2007, you were also convicted—back in 2007, you were convicted of a first-degree residential burglary; is that right?"

"Yes, it is."

"And that one also, with that case, you were also convicted of a grand theft of a firearm; is that right?"

"Yes, it is."

"I have no further questions."

What Chang did not ask Alisha about was her service to the state. Between her second conviction and this trial, she was a firefighter. She'd go out on megafires, populated by hundreds of federal crews, hotshots, helitacks, local engines, municipal crews. For three seasons, she went from digging dirt with a Pulaski to becoming a swamper, the leader. She hiked, she dug, she cut. She, like almost all the women I interviewed, worked so many fires she couldn't recall an exact number. But she remembered the soot that coated her nostrils after an out-of-county, how the smoke affected the way food tasted for days. How her body ached. How she could never wash away the ash. She remembered the smell and the choke of the air. But she also remembered the gratitude she felt to be in a position to help. Kids made signs on posterboard; families made cakes. She remembered the discipline of camp. How at Port, there were no drugs, there was no alcohol, it was a notoriously clean camp. She remembered how the structure and the militaristic demands of the job forced her to remain sober. But in this courtroom, only her past as a criminal counted.

The defense rested its case and Okamoto excused the jury for a fifteen-minute recess.

"Ladies and gentlemen, I told you that you'd have to come back tomorrow to closing arguments of counsel. Well, in the interim, they sent us five more cases that I need to call. This case will be concluded tomorrow. I'll give you final instructions. You'll hear final arguments on the part of the jury. And then tomorrow, this case will be submitted to you for your deliberation and verdict. So again, thank you folks for your patience. I want you back two o'clock tomorrow. We'll wind this thing up. Thank you very much. Drive carefully," Okamoto said.

Chang's closing argument hinged on the concept of what is reasonable. "How reasonable is it that someone, when someone was supposedly just threatened for their life, once they had removed themselves from distance from that alleged threatener, they didn't immediately run. That is not reasonable. How reasonable is it, if someone had actually just been physically assaulted, that they would not immediately tell the person that they first encountered, 'Hey, help me. I'm in danger.' So the question for you is what is the reasonable conclusion that you can draw from the evidence . . . Is it reasonable that she was so afraid for her life, that by the time she managed to get to the house, which she testified was some distance away from the car, she didn't immediately run? Is it reasonable that she decided, you know what, I'm gonna now go to a portion of the house where I'm completely out of their view, and at that point, I'm not gonna run. How reasonable is it that she thought, you know, I'm gonna create a diversion by breaking a window on the third floor . . . If she really believed her life was in immediate danger, . . . she would have run. If she really believed her life was in immediate danger, the moment Mr. Quiggle said, 'Hey,' she would have said, 'Help me.' If she really believed she was in immediate danger when both Mr. Quiggle and Ms. Ziegler were there, she would have asked for their help. Instead she ran. She ran. She ran. And she ran . . . The only reasonable conclusion is that the defendant is guilty of all these crimes and I ask that you find her guilty. Thank you."

Barrington argued in closing that Alisha "is an experienced burglar. The prosecutor did emphasize that. She had apparently nine counts of burglary back in 2013. What does that mean? That means that, apparently, she went on a burglary spree six years ago and was successful nine times before she got caught. Apparently, to some extent, she and this compatriot she was working with knew what they were doing. The prosecutor said this was a sophisticated burglary, that she had a painter's outfit and a ventilator and she was trying to impersonate somebody who was supposed to be there apparently. Was this a sophisticated crime? Does this sound to you like the work of a sophisticated cat burglar? It's 1:30 in the afternoon on Sunday. Manhattan Beach is a very crowded area where the houses are right next to each other." Barrington went on to describe the two men involved in the robbery. "You've been instructed that you're not to take into account the fact that these two people aren't on trial with Alisha. But you're allowed to speculate why the prosecutor didn't mention them at all during her case. The prosecutor didn't mention them in her case, and it was unusual. It didn't come out until the defense stated that there were two other people arrested with Alisha. It wasn't even mentioned. She clearly didn't want you to know anything about these two individuals." Half of Barrington's closing argument reminded the jury of Alisha's current and previous crimes. "As a juror, please remember, Alisha isn't on trial for all the bad stuff that the prosecutor was piling on top of her, stuff she openly admitted to, stuff like smoking meth, possessing meth, being with meth smokers, leaving the scene of a crime, running away from Mr. Quiggle. She is not on trial for her previous criminal history. She is not on trial for the things that she has done before. Just this. Don't go back there and find her guilty because you don't agree with what she was doing with her lifestyle. Don't convict her because you don't think she is a good person." Chang's final rebuttal ended with the sentence, "She ran because she knew she was guilty."

The jury deliberated for fifteen minutes and reentered the courtroom. Alisha stood. The foreperson announced a verdict: guilty on all four charges: vandalism, possession of burglar's

tools, attempted first-degree burglary, and first-degree burglary. Judge Okamoto thanked the jury for their service:
"You've been a great jury. We've reconvened after lunch at 1:30
for five days in a row. No one has gone to sleep. We appreciate
that." A date was set for sentencing; Alisha was turned over
to the custody of the sheriff's department and driven back to
County.

Four months later, Barrington, Chang, Okamoto, and Alisha met in Inglewood for sentencing. Barrington said Alisha
was sorry and that this offense was obviously drug-related.
He introduced her father, Eugene, to read a statement. Eugene
believed the words he wrote, but it was impossible for him to believe Alisha. He felt like for years he'd been lied to. For years,
he and his wife had shifted retirement plans to take care of
Alisha's daughter, Kayleigh, to try to explain to Kayleigh why
her father was AWOL and her mother was incarcerated. They
became her legal guardians; took her to Germany; took her on
cruises; brought her to swim practice and gymnastics; when
the pools closed, they bought her a wetsuit and boogie board
for ocean swimming; sent her to Georgia to see her cousins and
uncle. Eugene was embarrassed. He had worked in the LAPD
for thirty-five years and instead of bragging about his daughter's accomplishments, he was delivering testimony to shorten
his daughter's sentence on a third strike. "You like to talk about
your kids and how they're doing. I don't get to talk about my
daughter, my daughter who's in prison," he told me. Instead, he
read the following: "This is my daughter, Alisha. She does have
a daughter who is eight years old, which myself and my wife
take care of. My daughter is a good person, but I can tell the
court that she is an addict. I've been dealing with her and her
addiction in and out of rehab since she was sixteen, seventeen

years of age in high school. She has a drug problem. Thank you, Your Honor." Even though the statement was formal and brief, Alisha felt warmth. Her father's testimony meant more to her than it did to the court.

Chang read a statement from Ziegler; it was a letter Ziegler wrote to Alisha and she had asked it be read in court at sentencing.

Alisha, I thought about you often over the last year, wondering where you are going with your life and your choices. I've also wondered why you decided to break into our house on October 21, 2018. What would you have done to us if you had been successful? Are you a violent person? These are the scars that you left on us on that day. My husband crushed his ankle chasing you and needed surgery. It took months for him to be able to walk again. His foot is still numb and he has pain so he is reminded of you daily. The window you broke has damaged the floor in the stairwell and landing on the third floor of the living area. I think of you every time I walk up the stairs and see the gouges in the wood that could not be corrected properly. We both still jump when we hear a loud crash. It is an instant flashback to the window breaking. Actually, my heart is breaking now as I write this statement to you. We installed cameras and shutters in the back of the house because it does not feel safe to be in our own home without additional protection. We are hyper vigilant about locking the doors, putting the alarm on and watching people more closely. I grew up on a farm in central Illinois where we never locked our doors and never felt fearful like I do now. I'm not sure where the consequences of your choices will take you, but I pray for you, Alisha. I pray that somehow you will see that this life you've chosen for yourself is very destructive to yourself and to others who are victims. Hopefully, you will figure out another way to reinvent yourself.

Chang asked for thirty-six years to life. It was Alisha's third strike. Okamoto sentenced Alisha to thirty-six years to life in a state prison.

14.

SONYA: LIFE ON PAROLE

felt like an idiot because it happened every time. And with Sonya, it happened again. Of course I didn't recognize her. She had on makeup and jeans and a T-shirt and looked striking. Her hair was braided and her eye shadow was ombre-ed out like it had been applied by a professional. I remembered how adamant she was when we spoke on the fire road in Malibu. She was clear about what it looked like to be a Black woman, imprisoned, digging roads for the state. Now, in Escondido, we were eating burgers and fries at the Jack in the Box across the street from her job at the Dollar Tree. After we ate, we sat on the steps outside, on East Valley Parkway. It was blindingly sunny and hot for February. We talked about camp, sober living, fires, her kids, and vaping.

"I was smoking a pack or two packs of Marlboro Reds 100s every couple days at sober living and it was expensive," she said. "So, I started vaping. The only thing I spend money on is the coil, the glass, which is this piece right here, because I'm constantly dropping it, and the juice. It ends up costing about thirty-five dollars a month." She exhaled a sweet combination of Melon Milkshake and Incredible Hulk. It smelled like a puff of watermelon candy.

Sonya told me that if she went back to Riverside, she'd end up in prison again. "I chose to come out here because I needed different people, places, and things, a different environment," she said. She said that there was no way she would parole to a homeless shelter; she couldn't bear the idea of living in a shelter again. "My county, Riverside, it's hard for anybody to get out and actually succeed. There are not many resources out there for parolees. So, when I paroled, I went to a program, and I did ninety days in a treatment program, and I did another ninety days sober living." Sonya knew no one in Escondido, and that was by design. During the first thirty days in her treatment program, she was on blackout—no communication outside the facility, no leaving the building either. She went to group, she ate, she slept. She knew that she'd get "three hots and a cot." Three hot meals and a place to sleep. She could talk about her triggers, her feelings, she could talk about the "shit that you have buried deep inside that you don't even know you got stuffed in there, that could make you who you are today." She liked the groups. She liked the work. In those first thirty days she spent a lot of time in the rec room. Counselors would bring in movies. She watched *Black Panther*, *Thor: Ragnarok*, *Avengers: Infinity War*—all the movies she missed when she was in prison.

When Sonya could, she watched the news, specifically any segment about wildfires. July 2018, when Sonya paroled, was a record month for wildfire. A few weeks before, she was on those fires, camped out at night, cutting line, sometimes twenty-four hours straight. Now, she watched from the shared living room. Local reporters cut to video of charred destruction, scenes from the Carr Fire in Shasta County. Homes reduced to ash. Wind-whipped flames moving without regard to logic. Crowns of seventy-foot trees on fire, raining embers. Ruptured gas lines hissing in the background. A front that raged through the city center of Redding, jumped the Sacramento River, and engulfed a subdivision as sparks blew five and six miles ahead, creating spot fires. After a few days, media fixated on the centerpiece of this fire's destruction—the firenado, a vortex caused by a clash of fire, heat, and wind so extreme it created its own weather system. The firenado reached forty thousand feet in height. The system had a diameter of a thousand feet at its base, and was 2,700 degrees. Fire analysts compared it to EF3 and EF4 tornadoes. It spun, fueling its own power, chewing away at whatever was left to burn. It burned through mixed-conifer forest—California black oak, knobcone pine, manzanita, and annual understory. Sonya watched as Governor Jerry Brown, once again, declared a state of emergency, just like when she was on the Thomas Fire. The Carr Fire was faster and hotter than any that fire officials had seen; it represented what they called "the new normal." On news segments, local channels reported that crews from Australia, New Zealand, and all across the nation had been flown in to assist, all while inmate crews worked the line in their oranges in the background.

Sonya missed fighting fire, but she was glad she wasn't on this one. On her last fire, Sonya caught an out-of-county: the Thomas Fire. As predicted, the wet rainy season in 2017 led to a devastating fire season. When they arrived a couple of hours north of camp, Malibu crews didn't know what was already being reported—that the Thomas Fire was raging through Santa Barbara and Ventura Counties. During the first night, on December 4, five hundred residences were destroyed.

"That was a scary fucking situation. We were driving around trying to find a place to get in, to start fighting this fire. But because of the wind, the vegetation, everything surrounding the area, there was no starting point," Sonya said. "Fire has a mind of its own. It's such a beautiful natural disaster, and I would look at it and think how cool it is. But then you look a little harder and you're like, damn. You don't expect it, but it's a trip." It took five days for them to find a way in to fight the flames. Meanwhile, the fire engulfed more homes, surrounding and swallowing entire neighborhoods. In the first forty-eight hours, the fire began burning through the jagged Santa Ynez Mountains, threatening small communities along the Rincon Coast north of Ventura and spreading relentlessly into the Los Padres National Forest. "There were times when we were on top of the mountain looking for hot spots and spot fires, and we'd see a twister—a fire twister. All of sudden, it would go up. Everything would be bright one minute and then dark the next. We'd be like, boss, shut the fuck up. And then we'd have to go into it, hike towards it," Sonya said. For two weeks, they cut and sweat through what was, at the time, the largest wildfire in modern California history.

Sonya worked her way through the ridges of Ventura County, but she knew the reality of fire. "There is no way you can be protected from a fire. Like, seriously. We have our fire cover, but as far as, like, anything else, fire is an element. There is no way you can beat an element. You're not God. If it's your time to go, it's your time to go. That's how I honestly look at life. If it's my time, it's my time, no matter what I'm doing," Sonya said. "Do they train us to be safe at all times? Hell motherfuckin' yeah. They tell us our 10s and 18s. We have our watch-outs, we have our workouts, and we have everything.

We are forced to become aware of things at all times. You notice the wind, the wind changes, you know, you can feel it. And, if that fire is right there, and you see, even if it just moves just one way slightly different, you know, okay, this is what's gonna happen next." They secured homes, they arrived on scene to mop up, digging blackened earth to make sure no embers were left. And if they saw embers, they pounded them out.

The work was hard and dangerous. And not just for the inmates. The Thomas Fire was Sonya's last fire with Foreman John Brondyke. After the Thomas Fire, Brondyke was hospitalized. CDCR wouldn't tell the women what happened, but there were rumors. He had a lung infection; it was so severe that it was touch and go. They couldn't reach out. Fire and smoke came for everyone—inmate, captain, or foreman.

By the time the Thomas Fire was contained, it had burned 440 square miles, roughly 282,000 acres, and caused $2.2 billion in damage. Fire experts and armchair climate analysts noted the timing—it was a savage fire that began in what used to be the off-season, almost a month after seasonal wildland firefighters are let go from crews. Typically, rains came to Southern California in December, but in the past fifty years climate change has shifted weather patterns dramatically. November and December can still be dangerous and deadly months for wildfire in Southern California. The Carr Fire burned 230,000 acres, destroyed sixteen hundred structures, and caused more than $1.6 billion in damage. A week later, the Mendocino Complex Fire broke out, and Sonya watched that too. By the time her sixty days were up, the Mendocino fire was contained to 460,000 acres, the largest wildfire in California since record keeping began in 1932. News anchors kept repeating the same statistics: four out of seven of the largest fires in California happened between 2013 and 2018 and nine out of ten of the largest fires in California happened between 2007 and 2018. The new normal was megafires.

Sonya missed her crew, she missed being pushed to the brink with work and being physically challenged. She missed cutting line, beginning at a chunk of unruly brush and clearing it to mineral soil. But she did not miss feeling exploited. "I believe the work that those girls do, the work that I did, we should have gotten paid more. You know what I'm saying? Like the work itself, I appreciated the gratitude that I got from it. It's good. But we literally put ourselves on the line." But camp was structure. In the weeks before her release, Sonya worried that without the wake-up times, the meal times, the PT, the hikes, the cutting line, the days that were not hers to plan, that it would be hard for her to adjust to freedom. She worried about getting a job. But her goal remained the same: she wanted to be with her kids, she wanted to be a family and to figure out how to make her life a part of theirs. "It's crazy to go from being in prison, serving your time, to coming out and you're, like, literally on your own, you're just, like, what the hell? Where do I start?" Sonya started with a job—while she was waiting for a background check to clear after applying to the grocery store Sprouts, she picked up work at the Dollar Tree near the apartment she shared with a friend she met at the treatment facility.

When Sonya met with her PO once a month, he'd ask how she was doing. What she was up to. She'd list the groups—the many groups that she went to for support. AA meetings, NA meetings, women's meetings, where she'd talk about surviving toxic relationships, abuse, addiction, where others would listen and talk too. She talked about how she wished she'd seen the red flags in her marriage—the mental and physical abuse. She talked about her own addiction—the cocaine. She told her PO it was nice to have the support of women who were twenty-five and thirty-five years sober, people she could call when she wasn't working. She told her PO about the job at Dollar Tree. "My feet hit the pavement like a jackrabbit, I've been running, cause I don't want to make the mistake and fuck up again. You know what I mean, like it hurt my kids too much to be gone for that long."

She worked, went home, watched Netflix, went to groups. That was all. Her parole officer told her that her case was easy. "I don't do anything. I don't fuck up. I stay out of trouble. I comply with everything that they ask me to do. I don't plan on going back to prison anytime soon." She picked up as many shifts as she could within her status as part-time, open availability. She unloaded U-boats (carts that held boxes of inventory) at 5:00 a.m., unpacked freight during the 2:00 p.m. shift, worked the floor. With little notice, her manager asked her to come in at all hours. Sonya picked up around thirty-two hours a week at $11.50 per hour. It was hard for her to go from "damn near busting my ass for two dollars a day and be grateful" to working for $11.50 an hour and be grateful for that. "I am not sinking, nor am I swimming. I'm just barely floating." She felt underpaid in the camps, and underpaid once she'd been released. Sonya was trying to save up for her own apartment, to pay bills, to provide for her three kids, but money was always tight. "There's times when I just want all of my kids with me, but at the same time I can't have them with me right now." Not while she was still on parole. "Because of my actions and consequences, I get that, but we'll be brought back together. Right now, I need to focus on me. I gotta get me together because I can't be a good mom to them if I'm still fucked up in the head." Her oldest, now out of the foster care system, remembered the night when their family was broken up. When her parents were arrested. She was thirteen, and was immediately sent to group homes until she was placed with a family. "Nobody beat me up mentally better than I could beat myself up about this shit. Like I remember for a full year straight, I would ask my daughter to forgive me. And she'd be like, 'Mama, I forgive you. I love you. I'll never *forget*. But I love you.' I have to swallow that, there'd be times when I'd just be hiking and I'd cry. You know, just talking to God. Just, like, letting it all out."

15.

MARQUET: PREP WORK TO PULPIT TO FIRE SCHOOL

Marquet didn't want to leave fire camp at all. "I just felt like that's where God wanted me to be. I wanted to do all my time there, but I felt like my time was up. I got what I got out of it," Marquet told me. Marquet read about the seasons of the Bible and realized she was in a season. "When you try to stay in a season too long, you stunt your own growth." In February 2018, Marquet transferred from Rainbow to the CCTRP facility in San Diego, about a half hour from Marquet's aunt Sue's house in Southeast. It was a low-slung building with sliding windows, painted institutional pale yellow and peach, housing a couple dozen women. With its sloped roof, common area, and kitchen, it looked like some approximation of a home. She was required to wear an ankle monitor.

The routines of the CCTRP house made each day feel just like the day before. Marquet met with a counselor to look for minimum-wage jobs, and the schedule was stacked with groups—drug addiction groups, life groups, counseling groups, church groups, more addiction groups. CCTRP wasn't for everyone—a few months after Marquet moved in, another member walked out. She busted her ankle monitor and never showed up for her restaurant job. She was on the lam for six days, until she turned herself in and was sent back to CIW. Marquet was okay with life at CCTRP, but it was the opposite of fire camp. After landing a minimum-wage job at a fancy pizza restaurant in downtown San Diego, she realized how much she missed cutting. Now, she worked, she went to group, she went to group, she went to more group, and she slept. The monotony was reinforced by the lack of freedom. She was aware that the people she lived with were tired of her stories: all she could talk about was fire. She compared everything to camp, and to working in the woods. She missed her sister crew, the adrenaline, the feeling she got when she pulled and bucked, the satisfaction of a clean line. "I loved fire camp, I love fire," she'd say. She continued to tithe, sending money to the Bayview Baptist Church. While CCTRP was far from perfect, Marquet, the same Marquet who had been declared ineligible for fire camp in 2014, was staring at a release date: November 2018, only a few months away.

The first thing she did after release was go to her sister's house and squeeze her two kids. She could feel a future—football practices, good grades, bad grades, messy rooms, wild behavior, buying presents, meals together, what she had imagined when she was in prison. Then, she went to church. As often as she could. She participated in any way she could—the choir, community outreach, homeless services, super gospel performances, food drives. Every Sunday, she sang in three services, starting at 6:45 a.m. When she wasn't at church, she was living in a halfway home, watching movies on Pureflix, the Evangelical Christian answer to Netflix. She liked most of their programming, but *Fireproof*, starring Kirk Cameron as a firefighter fighting to save his marriage, was her favorite.

A few months after Marquet paroled, I met her at church on Sunday. Bayview was a lively place and it skewed young. The three DJs and eight singers were mic-ed up, red lights were flashing, and banners proclaimed "Come Enjoy the View," and "You're My Everything," and "Victory Belongs to Jesus." They had a YouTube channel, a livestream on Facebook, and Pastor T, a buoyant, funny preacher who conferenced in dial-in prayers every morning at 6:15 a.m. He greeted everyone, including me. He was young, handsome, spear bald, and exuberant. He wore a black T-shirt that read, "HBCUs Matter." "Good morning, streamers, good morning, Facebook, good morning, military personnel." He bounced in his bedazzled, tricolor slip-on sneakers, dancing with the choir director, who occasionally broke out into the Running Man. And he reminded the audience that to accept Jesus Christ, everyone could text "iBelieve" or "iUnite" to the church's main number. "How can y'all sit out there and NOT move when we're moving this way up here?" The stage pulsated in perfectly coordinated lighting and the choir jumped with each flick of the choir director's wrist. Marquet, who was already backstage when I arrived, sang in the semicircle behind the three lead singers. After an hour of announcements and music, Pastor T launched into his sermon. He spoke in a manner that could excite heart palpitations and devotion, without being entirely linear in his thoughts. He started by talking about *Thor: Ragnarok* and compared Thor to Moses. ("Y'all know who Thor is, he's a superhero, kind of looks like me except he's white, longer hair.") Behind Pastor T, Marquet sang, full-throated and swaying side to side. After his sermon, two members of the church, Safrina and Debra, climbed halfway up the display behind the stage. They dipped down into water to be baptized in front of the congregation. And with the shock of cold water, they accepted the Father, the Son, and the Holy Ghost.

After several months, Marquet quit her job at the pizza place. She worked two new jobs: one at an event space, Prado, in downtown San Diego, another prepping food at a Middle Eastern fast-casual restaurant named Tahini. The bus ride from Tahini was an hour and a half. If a party went past midnight at Prado, she'd walk home, two hours. She picked up as many hours as she had to give. While saving up for her own place, she also paid for basketball and football leagues for her kids. Six months after paroling, she was still living in the halfway house, with parolees upstairs, those on probation downstairs. There was a yard for smokers, a 5:00 p.m. curfew on weeknights, and an 8:00 p.m. curfew on Friday and Saturday. If you could prove you were at work or school, the curfews didn't apply. She shared a room with someone she knew from Rainbow.

Six months after paroling, Marquet enrolled in fire school to earn an associate's degree at San Diego Miramar College. She worried that the choice would seem selfish, that her kids wouldn't understand why she wanted a career that would send her to faraway places, especially after she'd been gone for so long. As we drove to Walmart to get fire boots for her program, she told me she hoped her kids would forgive her for her absence. She hoped they'd understand why she was compelled to pursue forestry. It had been more than a year since her time at Rainbow, and like Sonya, she watched crews—inmate, CAL FIRE, forestry, and international crews—battling walls of flames in large swaths of the state. At the time, the 2018

wildfire season was the deadliest and most destructive on record in California, with a total of more than 7,500 fires burning an area of over 1,670,000 acres, the largest area of burned
acreage recorded in a fire season. Marquet knew her skill set
and felt called to duty; she wanted to be on those fires. "I can
just picture myself at one of the fires talking to one of the girls
from Rainbow and saying, 'I used to be where you are. You
can do it if you really want to.'"

Saying that felt like a fantasy—but after sitting in San Diego County jail, then Chowchilla, then CIW, then Rainbow,
Marquet knew the power of fantasy. It could propel her toward a goal. Marquet was not afraid to ask for help, to look
for guidance in her family, in Pastor T, in friends. She applied
for financial aid so she could buy books, a uniform, boots,
and manuals, whatever supplies she needed for Fire 1. The
program would take at least two years, but Marquet wasn't
focused on how long, she just wanted to get through it in her
own time, get a degree, have a better chance of landing a job.
She knew getting a job in fire would be harder for her, a former inmate.

Miramar was her plan for the future and her escape from
the present. She liked sitting on the lawn of the bucolic campus before class, watching students walk by holding books
and carrying overstuffed backpacks. She observed other fire
classes—crews laying hose, doing push-ups on the asphalt like
she did in PT at CIW, climbing engine ladders, studying modules of various extreme fire scenarios. There was a whole section of Miramar devoted to fire protection technology (FIPT).
The classroom walls were decorated with operations maps
and posters of Smokey Bear warning, "Only YOU can prevent forest fire," a slogan that reflected decades of misguided

fire policy in western states. In Smokey's era, California led the way in fire policy. Suppression—the putting out of blazes whenever and wherever they popped up—was standard practice. More recent research makes it clear that periodic fire is necessary to maintain healthy forests; with naturally occurring fire, the understory burns but canopies and thick trees remain. Suppression led to unhealthy forests in some parts of the state; the theory for Northern California forests was that controlled burns could prevent megafires or at least minimize their damage. Every season forestry departments begged for resources to properly continue controlled burns in areas like the Sierra Nevada and Yosemite. But policy and funding were inconsistent; one year an area would be burned, but it would grow ragged with grasses and shrubbery the next season, when funds ran out for burn crews. Small towns built in high-risk fire zones lobbied against controlled burns—the optics of purposeful fire, after so many devastating years, were hard to overcome.

By April 2019, Marquet was enrolled in her first two courses and ready to learn, but also highly aware that she'd learned most of this information before—in PFT and in the field. She'd already done the work she'd be training for. "Because I was an inmate firefighter, I knew more than most of the men in there." During class, the instructor would lean on Marquet's experience, asking what she thought of certain scenarios, if they were still relevant in the field. How wind, slope, weather, and type of fuel might affect the way a fire burned. When they watched videos with interviews of firefighters in the field, Marquet was first to raise her hand with questions about logic and tactics. One video covered containment lines and a scenario of a fire that jumped line. Marquet raised her hand. "Did he say he lost all that line? They cut all that line just to see it torched?" Then the instructor led a discussion on the 2017 Lilac Fire, a 4,100-acre burn in north San Diego County that forced a hundred thousand people to evacuate. He explained that the Lilac Fire burned for a week, but flames were out and it was contained on the third day. Marquet raised her hand again. "But didn't it start up four days later?"

"I believe it did," her instructor said. Marquet knew that to be true, because she was called out to work that fire when she was an inmate. In the classroom, Marquet was attentive, inquisitive, informed. But she had basic technology hurdles to overcome—the class required a computer. She didn't have one, nor could she afford one, and she couldn't download the required fire module program on her phone. The library at Miramar was the only place she could use a computer for the course's modules. The library hours added another stressful dimension to her already impossible schedule. Though she knew the material backward and forward, she didn't have time to go through each slide for the tests—the S-130 and S-190— and just answer the questions. Everything took her longer, everything was weighted with the pressure of work, the length of her commute, the demands of her kids, whether or not she could make it to the library.

By mid-May 2019, Marquet and her younger sister decided it made more sense for them to live together—for Marquet to wake up with her kids every morning. "I wanted to actually be a mother to them." Marquet would pay rent—$250 a month. She could go to football practices and games. She taught her kids some of what she learned at camp—how to wash their clothes, fold them, put away their things. She did homework with them. She taught them to clean the bathroom. "We had a daily routine. I would wake up and put out their clothes. I'd put out their toothbrushes. They would wake up, get ready for school, brush their teeth, brush their hair. I taught them how to brush their hair. Then, they would fold their blanket and pajamas, put them away, and then eat breakfast." They'd watch *The Magic School Bus*. At 7:00 a.m., Marquet would leave for Tahini; her sister would drop the kids off at school.

For May and part of June, Marquet relished her time with her kids, but she was exhausted. She felt like a guest, and she was uncertain about how long her sister would let her stay in the house. She worked two jobs, at least six days a week, and if she took a nap on her time off, she felt judged by her sister for resting. About a month into the family experiment, she called her PO.

"Can you call the program, the house? I need to go back."

"They said they don't have room right now."

Marquet called the home herself and begged for a bed.

"I need to come back today, I can't stay out here."

"Can you come tonight?"

Marquet packed and was back within the hour. It was a safe haven, a place where she could work on herself and her needs. She missed the mandatory Monday meetings and the ability to save just a little bit of money. She would live with her kids, eventually—she felt that—but for now she needed a place where she felt more secure. "Every night, at my sister's, I went to sleep worried about whether or not tomorrow would be the day I'd get kicked out, and that's not safe. I can go to sleep in peace and wake up, and I don't have to be at work worrying about if I get home, if that person's going to be upset."

16.

WHITNEY: THE HOTSHOT

About a year after Whitney paroled to Massachusetts, she thought about fire again. She'd had odd jobs—cleaned stables, worked at a wood farm, sold illustrations—but nothing that felt like a future. She remembered an encouraging CAL FIRE captain at CIW. She looked for an email, a phone number, anything. There was no way to reach out. Technically, no one in fire was supposed to be in touch with women on parole, even if they'd been through camp and were looking for ways into fire or forestry. Whitney used a blank postcard and painted a watercolor of a fire scene, then added a note explaining her situation and her phone number. She addressed it to CIW.

One afternoon, Whitney was buying art supplies when "Unknown" popped up on her phone. She let it go to voice mail. It was the captain, explaining he couldn't leave a callback number but that he'd call again in a minute, and she should answer if she wanted help. He told her that she should reach out to Ted King, an engine supervisor in South Lake Tahoe. King would walk her through how to apply for a seasonal position, if she was still interested. Following King's advice, she posted an application on USA Jobs, which required her to go through all the basic training she had already done in prison. Forty hours of online classes with tests. Whitney was discouraged and frustrated. She'd already seen flames and fought fires, she had already taken these tests. Why did she have to prove herself again with recertification? "It's bullshit, inmate or not. We did that work. And I'm willing to jump through hoops again, because I feel like I owe it to everybody I put through this shit, to the family that I fucked up, to myself, but not everyone can. There are these women who come out, and they have kids to take care of—they can't be worried about S-190s."

She figured, if she was going to try fire, she wanted to be on the ground. Whitney being Whitney, wildland fire was not enough. An engine was not hard enough—she wanted a challenge. When she was at Malibu, she heard captains and foremen talking up hotshot crews. Established in the 1940s after a series of fires in the Cleveland and Angeles forests, men from the Civilian Conservation Corps were recruited to work the hottest parts of the fire. Now there are roughly 107 federal crews in the United States who have been specifically trained to respond to fires in remote regions with little or no logistical support. Within firefighting circles, they're thought of as the Special Forces of firefighting—elite squads.

The physical standard was high: a 1.5 mile run in 10:35 minutes or less with a forty-five-pound backpack, forty sit-ups in sixty seconds, twenty-five push-ups in sixty seconds, five chin-ups, all of which was fine with Whitney. She had met those standards before. She'd hiked with that weight through fire. She sent sixteen applications out to hotshot crews in Northern California. Before the accident, she'd lived in Reno, and she remembered liking the area. Her crew list was narrowed down by geography. Fifty-K runs near South Lake Tahoe beckoned. The wooded trails and biking and space seemed like freedom. She called King and asked if it would help if she flew out for interviews—if crews would be more willing to hire her if they could see her face-to-face, talk to her?

Whitney asked her parole officer if she could travel from Massachusetts back to California to interview for jobs. There weren't many inmate firefighter alums who actually made the transition from camp to paid crews. That's because it was nearly impossible to get a job. "It's all about resources," Danny Ramirez, a CAL FIRE foreman at Rainbow, told me. "Some of these girls leave very interested in what they got exposed to, like, 'Oh, I never knew this exists, how do I keep on doing this?' And it's hard when they get out there, because they do have a lot of walls." Municipal fire departments don't hire ex-felons; CAL FIRE makes it nearly impossible to qualify for jobs by requiring EMT and EMS licenses, which felons weren't eligible for in California until a bill passed in 2020. That left Whitney with federal wildland forestry, one of the only fire-related departments that hired ex-felons at the time.

In one of her first interviews, with the American River Hotshots, the captain and superintendent glanced at her résumé and saw that she had worked for an L.A. County hand crew.

"Oh, where were you?" the captain asked.

She said Malibu.

"So, you were running the crew?"

"No, I was an inmate," she said.

There was a pause. And then he asked what had happened,

what she had done. She explained that she had been in a car accident, that she was drinking and driving, and that she hit someone and killed him. After the interview, she went for a run with the crew to gauge where she was at, if she was physically fit.

The superintendent, Andrew, called and left a message the next day. When they talked, he explained that he knew she was also interviewing with Tahoe. That's where he had gotten his start. He wanted to tell her that the Tahoe Hotshots had had their own experience with drunk driving within the camp. Andrew didn't want her to be blindsided by it during the interview or if she decided to accept a position there.

It ended up not being an issue. When she drove out to meet the superintendents and captains of Tahoe, they were all on the Thomas Fire. The camp was empty. But she saw the towering trees of Tahoe National Forest, and a lake just below camp with trails around the ice-blue water of the New Bullards Bar Reservoir. She saw wood-paneled housing and the main buildings, where the buggies would normally be parked. She could breathe here. Andrew knew the crews were gone. He lived nearby and offered to give her a tour of Nevada City. He wanted to show her where some of the other running trails were. She didn't mean to get into a relationship. She didn't want to focus on anything except recovering who she was and figuring out who she might be. But Andrew and Whitney started talking and running. She chose Tahoe, instead of the American River crew, for a number of reasons, one being that she couldn't date Andrew if they were on the same crew.

Another reason: the Tahoe Hotshots was the hardest crew to get on, and it had a long history. After the Great Depression, in the 1930s, the Hobart Work Center near Truckee was built as part of the Civilian Conservation Corps. Work crews laid winding roads, logged thick virgin forests, and suppressed fire. By 1961, the center had transformed into the Hobart Mills inmate crew. A decade later, it became a thirty-two-person brigade made up of students from the Stewart Indian School, an educational institution for Native Americans that emphasized assimilation. In 1973, the crew became the second to acquire hotshot status in the northern region of the west. When Whitney finally spoke to Hector, the supervisor of Tahoe, she knew this was the crew she wanted to be on. Hector had come to fire the same way Whitney did—via inmate fire camp. He was at Washington Ridge inmate camp near Nevada City, just south of the Tahoe Hotshot camp. When he got out, he picked up seasonal work on an engine and ended up applying to the entry-level academy apprenticeship in Sacramento. For two years, he spent a month training in the capital during the off-season, until he was officially certified. Then his status was converted to full-time, a permanent position. When he interviewed Whitney, he told her it was possible. He had done it, so could she. His theory: "It was all about giving people a second chance."

On July 19, 2018, four years to the day after Whitney's car accident, the Tahoe Hotshots drove to the Sierra National Forest in Mariposa County to fight the Ferguson Fire. Whitney sat in the buggy looking out the window. The smoke clouded the horizon lines of Yosemite National Park, described in 1912 by John Muir, the advocate and naturalist who lobbied for Yosemite's protection, as "mountain streets full of life and light, graded and sculptured by the ancient glaciers." The mountains, the ponderosa pines, even the road ahead was visible for only a half mile beyond the window. She could barely make out the terrain—but she already knew it was steep and rocky. This was an area she'd been to before. Whitney had visited Yosemite with her family, on a tour of national parks when she was in eighth grade and still wearing neckgear for her braces. On the same trip, the family went to Sequoia National Park and saw California's towering redwoods. Now, she was saving the giants, wrapping line in the meadows, trying to predict which part of the overgrown, dry, and drought-weakened understory the fire would destroy. These parks were different from when she visited the first time—the forested hillsides were scarred by recent fires. Even the giants were showing signs of fatigue, their crowns turning golden brown. She knew the significance of Yosemite to California. It wasn't just the brutal and towering beauty of Half Dome and El Capitan, it was also the sacred trees that surrounded those ancient formations—the cypress, juniper, pine, hemlock, fir, and giant sequoia.

These forests held California's past. The oldest sequoia was three thousand years old, give or take a couple hundred years. The trees had seen humans come and go, slaughtering, stealing, and warring over resources and space. The trees had seen the Ahwahnechee perform controlled burns in the valley to coax acorns from black oak. For nearly a century, they'd seen humans gather bark nightly and release embers at 9:00 p.m. from Glacier Point to the valley, three thousand feet below: firefall for the tourists. What a bizarre spectacle, a waterfall of glowing oranges and reds, sparks that vertically streaked the wall of rock. When Whitney saw Yosemite and the sequoia, she knew what she was protecting was more than just trees and rock, more than a tourist destination. The trees that blurred by—out the window, shrouded by smoke—were the ones left. But climate crisis was threatening even them. Fire wasn't supposed to affect sequoias—their trunks too wide, bark too thick. Sequoias, hundreds of feet tall, usually die from old age, collapsing under their own weight, but now some were dying from dehydration, rotted inside and out.

———

They were heading to a spike camp where the elevation was above four thousand feet, and again, the terrain was steep. This was Whitney's fifth fire since she'd been hired as a hotshot in May. She knew that this was a big fire, that they'd probably be out for the "full fourteen," a complete two-week assignment, which meant her crew would get a couple of days off. This time, it seemed like they'd be on the ground for the duration. Whitney's fingernails were blackened from previous fires, from clawing at charred soil.

She was still being treated like a new guy, the rookie, not so much hazed as pushed to the brink, tested. The new guy from the year before was especially hard on her. Being on crew was hard. If she lagged even a foot behind, if she was struggling, they'd yell, "Close the fucking gap," "Fuck you, you're fucking up." There weren't many women on hotshot crews. For Whitney, this was the first time anyone had questioned her physical abilities or stoked her competitive instincts with verbal abuse. She didn't respond well to that. In fact, it shut her down. Made her feel like she shouldn't be there. At Malibu, she was a leader.

Now, most of her crew seemed skeptical of her, and she didn't like it. She didn't like the feeling of not being enough, of having to prove herself again and again. She remembered her first fire with Tahoe, the Mendocino Complex, when she was so isolated from the crew, she didn't even tell them it was her birthday.

The Ferguson Fire started after an overheated car's exhaust pipe spat out gases containing hot metal fragments from the catalytic converter. The fragments landed in dry grass and leaves and ignited the parched area. A smolder turned to flame, which turned to more flames; embers chased tree branches, burning tree branches collapsing on more dead wood. For the first four days, the fire doubled in size each day. Local agencies warned that it had the potential to spread to Yosemite National Park and nearby communities. Whitney knew being a hotshot would be a challenge but, she told me, "This season felt especially gnarly." And it was only eight weeks in. By the end of the month, three thousand people from around the world had been dispatched to fight the Ferguson Fire, including three hotshot crews—Tahoe, Arrowhead, and Elk Mountain. They fought fire with back burns, setting flames from the containment line that would diminish fuel in front of the main fire front. In areas where the fire had already coursed through, they mopped up, sifting blackened terrain to make sure there were no sparks left. One spark could smolder and turn to embers; embers could catch dry wood; dry wood could ignite a spot fire; and a spot fire could extend the life and reach of wildfires. Mop-up was meant to squash any potential extension.

To start, Tahoe split into its two mods—8 Ball and 7 Ball. Whitney was on 8 Ball. They hiked in, holding the line. For this shift, they hiked down toward a river where they were going to take a trolling boat out. The expectation was that they wouldn't be hiking back up this mountain of granite. Just as they arrived at the river, Whitney's captain got a call that a spot fire had flared up at the top of the hill they had just hiked down. Although 7 Ball was still there, they needed both mods, so 8 Ball booked it up the mountainside they'd just slid down. The crew member who gave Whitney the most shit, the one who made her veins pop out in her neck in anger, was hiking slower than she was. He was "gaping." The line was lagging because he couldn't keep up. Her squad boss yelled to Whitney, "Pass him." She knew she had it in her. This was the first time she had kept pace with the saw teams up front. When she got to the top, which required a brisk quarter-mile vertical run, 8 Ball's lead saw complimented her.

The next morning, Tahoe hiked back down the valley and cut line around a two-acre spot fire. The morning after that, Whitney heard yelling, and the crash of a tree. The tree sounded bigger than the ones they'd dodged while hiking. The yelling and shouting Whitney heard wasn't a warning. It was panic. Captain Brian Hughes, of the Arrowhead crew, had gone out, just beyond where Tahoe was working, to scout for snags—trees or branches that posed a risk to the fire line. One in particular stood out—a 57-inch-wide, 105-foot-tall ponderosa pine, burning approximately 10 feet from its crown. A steady stream of embers cascaded to the forest floor, and winds were picking up. The snag was a major problem. The crew wouldn't be able to safely work the line. So Hughes and the sawyer planned for the tree to fall uphill into an opening between growth. Instead, the tree fell downhill, grazed another standing dead snag as it fell, and crushed Hughes. Whitney heard on the radio that it was a Code Red, so

8 Ball hiked toward the sound. When they got there, the scene was chaos. Hughes's body was already strapped to a stretcher. Crew members alternated administering CPR. After trying to resuscitate him, all three crews were instructed to chain him out. CAL FIRE couldn't land a helicopter close enough. One group of people would hold the sides of the stretcher and hike, as the front person in line ran behind to relieve the last person. They got halfway up the mountain when a local wildland fire crew—one that Hughes had worked on before he became a hotshot—said they'd fly through the smoke to assist. Hughes was scrambled back down to flatter land. The person holding the emergency IV leaned on Whitney for support. She hiked with Hughes all the way to the helicopter, trying to keep her footing straight on ground that was uneven and rocky. After Hughes was flown out, Whitney spotted two women from Arrowhead, one crying. She squeezed her shoulders and cried with her.

The pause for emotion was brief; then thoughts shifted to what-can-we-do-now mode. Tahoe captains took over. They had to get the whole Arrowhead crew—still in shock—out. Each person grabbed packs and saws and tools from someone on Arrowhead. Whitney hiked out with a pack and a saw. The other new guy on Tahoe had two packs and two tools.

"I felt more a part of the crew than I ever had before, and was getting respect, but mostly it was the coming together as a crew. When stuff like life and death and extreme moments like that happen, all of that new-guy shit just falls away. I remember getting to the top, where our buggies were, and one of the guys came over and gave me a big hug cause he could see, you know, like women obviously also kinda show emotion a little bit more. I wasn't, like, a mess, but I was definitely upset. To have him come over and give me like a real hug, and like you're just, like, we're there for each other."

Brian Hughes died while being transported to the hospital. He was thirty-three.

⎯⎯⎯

When I met Whitney for the first time outside of prison, it was for breakfast in Yuba City. I recognized her, but only because she was wearing her Malibu 13 trucker hat pulled low. It was brown, silk-screened with an eighties logo: a yellow wave that looked like a surfboard fin, a "13" tucked under the wave, and below that the word "Malibu." If it wasn't prison garb, it might have been stacked in the back of an Urban Outfitters. Whitney's hat was puckered with dirt and salt rims, residue from her time at camp. Before she paroled, on December 3, 2016, she stuffed a pair of orange CDCR pants and two hats into her CamelBak. She planned to sprint out, as she usually did, on her last run. When crew 5 took its morning hike, Whitney's last, on the Backbone trail heading toward Mulholland Highway, she broke away from her crew and stashed the souvenirs near the road. She marked the bush, and continued running. When her mom picked her up, they went directly to the marked bush, where she retrieved her contraband—two hats and a pair of pants that could never be bought.

It was now December 15, 2018, and I was driving up to Paradise, in Northern California. Whitney was living in Nevada City, so we met at a diner forty-five minutes north of Sacramento. She ate a high-protein scramble with veggies and no carbs; I had eggs on toast. It had only been a little more than a month since the Camp Fire in Paradise had started, and only a couple of weeks since the fire had been contained. The Camp Fire changed the conversation about wildfire, and it was impossible not to talk about, especially because of Whitney's new hat. This one was red, also caked in dirt and sweat, and the patch on it read, "Tahoe Hotshots, Region 5."

Like most hotshots employed in forestry by the federal government in forestry, Whitney was a seasonal worker. Her season was determined by the pattern of fires in California from previous decades—June to November. On November 8, just as the Paradise Fire ignited, seasonal crews, including hotshots, were getting ready for their planned layoffs. Whitney worked the first thirty-six hours of the Camp Fire, providing structure protection, cutting line, and chasing spot fires. She told me that when they first approached the fire, "it was like Mavericks"—the homicidal big-wave surfing spot off Half Moon Bay, just south of San Francisco. "It was a wall of smoke—the biggest smoke column I'd ever seen. Grasslands are not supposed to burn hot, but the heat was hotter than I've ever felt."

The Camp Fire was unpredictable, but absolutely predicted. The night before the fire started, weather channels announced red-flag conditions—extreme weather, no humidity, and persistent winds. There was a 76 percent chance that a single spark would ignite a fire big enough to require fire crews. That morning, a fire station recorded gusts of up to fifty-two miles per hour. Paradise was built in a high-risk fire zone. In 2005, a state fire-planning document had predicted the possibility of an ember-driven firestorm similar to the one that fourteen years earlier had ripped through the Berkeley and Oakland hills, killing more than two dozen people and destroying more than two thousand homes.

The morning of the fire, all 26,561 Paradise residents could evacuate on only one road. The sky went from sherbet orange to ash to black. The morning looked like the middle of a starless night; the air was impossible to breathe. Eighty- to one-hundred-foot flames crashed buildings and leveled the town, leaving concrete slabs that looked like floor plans where houses had been. Helitack teams attempted water drops, which did nothing to impede the fire's progress. Heat pockets melted tires. Propane tanks exploded. Cars turned to ghostly skeletons. The Camp Fire burned as aggressively at night as it did during the day. White metal fences buckled under the heat.

Though Whitney volunteered to stay longer, she was sent home. By mid-November, roughly fifteen hundred inmates had been deployed throughout the state. Two male inmate firefighters, ages thirty and twenty-seven, were among those sent with a CAL FIRE crew to protect Butte College in Oroville, where they scouted areas for back fires along Rattlesnake Flats Road, a one-lane, dirt farm road flanked by barbed-wire fences. As they were hiking out, the winds switched directions. Fire raged toward the crews, trapping them. One inmate firefighter ran toward the flames but was halted by the fence and was burned. The second inmate firefighter tried to jump the fence, but his tool caught on the barbed wire. He was burned on his face and neck. When a CAL FIRE captain received serious burns to his hands, arms, face, and neck, the inmate firefighters gave him medical care. The number of seriously injured firefighters in the Camp Fire was low compared to the deaths and devastation of the town. Those three were among a total of five firefighters whom CAL FIRE considered seriously injured from working the Camp Fire.

When Whitney went home to Massachusetts for Thanksgiving, she debated whether or not she'd return to fire. She knew she wouldn't be a Tahoe Hotshot, but not because her captain didn't want her to return. In his stellar review, she was surprised by how much he valued her and noticed her improvement. He even gave her a metal belt buckle that read, "Hobart Hotshots Tahoe," with the traditional imprint of a diagonal ax, a gift usually reserved for those who return for a second year. When her boyfriend, Andrew, was offered a position as captain for Tahoe, they decided they shouldn't work together. Whitney still wanted to stay in the area, so she applied for an engine crew. Before her training started in spring 2019, a free EMR course was offered as part of the certification for a first responder. She took the course, studied every day for a couple of weeks, passed the required tests, and, when it was requested, sent in a copy of her fingerprints. Her certification was denied, because Whitney had a felony on her record. Her lawyer appealed the decision. But even though Whitney had already worked a season as an inmate firefighter, and one on an elite hotshot crew, she wasn't allowed EMR certification.

On the first day residents were allowed back in Paradise, I decided to stop near the fence where I thought the two inmate firefighters had been burned. It was six miles south of the actual town of Paradise—there were no homes or structures off the road. I wandered around the coordinates described in CAL FIRE's Green Sheet—where the east side of Clark Road meets the north side of Rattlesnake Flats Road. I couldn't locate exactly where it happened—CDCR and CAL FIRE released only scant details about the injuries. But now, as I looked around at vast golden fields and some trees in the distance, it made me think about what several fire analysts have told me, that fire season in California is certainly affected by climate change, but also by a relatively new awareness of the fires, via cell phones, the internet, and cable news. We see fire more. We breathe it. A fire in California can be so intense, it affects the air quality on the East Coast. We see the overwhelming devastation and walls of flame in videos, as it's happening. In real time, we hear the panic of people realizing there is no escape. We see the carcasses of their homes and cars and communities. Fire is closing in more so now than before.

As I drove on, the road became steep; pastures turned to inclines. Cars were backed up along the 191. The tie-up stretched for miles, inching along. The trees got denser. I tried to imagine being stuck in traffic while hundred-foot flames advanced. The first sign I saw of the fire's remnants was an entire hillside covered in an unnatural film of mint green, the color of a chemical substance that had been dropped to stop the flame's progress. After hours of stop-and-go, I got to a sheriff who was restricting access to residents only. I told him I wasn't a resident but that I was hoping to write about the area. He sighed and let me through with a warning: "I hope you brought a mask or respiratory gear." I hadn't.

When I entered Paradise, there were dozens of PG&E trucks careening down the streets of a leveled community.

It was as if a giant beast had scooped up Paradise and left a charred imprint in its place. There weren't many people. The people who were there were wearing white hazmats and respiratory masks, sifting through burned belongings, trying to figure out if they could save anything. A blistered photo? A half-melted heirloom? A dress? A passport? Houses were reduced to hints of where a bedroom had been, where the garage might have been. Brick chimneys still stood, but not much else. Car windows were melted. Blackened washer-dryer units stood like useless sentinels. Claw-foot bathtubs held piles of debris. The Elks Club bingo sign survived, announcing the game: "Sundays, open to the public at 1:30, play at 2:30." The fire's brutal wake left rubble, like the wreckage of war.

Except for one thing. Only weeks after the fire, perennial bulbs were poking through what used to be front gardens, alert and ready to bloom. Their neon green was so striking against the blackened soil that the shoots seemed almost alien. The plants were already rebuilding.

The courtroom in Oroville on June 16, 2020, was mostly empty. A line of half a dozen lawyers, wearing masks, faced Judge Michael Deems. The lawyers sat behind a long, nondescript pale wood desk. A masked bailiff stood at a door behind empty rows of plastic chairs. A grid of faces loomed, projected onto a wall. These eighty-four faces belonged to people killed in the Camp Fire. The former chief executive of PG&E, Bill Johnson, stood, unmasked, with his hands clasped around the base of his belly.

"On behalf of PG&E, how do you plead to a violation of penal code section 192(b), involuntary manslaughter as a felony, concerning the death of Joyce Acheson, as alleged in count two [of the indictment]?" Deems asked.

"Guilty, Your Honor," Johnson said.

"On behalf of PG&E, how do you plead to a violation of penal code section 192(b), involuntary manslaughter as a felony, concerning the death of Herbert Alderman, as alleged in count three of the indictment?" Deems asked.

"Guilty, Your Honor," Johnson said.

"On behalf of PG&E, how do you plead to a violation of penal code section 192(b), involuntary manslaughter as a felony, concerning the death of Teresa Ammons, as alleged in count four of the indictment?" Deems asked.

"Guilty, Your Honor," Johnson said.

"On behalf of PG&E, how do you plead to a violation of penal code section 192(b), involuntary manslaughter as a felony, concerning the death of Rafaela Andrade, as alleged in count five of the indictment?" Deems asked.

"Guilty, Your Honor," Johnson said.

Judge Deems went on for almost thirty minutes, reading each count, each name, until Johnson replied with, "Guilty, Your Honor" eight-five times.

The defendant, PG&E, had a lengthy history of priors. The company was still under federal criminal probation until 2022 for felony convictions stemming from a 2010 San Bruno gas pipeline explosion that killed eight people, injured fifty-eight, and destroyed thirty-eight homes; in 1997, PG&E was convicted of 739 counts of criminal negligence for failing to trim trees near its power lines; in 2017, a judge determined PG&E to be at fault for a downed tree that made contact with a PG&E electrical wire, sparking the Butte Fire, which burned more than seventy thousand acres, destroyed 365 homes, and killed two people. The list went on.

In January 2019, just after the Camp Fire, the privately owned PG&E, the nation's largest utility, filed for chapter 11 bankruptcy. It faced at least $30 billion in potential damages from lawsuits stemming from wildfires in California in 2017 and 2018. Advocates for a public utility, one not owned by shareholders expecting profits, argued that PG&E cut corners on infrastructure and maintenance, that when a power line fell, it was an example of corporate negligence. Part of the reason the company agreed to plead guilty to eighty-four charges of involuntary manslaughter, and one charge of illegally setting a fire, was that by doing so, it would meet Governor Gavin Newsom's June 30, 2020, deadline to exit bankruptcy. If PG&E could exit bankruptcy by the deadline, the company could take part in a $20 billion wildfire fund established by the state of California to pay future damages relating to wildfires. In other words, the company, with new leadership, could continue to function as a monopoly and would be protected from future liability if it agreed to the terms of the plea deal.

Judge Deems ordered the maximum penalty allowed by state law: $3.5 million in fines, plus $500,000 in additional fees to cover prosecutors' investigative costs. Under California law, executives couldn't be prosecuted for actions about which they lacked direct knowledge. The district attorney said that it "would have been impossible" to prove criminal charges, therefore no executives were charged in the case.

"If these crimes were attributed to an actual human person rather than a corporation, the anticipated sentence based on the applicable statutes to which the defendant has pleaded guilty would be ninety years to be served in state prison," Judge Deems said. "As a corporation, PG&E cannot be sentenced to prison."

On the same day the Camp Fire began, just eight hours later and five hundred miles south, the Woolsey Fire ignited in Simi Valley, on Boeing's shuttered nuclear and rocket engine testing site. Again, the initial spark was caused by faulty power lines, this time operated by Southern California Edison, the second-largest utility provider in California. As was the case in Northern California, it was a hot and dry day; the Santa Ana winds were coursing through mountainous terrain, a classic red-flag day, and the National Weather Service deemed it so. The Woolsey Fire started on private land that was considered a mutual coverage zone—Ventura County, L.A. County, L.A. City Fire, and Boeing's own private fire engine were all responsible for what was initially thought to be a blaze that could be contained to unpopulated areas. But there were so many responsible agencies involved that the response time was complicated and consequently delayed.

As in Paradise, the Woolsey was a hot, fast-moving fire. Because of the forty-to-fifty-mile-per-hour winds, it went from a brush fire to sheeting across steep hillsides within hours. Several crews from Malibu 13 were dispatched, with the initial strike team heading to Simi Valley to cut line. Captains and battalion chiefs tried to anticipate where flames would travel next. Fueled by wind gusts that had grown to seventy miles per hour, the fire front ate through Agoura Hills, Oak Park, and Thousand Oaks. By the next morning, the Woolsey had reached the 101 freeway, and around 5:30 a.m., the explosive front jumped its twelve lanes. At first, the crews that remained at Malibu 13 evacuated to Zuma Beach, where they sat in their buggies, waiting for instructions. They didn't know if they'd go back to camp, to Rainbow or Port, to CIW, or be dispatched to the fire. Flames burned 88 percent of federal parkland in the Santa Monica Mountains—fire roads they built, hiking trails they hiked, their backyard. By 10:15 a.m., Malibu 13 was engulfed in flames. The crafts area, the memorials, the black oak that was planted for Shawna. The fire blanketed camp. The women of Malibu 13 were sent to Rainbow and Port, then, days later, back to Malibu to work the fire.

After two weeks, the Woolsey left a charred footprint of over 150 square miles. The most destructive fire in L.A. County's recorded history, it burned 96,949 acres of land, destroyed 1,643 structures, killed three people, and forced the evacuation of more than 295,000 people. Malibu 13's camp was empty for months. The structures survived. A couple of foremen remained, joking about where the women would stash drugs now that the bushes on the perimeter of camp were burned through. One told me, "When they came back to work Woolsey, they were even more dedicated. It was their backyard they were protecting. Their home too."

The chaparral stands and live coastal oak were torched to ash. Everything that made Malibu a wooded retreat burned. Beyond the loss of trees, the camp was minimally damaged. When the crews returned to move back in, the mountains around camp were naked and ashen. Tree stumps and gnarled branches were pockmarked and blackened. In Malibu, estates were reduced to rubble. As in Paradise, new growth penetrated the darkened earth, covering the Santa Monica Mountains in neon green. Grasses would grow again. Fire would burn those grasses again too.

17.

THE FIREFIGHTERS

As far as fire seasons go, the year after Paradise and Woolsey was mild, and Californians did what they normally do. They forgot their state is constantly threatened by fire, that climate crisis has exponentially amplified that threat, and that the next year could be another "worst on record" season. But life goes on, and for most of the women I interviewed, it was life on the outside.

In 2016, when Selena paroled to Los Angeles County, her restitution was paid off from fire service wages. CDCR issued her the legal maximum release funds—$200 in gate money for reentry. Since she didn't want to go to a homeless shelter, Selena crashed with a friend in MacArthur Park. She knew that the shelter might provide a link to housing or some kind of section 8 benefits, but she didn't trust the system.

Selena would see people from her previous life. She'd nod, say hello, and keep moving. She didn't affiliate with the people from before; she couldn't. Selena wasn't intending to go back to prison. Within a few weeks, she got a job at a warehouse—one that specialized in Filipino pastries and bread. She worked the line for minimum wage, 8:00 a.m. to 4:00 p.m. She baked buko bread, biscotti, ensaymadas. "The stuff we baked had hella butter on it. You put your hand in the can of butter and you just smother it all over the bread. That was their main ingredient on all of their bread. I mean, the biscotti was just bolillo bread with butter and sugar and you put it in the oven until it gets crispy." Selena met her boyfriend while they were both on break at the warehouse. But when she was promoted to machine operator in charge of bread packaging, they had different lunch hours. Selena would take her break and then tell her line of workers she was going to the bathroom, and sneak out with her boyfriend to the liquor store for a second break. They'd grab a beer and she'd drink hers quickly. After ten months at the baking facility, she was fired.

Selena's PO sent her to job fairs to fill out applications and required classes that covered how to write résumés and how to approach job interviews. Nothing led to actual work, but she would go because guys on parole would be there too. Selena did what she always did and hustled for work. In the two years after her release, Selena held six different temp jobs, each paying minimum wage. She baked doughnuts and cookies for 7-Eleven; she worked the floor of the Fashion Nova warehouse in Santa Fe Springs, just twenty minutes east of Lynwood. She worked twelve-hour days, six days a week, and never received overtime. In 2019, federal officials investigating low wages in factories found Fashion Nova—the fast-fashion label that collaborated with Cardi B—had been cited in fifty investigations for paying less than the $7.25 an hour minimum wage or failing to pay overtime. "There were a lot of people saying we should file a lawsuit, but I needed to work and make money. I couldn't wait for a lawsuit."

254 | BREATHING FIRE

Eventually, the owner of her apartment building offered her free rent if Selena agreed to be the manager of several of the properties. She could stay home and respond to tenants' calls. The company office asked if she had a criminal record, and she said no. They asked for her personal information to run a criminal background check and several days later offered her the job. She told me, "Now I have a one-year-old and a two year-old, and my one-year-old does everything the two-year-old does, so it's like two two-year-olds. Having kids is the most challenging thing I've ever done, mentally and physically. I think I'd prefer fire camp at this point." She laughed. When the United States started to address COVID-19 in March 2020, Selena said, "This is my time to shine. Nobody else is working." She got a job as a cashier at a 7-Eleven near her apartment.

<hr>

Laurie paroled to Santa Clarita, halfway between Simi Valley and Palmdale. She chose Santa Clarita because there was an in-house drug treatment program that offered a real chance to avoid a relapse. It was a tortured decision. Her dad was dying of cancer and she had to choose her rehabilitation over staying in Palmdale. When Laurie was in County, she met a woman who introduced her to religion, and to Hannah's Gift, a Christian ministry that helps incarcerated women foster better relationships with their kids on the outside. Her friends would visit her at CIW and pray with her. In the program, she could get a job, get grounded, reconnect with meetings and God. She could stay sober.

Laurie did stay sober. She met a partner, got an associate's degree in art, took care of her kids—trekking to and from school events—and bought a house. She also applied to jobs. So many jobs that she lost track. And every time her potential future employers, like Northrop Grumman, ran a background check, her felony would pop up. "Getting that job would have changed my life. It completely holds me back. So much for rehabilitation. That's the thing—I'm like, I did my time, I did plenty of time for this stuff. And now I'm doing everything right. So, I don't understand why they keep punishing me for something that I've already done my time for."

By early 2020, Sonya had been promoted to assistant manager at Dollar Tree. With it came a pay raise and afternoon hours. When COVID-19 spread through California, Sonya, as a grocery worker, was deemed an essential employee. So she strapped on a face mask with a jaw skeleton silkscreened on it and showed up for work every day as the pandemic cases multiplied. She disregarded her history of asthma and whatever lingering respiratory damages she suffered from fighting fires. "I look around, and, like, if I can handle life in prison, then I can handle this." Every two weeks, she took home $950 after taxes. "I'm not making enough," she said, especially now that her eldest daughter was pregnant and had moved in. They shared the master bedroom of a one-bedroom apartment while Sonya's roommate slept in the living room. In Sonya's room, they had two beds, a crib, a mini fridge, a microwave, a TV, clothes. "We make it work." She texted and talked with a new love interest whom she met on a Facebook chat. "I have a guy that I talk to but he's in South Carolina. We've been talking for a good year now. It's frustrating, he's an EMT first responder and also works for Taco Bell. I get it, he works a lot, go get your money, it feels like he works twenty-four hours a day. When I want to talk to you, *I want to talk to you.*"

In June, when George Floyd was killed in Minneapolis, we talked about the protests unfolding throughout the nation's streets and near where Sonya lived. Even in San Diego, a conservative stronghold, there were people in the streets, chanting about Floyd's and Breonna Taylor's murders. "More Black lives are being lost behind crooked cops and fucked-up government and just fucked-up people in general, like, ignorance is real. How can they sit here and say that his life didn't matter? He didn't do anything. You know, like legit, there was nothing in that man's hands for the cops to sit there and continue to take his life. They had already detained him. So, what was the need for the extra force?" Sonya told me, "If you're a cop of the Caucasian descent and you do something like this, you get a slap on the wrist. And it's not just with these two instances, you know what I mean? Like, it's been going on since I was a little girl, there's literally no justice."

And when her pregnant daughter wanted to march and protest, Sonya supported the sentiment but told her daughter she was too pregnant to take to the streets. By the end of July, protests were still going, and Sonya had become a grandmother to Trey. He had big brown eyes, and round cheeks, and Sonya was in love. This child was her do-over. If there was ever a question about mothering, she offered up solutions. "I can answer any questions she has about the baby. One time he was constipated, and I got him some apple juice and put it in the bottle to flush out his system. I can just help her with things I learned when I raised her." Trey slept in his crib and at three months was gurgling and making noises. "He's already trying to talk," Sonya said. "He's definitely got something to say."

She saved money to move from Escondido back to the desert, where the cost of living was more affordable, where she could provide a better life for her daughter and Trey. Sonya applied for jobs at Home Depot and GameStop and waited while both ran background checks. "I'm not putting too much into it because I don't want to jinx myself." But she was tired of working the floor at Dollar Tree and she was tired of the toll the pandemic was taking. "The rudeness, the ignorance, like the sheer, just, *I gotta have everything my way and I got to have it now*. The demandingness of the attitudes and I'll be at work and then the way people talk to me, it's not what you say, it's the tone and how you say it. And I literally sometimes just want to smack the dog crap out of people. It's like, who are you to sit here and talk to me like that. Like, I've had some people say thank you for staying open. Like, I appreciate you guys, you're out there working amongst it all, and then I got some people that just sit here and act like, 'Oh, well, that's your job. That's what you're supposed to do.' Uh, no, the hell I'm not."

When a grand jury declined to charge any officers in the killing of Breonna Taylor, Sonya was angry but not surprised. There were parallels between Breonna Taylor's murder and her own arrest; she was all too familiar with law enforcement busting down a door in the middle of the night. Sonya's daughter wrote on Facebook, "When will there be justice? They expect us to remain peaceful in a society that turns the other way when time and time again, wrong is done to us. There is only so many times you can provoke someone and expect them to be calm, expect us not to do anything (surprised a Rodney King riot hasn't happened yet) but it's only a matter of time . . . we are tired of living in fear how are we supposed to raise Black children in a society that sees no wrong in killing us . . . it's hard not to have that anger and hatred so the next time a Target get burned down or a store gets looted be grateful because this generation, we can do a lot worse, it's only a matter of time and I'm not saying that burning down stores is the right thing to do but be grateful the anger is being taken out on that instead of beating y'all asses and doing y'all how y'all do us."

For most of 2019, Marquet balanced two jobs, church, her family, and fire school. She quit Prado and got a second job at WIS International, an inventory and data collection company. Marquet worked thirty-six hours a week at Tahini, and thirty-six hours a week at WIS International. She was so focused on making money for an apartment, there wasn't time for fire school. She quit, intending to reenroll. Then the coronavirus pandemic hit. By March 2020, Marquet's hours at WIS International were cut to five a week, and her hours at Tahini were reduced to twenty a week. There was no way she'd find an apartment with such little financial security. She moved back in with her sister and returned to her daily routine with her kids. And every Sunday Marquet would listen to Pastor T, who preached like he still had a physical audience. He preached exercise. He preached taking care of your body. To help with depression, he preached looking to religion, to God. Relating to a passage from Kings 19:8, he said, "Watch your diet, get more sleep, establish an exercise program. That's how you dig yourself out of depression. When you take care of the physical, you can relinquish your frustration."

Marquet listened but couldn't hear what Pastor T was saying. "I was juggling too much. I had a setback and lost my way for a second," she told me. "I started questioning my faith and God. I stopped praying and I stopped believing in God. I let the struggles of life cloud my judgment and I made up all these excuses. *I can't sing that well anyways. They'll do better without me. They don't need me.* It was just a battle, a struggle. I miss choir." After applying for every job she could—housekeeping at a hospital, janitor for an apartment building downtown, cutting down trees—Marquet was feeling desperate. Her sister could no longer take care of her sons, and Marquet filed for custody, hoping to prove she could provide care. It was a bad time to be minimally employed. "It's stressful. Right now, I have to wait for the courts to investigate for whether I'm a fit mother. They're looking for security, making sure the home is fit, I'm fit, making sure they have a bed, making sure everything is set for them. It's stressful because any moment something can mess up, something can go wrong, and then they're gone. They'd go into the system," Marquet said. "It's just tiring sometimes, when you take ten steps forward, then you take ten steps back. Sometimes I want to throw my hands up and say I'm done. No one said it would be easy and no one said it was going to be this hard. I'm trying and I'm trying and I'm trying and I don't think that they see that. I have to trust that God's going to work it out. I have to hold on to that hope."

She still had her family and her church, and since August, Marquet had been involved with a new love, an old friend. He got in touch with her through his sister's Facebook page. He was in prison at the Sierra Conservation Center, a state prison just north of Modesto. He wrote her letters and called. "He's been in prison for four years," she said. "A lot of people think I'm crazy, like, why are you dating someone in prison. I feel like everybody deserves a chance. A lot of people in prison are alone, because people gave up on them, they think they're trash. We have a lot in common. He was locked up; I was locked up. His mother was a drug addict; I was a drug addict, my mom was a drug addict. He has a son; I have sons. A lot of people call me gullible, but I have a big heart and I refuse to crucify someone for their mistakes."

Marquet's remaining fire classes were all in-person and impossible to complete during the pandemic. She told me she still intends to finish and still intends to apply for a job in forestry. She wants to get on a crew again. She knows the path is more complicated for someone with a criminal record, but she's hopeful and persistent. By mid-October, Marquet had gotten two pieces of good news—she was offered a job as a cook at a hospital, and she got her own place. Good news was tempered with bad; after she was offered the cook gig, it was quickly rescinded. Her assumption was the company ran a background check, saw a criminal history, and opted out. But while she was driving to a shift at Tahini, her phone rang. Her PO told her, "You're off parole." She was shocked; she was supposed to be on parole until 2023. She told me it felt like "chains breaking."

———

For the 2019–2020 fire season, Whitney was bored on the engine crew in Camptonville. Part of that boredom stemmed from the slow season. She trained, she ran, she went out on small two-hundred-acre fires, mostly local, but nothing as intense as the experiences she had as a hotshot or even when she was at Malibu. On slow days, her crew would practice drills for how fast each member could unfurl a fire shelter. She'd line up with her pack on, run a hundred yards full-tilt, then drop and unpack the aluminum foil and glass cloth laminate. The end result resembled a human-size burrito. The drills looked and felt like carnival races. But if anyone was trapped by flames, this would be the last line of protection. She got less overtime, less actual fire work, which she'd joke was a good thing for the state, the trees, and the world, but less good in terms of making money. Seasonal firefighters make between $28,700 and $43,000 a year, depending on overtime and length of the assignment.

In May 2020, Whitney started her third year of fire work on Tahoe Helitack, crew 514. This season was predicted to be bad, the worst on record potentially. The winter before had been bone-dry, and there were already flares before seasonal workers were even officially hired. Her crew, like all the fire crews, had to accommodate the CDC restrictions established because of the coronavirus. There were no more base camps; crews stayed in hotels. Social distancing was practiced, even while fighting fire. Firefighters had to contend with COVID-19, a potentially fatal disease that significantly affects the lungs, on top of what they have always dealt with, chronic respiratory illness.

———

In mid-March 2020, CDCR halted all family visits and programming in state prisons, and when the first confirmed COVID-19 case was reported at CIW on April 6, women were subjected to a twenty-three-hour lockdown in their cells. Any prisoners who were confirmed COVID-19 cases were sent to medical isolation, a place so feared that many people didn't report symptoms at all. Amend, a group affiliated with the UCSF School of Medicine, warned, "Keeping people socially isolated in a closed cell without a meaningful opportunity to communicate with family, friends, and loved ones or to participate in exercise, educational, and rehabilitative programming (solitary confinement) causes immense, and often irreparable, psychological harm."

The pandemic highlighted what has already been known for decades—CDCR is not capable of providing mental or physical health care. "Rather than treat their mental health," the entire correctional health care system has shifted the priority during the pandemic to "basically, just trying to keep people alive," Michael Bien, lead counsel in two years-long class action lawsuits against CDCR, told *The Washington Post*. According to the *Post* article, since May, "mental health staff walk through the women's general housing units once or twice a week, passing out connect-the-dots puzzles and Hello Kitty images to color."

In an attempt to contain the spread of COVID-19, CDCR released 3,500 people who were within sixty days of parole or their release date, and Governor Newsom said that California would release up to 8,000 more. By the end of July, 280 women at CIW had tested positive for the coronavirus, and one had died. The coronavirus ravaged prison and jail populations—in all of California's prisons, 7,481 incarcerated individuals had tested positive, and 42 had died as of July 2020.

Meanwhile, the forestry program at CIW froze—no new crews would be sent to camp, for fear of spreading the virus. Most of the crews at camps would be released because they were serving shorter sentences for low-level crimes. By mid-April, Malibu 13 was down to sixteen or seventeen firefighters. In early June, a small two-acre fire erupted about a mile south of CIW, in what was basically an empty field down the street. Female inmate firefighters from CIW were sent to protect their own prison, which they did.

As of mid-June, there were at least 59,000 COVID-19 infections in jails, prisons, and other federal facilities across the country, and at least 557 inmates and prison workers had died of COVID-19. Though California's prison medical system was still under the 2006 federal receivership, CDCR was in charge of a catastrophic health crisis.

CDCR officially paused interprison transfers between March 24 and May 30, 2020. One of the first publicized outbreaks in California prisons occurred at the California Institution for Men (CIM) in Chino. By early May, one inmate had died and 247 prisoners had tested positive for COVID-19, along with 44 staff members. The prison quarantined according to CDCR rules but the dormitory setting made a true quarantine impossible. Coronavirus spread. Movement between buildings slowed significantly but didn't stop outright. CIM still required inmates to do essential work in the kitchens and laundries, which put them in contact with other inmates. In late May, 121 CIM inmates, many of whom had not been tested for weeks, were transferred to San Quentin. The transfer sparked an outbreak that swept through roughly one-third of San Quentin's inmate population. A week later, three inmates from San Quentin were transferred to the California Correctional Center in Susanville, triggering another outbreak.

Susanville, in Northern California, typically houses more than 3,000 minimum- and medium-security inmates and serves as training grounds for men entering California's prison wild-fire program. Right around the same time as the transfer in late May, several members of inmate crews tested positive for the coronavirus. By early July, twelve Northern California conservation camps were under quarantine. With the ongoing COVID-19 outbreak, newly trained inmate crews could not be transferred to camps. As a result, just weeks before the state's first major fire, Governor Newsom announced the hiring of 858 seasonal firefighters to replace prison crews. Suddenly, the state had money to pay for the same inmate labor it had previously claimed it could not fairly compensate.

After sentencing, Alisha was sent back to Lynwood. Because she was appealing her sentence, when the pandemic hit, Alisha was stuck in Lynwood, where a lockdown was enforced for the first couple of months of the pandemic. "Sometimes I get very depressed here and I think I'm never going to go home. I think about suicide at this point. You're in a cell for twenty-three hours a day. You're alone with your thoughts a lot and you can't really communicate with other people here, there's a lot going on. Everything I went through . . . I should have made better choices, and I think about what my captain would say." Alisha watched other women get psych evals and prescriptions for Seroquel. "Everybody buys each other's pills, everybody takes Seroquel because everyone wants to sleep here," she said. Alisha took meds too, and slept all day.

She told me over the phone that what she learned at Port was life-changing—that she was leading a crew of seventeen women, all of them looking to her for direction. "I went through all that, I fought fire," she said, as if she couldn't believe that previous version of herself ever existed. Her captain was like a father figure, someone she kept in touch with after release. Once she relapsed, though, she stopped updating him on her life.

"I know he would have been very disappointed."

She told me some of the captains at Port would talk about creating a link from camp to civilian life at Port—like a halfway house—where women from crews who wanted to work in fire could train and eventually be folded into jobs at CAL FIRE. It made me wonder whether Alisha would have relapsed if a program like that had existed.

Every day at Lynwood was another day of waiting to start her real sentence. As she anxiously asked COs about news of transfers to Chowchilla, COVID outbreaks seemed like the norm. And until those outbreaks stopped, there would be no transports. Deputies told her the sheriff's department couldn't afford tests for incoming bodies. Some weeks a person on the kitchen staff would get sick, requiring inmates to be shuffled around modules and the triple-bunk cells. No kitchen staff meant most meals were frozen burritos and whatever Alisha could afford from the vending machines—Little Debbie cakes and potato chips. On the bus to court, where she filed her appeal, one woman was so sick, she threw up several times. But if anyone reported being sick, the whole bus would be sent to the hole and put in quarantine, meaning no one could go to their court appointments and, effectively, they'd be placed in solitary. "I don't want to die in here," Alisha told me. "But I understand not wanting to tell anyone if you're sick. If it happens, it happens. I can't protect myself and I can't choose where I go."

When news of George Floyd's killing was broadcast in

the common room at Lynwood, women organized moments of silence and knelt in protest in the dayroom. Alisha talked with Kayleigh on the phone, though most conversations were painful. Alisha knew Kayleigh was cared for, but she couldn't be there for swim meets or school or breakfast pancakes or pizza days. For her thirty-first birthday, Alisha's cellies made a cake. Alisha couldn't believe she had spent the majority of her twenties in prison and now she was back facing old age while being locked up. The numbers were daunting—thirty-six years to life felt impossible and overwhelming. Because of COVID, there was no programming, no NA meetings, no AA meetings, no classes. She volunteered to be the "trustee" for her module, distributing food and clothes to the women who were housed in her block. And she slept. When she wasn't sleeping, she watched the fire season escalate on the news. She thought about her girlfriend from Port, who was on a helitack crew in Sequoia. She was probably on the Creek Fire or the SQF Complex. Alisha could picture her rappelling from a helicopter into targeted areas of wildfires, sawing, cutting at growth. Because this season was so bad, epically and historically bad, millions of acres burned and decimated, thousands of people evacuated, newscasters focused on the future of the state. Experts testified that CAL FIRE's approach was no longer working. Suppression was no longer a viable long-term plan. Unhealthy forests needed to burn. Alisha watched and wished she could be out there, at one of the thousands of fires that ripped through the state. She was trained and ready.

After a couple of false alarms, CDCR began transferring County bodies to State in October. Alisha was on the second bus to Chowchilla with about thirty-five other women. They moved through processing fast because of the backlog. She saw psych, where they asked about suicidal ideation. She lied and said no, she had never attempted or considered suicide. They gave her a standard evaluation and asked about her history and what meds she had been on, in and out of prison. After they switched her to Celexa, Alisha no longer felt like she needed to sleep all day. She worried about forgetting things and wondered if that was a side effect. "I notice that I'm talking and totally forget what I'm talking about. I don't want to be a wet brain, but I think it's helping," she told me. With new meds, Alisha got up early for breakfast. Chowchilla had better food than Lynwood. One morning she got a plate of hash brown patties, eggs, and oatmeal; another morning it was a bundle of raw green onions, coffee cake, oatmeal.

Now that Alisha was at Chowchilla, her appeal could move forward. She talked with her counselor from the Appellate Project. "I'll find out in the next couple weeks if they're making me a violent third-striker or nonviolent. My counselor thinks I'll be nonviolent since no one was hurt," Alisha said. There was an optimism in her voice, but then it dropped slightly. "I'm eligible for parole board in 2037. And they said my parole date is 2042."

Calls with Alisha became shorter and less frequent—she was new at Chowchilla and had less seniority with the phones. When we talked, she was rushed. On January 9, 2021, she ecstatically shared some news—it sounded like her crime might be considered nonviolent, which, she told me, meant she'd serve only five years. She explained why she was tired and hadn't spoken to Kayleigh or anyone in weeks. There was an outbreak of COVID—at least one hundred women tested positive. The entire prison was on lockdown with no yard time.

The COVID-positive cases were quarantined to one building on C Yard. Her neighbor across the hall was sick. The kitchen staff was sick. There was no one to work, so Alisha volunteered for kitchen duty, working sixteen-hour shifts, seven days a week. It was exhausting and terrifying. On top of that, her cellie played music too loud one night and a guard who was known for violence cuffed her cellmate and slammed her body to the floor. "Her face was leaking, there was just blood everywhere and the other guard just stood there and said, 'I hope this doesn't ruin my boots.'"

By mid-January 2021, 175 incarcerated people and 16 CDCR staff had died of COVID-19. The next month, Alisha tested positive and was sick for a month in isolation before recovering.

There are a few Facebook groups that connect women who served time in the conservation camps with one another. The one dedicated to Malibu alums is especially active, with almost six hundred members and daily updates. Women would post pictures of themselves hiking in Malibu, describing the feeling of choosing to hike rather than being forced to hike. They'd shout out the most painful trails, the most intense foremen, the salacious gossip, and their crews. Some women would post faded pictures of themselves, in oranges, in front of flames or at base camps. News of current fires and prayers to the crews were often posted. Memes were shared, marriages were announced, along with births, businesses, and deaths.

On December 27, 2020, a GoFundMe page shared on the

Malibu group raised over $6,000 for a funeral. Maria, the dragspoon on crew 13-3 at the time of Shawna's death, had died. There weren't many details except that Maria had been at Malibu and Port, and that her wife, Noeli, was hoping to pay for a coffin, a burial site, and a memorial service. When I called Noeli, she was driving from Santa Barbara to Indio to claim Maria's body and find a mortuary. "I've never done anything like this before. I'm twenty-eight."

Noeli and Maria met in March 2016, just after Maria was transferred from Malibu to CIW and then to Port. She told Noeli about the day, about giving Shawna mouth-to-mouth, about how she couldn't stay at Malibu after the death. Every hike reminded her of Shawna's limp body, that Shawna's death was her fault.

"She was a real serious person and she had this real serious face, this don't-effin-talk-to-me face. But you could tell in her eyes that she looked broken," Noeli said. When Maria had first transferred to Port, she kept to herself.

Noeli asked if Maria wanted to eat together in the cafeteria. "I wasn't even attracted to girls, I wasn't pursuing her in that way. I felt like she needed a friend. Little by little we just started talking and then being in prison, you cling on to someone and you get to know someone on a whole different level. One day I gave her a hug and I kissed her on the cheek and she said, 'Hey, if you're gonna kiss me, kiss me right.' I didn't even know how to do that, I just pecked her on the lips and I was like, 'Okay, bye.' And I took off and I avoided her for a week."

Maria collected a bouquet of wildflowers on one of the hikes behind Port and asked Noeli if she had done something wrong. "She brought them to me. And she got me. That whole time, on that hike, she thought about me and people don't do that, at least not where I'm from." For a year and a half Noeli and Maria were inseparable. Noeli was on crew 3, Maria on crew 4. Most of the time, the night guard skipped final count and Noeli would sneak into Maria's bed. "We would eat together, sleep together, shower together. If we went on out-of-counties, we would write journals to each other and give them to each other." They made plans for their life together upon release.

Maria paroled in August 2016, Noeli in May 2017. The day after Noeli got out, they got married in Bermuda Dunes, in Palm Desert. They applied for forestry jobs together—on helitack crews, hand crews, hotshot crews, smoke jumpers, anything that was grade three. "We did the whole application. It was crazy, it was so long," Noeli said. "They sent us an email that a training session was gonna start in December and they would get back in touch with us, but we never heard anything." Within a few months, they started smoking meth again. In 2018, Noeli was arrested and convicted of stealing a car. She asked for one thing: that Maria go to rehab.

Noeli tried to get endorsed to return to fire camp when she was back at Chowchilla, but CDCR said her labor was needed elsewhere: to harvest the almonds in the orchards surrounding CCWF. "It was hot. I'm short and I had this long stick and I was shaking the tree to get the almonds down." After a while, Noeli stopped hearing from Maria. She stopped paying for phone calls and sending packages and putting money on her books for hygiene and clothes. Noeli heard Maria was still using and that she was pregnant. "It was with a man. She was heavy on drugs," Noeli said. Then she started crying. "It wasn't her. My wife, the woman that I married, was so amazing and so beautiful and to see what she became. That's not her."

In January 2020, Noeli paroled to Santa Barbara and got a job in Oxnard making $15 an hour compounding Kylie Jenner makeup. She heard Maria was living in a trailer, pregnant for a second time. Maria's family had never approved of their relationship and Noeli lost touch with Maria. They didn't speak for all of 2020. Maria posted pictures of her partner and her pregnant belly.

By December 23, 2020, Maria was sick. Her hands and feet were swollen; she couldn't walk; she was coughing up blood; she couldn't breathe. The intake staff at JFK Memorial Hospital in Indio had seen many COVID-positive patients and Maria's symptoms fit the diagnosis. They separated Maria from those in the waiting room. It took ten hours to see a doctor. Then she was transferred to Desert Regional Medical Center in Palm Springs, where she waited for another four hours until she was admitted. At 2:03 a.m. on Christmas, she passed away from cardiac arrest. No one was with her. The baby didn't survive.

After I met Diana in 2016, I'd tried to drive out to Lancaster to see her whenever I was in California. With each visit, it seemed like the loss of Shawna had carved a bigger hole, leaving Diana more scattered, more stressed out than she'd been previously.

The year 2017 was bad. Diana's boyfriend gave her a black eye; she filed a restraining order. Diana moved back in with her estranged husband out of convenience. A night out to dinner led to a fight, which led to Bobby approaching Diana from behind in their bedroom. He grabbed her neck, choking her until she couldn't breathe. He screamed at her, twisting her neck until she was gasping for air. Ashley's boyfriend kicked the door down and Ashley saw her mom's face covered in blood.

Police arrested Bobby; he was sentenced to two years in County and served ten months of his two-year sentence. Just as he got out of jail, Diana started having suicidal thoughts and checked herself into a VA hospital. She stayed there and "slept" for three days. She was prescribed antipsychotics, but she refused to take them. Her liver damage made it hard to find the right meds; she figured no meds were better than ones that were going to destroy her internal organs. Her husband was abusive; her boyfriend was abusive. She self-medicated with alcohol. One night she took a knife to the meatiest parts of her forearms, slashing four cuts. She felt the pain, she saw the blood gurgle over her skin, but couldn't dig deeper. She realized she was still hurting and was just trying to make something else hurt worse. She lost her job at the Trap. After Shawna's birthday in December 2018, Diana told me, "I don't want it to be 2019. I don't want time to keep passing without Shawna. I don't want to forget. I just don't want the world to keep on going. And it does, time just keeps going by, the New Year is just a couple weeks away. And I don't want it to be 2019."

The last time I saw Diana was in May 2019. Because it had been a wet winter, the poppies popped and a mass migration of painted lady butterflies crowded the skies with a flurry of orange wings, a kaleidoscopic vision. The pollinators migrate seasonally from Mexico's dry deserts, passing through the Antelope Valley to the Cascades in the Pacific Northwest. Ashley was about to graduate high school, and the three of us sat down for salads and smoothies. Diana was exuding pride—Ashley had straight As and told me she wanted to go to MIT or Cal Poly. She already knew she was going to major in mechanical engineering, but she wanted to work as an aerospace engineer.

"I don't want to just build planes. I want to do something new and explore it."

"I don't know where this kid came from, not me," Diana said.

Ashley is strong, self-assured, and pragmatic. She's inquisitive and determined. She asked a lot of questions about why I wanted to write about Shawna, about the incarcerated-firefighter program.

Ashley missed her older sister, missed having someone to advise her on prom dresses, boyfriends, good trouble versus bad trouble, skateboarding, beach volleyball, museums. All the things Shawna promised they'd do together when she got out. Ashley told me about her visit to Malibu and how pretty it was there and how proud Shawna was. Every time Shawna got bumped up on her crew, from tool to bucker to saw, she felt like she had accomplished something. She could run up the mountains; she could keep pace; she could fight fire. Ashley felt like Malibu was peaceful, a certain kind of perfect. Birds composed the soundtrack, the smell of damp oak permeated the air. It was like a Disney version of prison. Ashley felt like Shawna was safe.

She told me about how Shawna would terrorize her as a kid, playing Insane Clown Posse's "Boogie Woogie Wu" before bed. Ashley would shudder at the thought of going to bed after hearing the lyrics "You fall asleep and you wake up dead / With a broken broom sticking out of your forehead."

Shawna was nine years older than Ashley, and tormented her the way an older sister might. She remembered the Faygo cans stacked in Shawna's room. She missed being harassed by her older sister, even the Insane Clown Posse phase.

When Ashley saw Shawna in the hospital, the nurses told her they were waiting for brain activity. She didn't know that meant Shawna was brain-dead. Not barely hanging on, but already gone. Then Ashley told me about how it felt after Shawna died. That she felt weird being the strong one, the older one, the one who had to take care of Diana. Ashley had to explain to Diana that she needed a mom, that she had felt abandoned and left out when Diana would disappear with Shawna. And now, with Shawna gone, they were both in mourning. They needed each other. "I was just never taught how to be a mother. I'd been on my own since I was thirteen. I didn't realize I hurt her so bad," Diana said. Ashley showed me her prom picture—she wore satin gloves and a black hourglass dress that looked like the red one Julia Roberts wore to the opera in *Pretty Woman*. When Diana started weeping about Ashley's success, Shawna's death, how she spends most days vacuuming the house carrying a small bottle of tequila, I apologized for dredging up pain. "No, I want to talk about Shawna, no one asks me about Shawna anymore. I don't want to forget Shawna."

By 2020, Diana was doing better. Instead of Shawna's memory fading, Diana was starting to remember details that had been shrouded in grief. She'd gotten a full-time job at Altman Plants, taking care of three different Home Depot Garden Centers. She was thrilled when Bailey, crew 13-3's foreman, and Chaplain Jake showed up in Lancaster for breakfast at Otto's and to see her Christmas tree, decked out with ornaments to honor firefighters.

The last time I saw her, she invited me into her house to show me the green marble urn that held Shawna's ashes. The same ashes that were driven from the coroner's department to Eternal Valley Memorial Park & Mortuary, in an empty rented casket. That day, a fire crew was on every overpass, standing on their trucks, saluting in full uniform as Shawna's procession drove underneath. Outside her funeral, rows of sheriffs and deputies stood at attention, right hands at their brows. Two fire trucks were parked at the entrance with their ladders raised, crossed in tribute to her. A flag was draped on the casket during the memorial, then folded tightly and handed to Diana.

Shawna Lynn Jones lived as an inmate and died an honored firefighter. Carla, Selena, Marquet, Sonya, Nichelle, Lilli, Whitney, Laurie, and Alisha were inmate firefighters, forever tagged as felons. Every criminal background check will reveal their history. In death, Shawna was granted freedom and honor; in life, the other women have to navigate a system stacked against them. A few months after Shawna's funeral, at a CIW graduation of inmate firefighters, the mood was celebratory, almost exultant. One speaker brought up Shawna and asked, to great applause, that her life and her death not be in vain. He said, "She gave her life for this program, and L.A. County made sure she did not leave without full dress." In the same ceremony, a captain told the women who hiked mountains in their oranges, "Just go out now, and serve the state of California. They rely on us, okay? You guys are trained, ready, professional."

EPILOGUE

Starting in the 1850s, women were subject to incarceration—they lived on the *Waban*, in a shack next to the captain's quarters. "The heavy doors and slatted windows failed to keep men out, including guards and the ship's captain, who had sex with the female prisoners," Kathleen Cairns wrote in *Hard Time at Tehachapi: California's First Women's Prison*. At first, women were of little concern to the prison industry because there weren't that many women prisoners—roughly thirty in the late 1800s. They were isolated, tasked with sewing jute bags and doing the laundry and cooking for the male prisoners and employees of San Quentin. By the 1920s, the female population had grown to several hundred—some women were sentenced to life for gruesome murders, others were imprisoned for prostitution or forgery or fraud. Organizations such as the Women's Christian Temperance Union, the League of Women Voters, and the California Federation of Women's Clubs "began pressing for separate facilities, partly because they believed in redemption, but partly because they had a very narrow view of 'womanhood' that leaned heavily toward piety, virtue, and domesticity," Cairns told me. They wanted to protect the women but also to reform them and prepare them for "civil" society. They lobbied for the right to house women separately from men and for a board of trustees separate from the board at the men's correctional division. Eventually, after years of contention, they convinced the state to agree to a new facility in a rural farming area in Cummings Valley, just west of Mojave and halfway between Bakersfield and Lancaster.

Tehachapi, the original California Institution for Women, was built on 1,600 acres. Its grounds were meant to be more like a college campus—they included gardens and cottage-style residences. The campus dorms were two-story homes with red-shingled roofs—each had a kitchen, dining room, and communal area. Many inmates had individual rooms and could wear their own clothes. Women had access to tennis courts, badminton courts, baseball diamonds; there was lawn bowling, croquet, horseshoes. The prison had a women's softball team named the Bomb-A-Dears. A *Christian Science Monitor* article described Tehachapi as "more like a country club than a prison." There were no fences, and prisoners escaped frequently. They didn't get very far, however, since the prison was in a dry, isolated valley. At its peak, Tehachapi was home to 426 prisoners.

In Tehachapi women performed agricultural tasks on a working farm and also produced theater performances. Inmates had their own newspaper, *The Clarion*, which provided a forum for profiles, anecdotes, poetry, and in-depth analysis of the prison-produced theatrical performances. ("What shall we say of the recent performance by a director and a cast within our midst? Simply that it was astonishing!" Navas

Rey, an inmate, wrote in a review. "Without a real stage, with makeshift arrangements on every hand, a great deal of back-breaking work and very little opportunity to devote time and energy to rehearsing, the director and her cast succeeded in putting on what any fair-minded individual would qualify as practically a professional performance.")

When the women of Tehachapi held county fairs with parades, townspeople were allowed into the prison. During World War II, the women sewed twenty thousand pillowcases and fifteen thousand mosquito nets for the navy. Attending vocational and educational classes was an essential part of life in Tehachapi—the goal was to train women for a profession. In the 1940s, the recidivism rate at Tehachapi hovered around 10 percent.

By the 1940s, Tehachapi had also become a reference point in popular movies. In *The Maltese Falcon*, Humphrey Bogart told Mary Astor, after accusing her of murder, "If you get a good break you'll be out of Tehachapi in twenty years, and you can come back to me then. I hope they don't hang you, precious, by that sweet neck." The prison was also mentioned in Billy Wilder's *Double Indemnity*, when Fred MacMurray tried to convince Barbara Stanwyck to murder her husband by explaining, "There was another case where a guy was found shot, and his wife said he was cleaning a gun and his stomach got in the way. All she collected was a three-to-ten stretch in Tehachapi."

The female-controlled parole board lasted only until 1944, when the prison was folded back into the men's correctional board. Then, after an earthquake in 1952, Tehachapi's buildings were mostly leveled, destroying the prison. After it was rebuilt as a men's prison, the women were transferred to the new CIW in Chino. The female inmate fire camps are the closest CDCR has come to replicating the intentions of Tehachapi. The difference? The society women of the 1930s and '40s were laser focused on reintegration and rehabilitation, meaning the jobs they trained for in prison were available upon release.

On Friday, September 11, 2020, Governor Newsom held a press conference in Oroville, at the site of the North Complex Fire—a series of fires in Northern California that had burned for the previous four weeks straight. He spoke of 2020's fire season—the 3.2 million acres that burned and the 7,700 fires that coursed through California. "If you do not believe in science, I hope you believe in observed evidence," Newsom said of the climate catastrophe unfolding in California and the western half of the United States. As a result of the North Complex Fire alone, nine people were dead. The flames had chewed through 252,313 acres of land from several directions, the fire was only 21 percent contained, and it was closing in on the scar of 2018's Camp Fire in Paradise, just a few miles away. The governor spoke through a bank of brown smoke that made the ground, the trees, and his hunting jacket indistinguishable. Newsom thanked "those prisoners who are out there, on the frontlines . . . who actively participated in heroic ways." Then he signed a bill that had been introduced in February by the assembly member Eloise Reyes—AB 2147, legislation that would provide a potential pathway to employment for incarcerated firefighters. "This bill will give those prisoners hope of actually getting a job in the profession that they've been trained," Newsom said.

When I started reporting about incarcerated firefighters in 2016, there was no pathway to a professional career through CAL FIRE or municipal fire departments. Despite their experience working on the frontlines, sometimes for several seasons, ex-felons could not qualify for EMT or EMR licenses, which are required in order to be hired on a professional crew. This bill seeks to remedy that by allowing incarcerated firefighters the chance to petition for expungement relief immediately upon release. If relief is granted, those individuals won't have to wait until they're off parole to apply for state jobs—not just firefighting jobs, but government jobs in roughly two hundred different careers.

The day after Newsom signed the bill, I talked to Alisha. "Oh god, that's so dope," she said. "I wish I was out." Now, with a life sentence, she can't even qualify for fire camp. It's unclear whether or not AB 2147 would have helped Alisha. First, she would have had to get a certificate from CDCR confirming she completed the fire camp program. (Although CAL FIRE captains and foremen are the supervisors who actually see inmates in the field and on the frontlines, correctional officers will be signing off on certification.) Next, she would have had to go before a judge, who can deny an application for expungement. But even if a judge had granted the application for expungement, a district attorney could have opposed it. A judge would then have had to hear that argument. And finally, CAL FIRE, or whichever hiring agency is in charge of the interview process, would have to choose to hire individuals with criminal records, which will still appear in background checks, even after a successful petition for expungement. (Many municipal firefighting agencies get three hundred applicants for every firefighting position, and often point to that statistic as the reason an individual isn't hired.) The bill, though progress by any measure, provides no mechanism to monitor any of these steps and no formal attempts to gather data on whether or not formerly incarcerated firefighters will benefit from the bill.

Even with the most progressive application of AB 2147, and if it had been in effect when Alisha was released the first time, she would have had to navigate reintegration into a world beyond prison while negotiating several levels of legal petitions in order to expedite an expungement of her record. And the law still doesn't guarantee a job, despite her three years of experience on the frontlines.

This law also does nothing to address the fact that California still relies on thousands of inmates, who are paid two to five dollars a day in camp and an additional one dollar an hour when they're on a fire line. AB 2147 does nothing to reform or recognize the inherent flaws of using inmate labor to save the state. The bill is also discriminatory—the expedited expungement process is available only to former incarcerated firefighters and not to any other ex-felons.

California is always on fire—climatologists predict the best-case scenario for the future of the American West is decades of megafires. Arguably, inmate crews are working the hardest, most dangerous job in California right now. They are a literal army, fighting to save the state from a climate catastrophe. Dozens of current and former inmate firefighters, including Alisha, told me about the benefits of the program and how it changed their lives, but imagine if, instead of a prison camp, those who qualified for camp were part of an apprenticeship program that paid competitive wages. Ideally, it would be a forestry camp run through the California Conservation Corps and CAL FIRE, eliminating the presence of correctional officers altogether. Imagine if these fire camps included social services. And then, imagine that the apprenticeship led directly to a job as a California firefighter. The future of the fire camps is unknown—in 2020, Newsom eliminated eight camps, including the first one established, Rainbow. But there are still thousands of inmate firefighters serving the state while serving a prison sentence.

The bill reminded me of what David Fathi, the director of the ACLU National Prison Project, told me when I first started reporting on this issue: "I think one important question to ask is, if these people are safe to be out and about and carrying axes and chain saws, maybe they didn't need to be in prison in the first place."

A NOTE ON SOURCES

The majority of this book is based on five years of interviews with women who have participated in California's Conservation Camp program, and on my firsthand reporting. Their stories are nonfiction; there are no composite characters. Some names have been changed, when requested, to protect individuals. I used first names throughout, even though most women were known to captains, foremen, and peers by their last names. When possible, I cross-checked information and spoke to multiple sources to verify stories of camp and personal histories. When it came to relaying conditions inside jails and prisons, I relied primarily on these women's experiences, court documents, and reported investigations.

Throughout the book, I depended on local reporting about fires and prisons from the *Los Angeles Times*, *The Sacramento Bee*, *The Fresno Bee*, *The Mercury News*, the *San Francisco Chronicle*, and *The San Diego Union-Tribune*, among other publications. Oftentimes, reporters break stories about incidents within jails and prisons or white-collar crimes within power companies. Without dogged local reporting, many of these crimes would be unknown. Local newspapers that produce original investigative journalism are a critical and necessary pillar of society, one that cannot be lost to corporate conglomeration, tech monopolies, and billionaire interests.

Many books informed my thinking on how to approach telling this story. Some served as inspiration, while others provided necessary historical and social context and crucial academic research. Many authors and scholars paved the way for me to be able to tell these women's stories. These are a few:

Alexander, Michelle. *The New Jim Crow: Mass Incarceration in the Age of Colorblindness*

Baldwin, James. *The Fire Next Time*

Bazelon, Emily. *Charged: The New Movement to Transform American Prosecution and End Mass Incarceration*

Cairns, Kathleen A. *Hard Time at Tehachapi: California's First Women's Prison*

Coates, Ta-Nehisi. *Between the World and Me*

Davis, Angela. *Are Prisons Obsolete?*

Davis, Mike. *City of Quartz: Excavating the Future in Los Angeles*

Desmond, Matthew. *On the Fireline: Living and Dying with Wildland Firefighters*

Didion, Joan. *Where I Was From*

Faragher, John Mack. *Eternity Street: Violence and Justice in Frontier Los Angeles*

Finnegan, William. *Cold New World: Growing Up in a Harder Country*

Gilmore, Ruth Wilson. *Golden Gulag: Prisons, Surplus, Crisis, and Opposition in Globalizing California*

Hernández, Kelly Lytle. *City of Inmates: Conquest, Rebellion, and the Rise of Human Caging in Los Angeles, 1771–1965*

Hinton, Elizabeth. *From the War on Poverty to the War on Crime: The Making of Mass Incarceration in America*

Knight, Etheridge. *The Essential Etheridge Knight*

Lorde, Audre. *Sister Outsider*

Manion, Jen. *Liberty's Prisoners: Carceral Culture in Early America*

Muir, John. *The Yosemite*

Murakawa, Naomi. *The First Civil Right: How Liberals Built Prison America*

Penn, Ozroe. *California Inmate Firefighter*

Pyne, Stephen J. *California: A Fire Survey*

Sherry, Michael S. *The Punitive Turn in American Life: How the United States Learned to Fight Crime Like a War*

Stevenson, Bryan. *Just Mercy: A Story of Justice and Redemption.*

Taylor, Quintard. *In Search of the Racial Frontier: African Americans in the American West, 1528–1990*

Thompson, Heather Ann. *Blood in the Water: The Attica Prison Uprising of 1971 and Its Legacy*

Villavicencio, Karla Cornejo. *The Undocumented Americans*

Ward, Jesmyn. *The Fire This Time: A New Generation Speaks About Race*

ACKNOWLEDGMENTS

Thank you to everyone who trusted me with their stories—I don't take that lightly. Your generosity, candor, and willingness to sit down and talk has shaped this book and has altered me. You've not only shared insights about the insides of places that remain walled off, you've shared pieces of yourselves.

Thank you to the experts on social justice, mass incarceration, the court system, firefighting, the history of California, and climate science who advised me along the way and provided necessary context.

Thank you to my agents, Jud Laghi, for being my champion and friend for fifteen years, and Jason Richman, for advocating tirelessly for this project in all forms.

Thank you to my editor and publisher (and now friend—you are my friend whether you like it or not), Sean McDonald, who delivers hard truths about first drafts with a soft touch and provides editorial prowess through grace, wisdom, heart, and a love of the Lakers and Dodgers (2020 Champions, fuck yes). Thank you to the team at MCD / Farrar, Straus and Giroux, especially Olivia Kan-Sperling, who brought impeccable insight, organization, clarity, and calm; Hannah Goodwin for production editorial wizardry; Frieda Duggan for deft copyedits; Lauren Roberts for publicity magic; Danny Vazquez for early support; Nina Frieman for production excellence; Gretchen Achilles for the book's design; and June Park for an alarming, breathtaking cover. Thank you to Jessica Suriano for her sharp eye and fact-checking expertise, above and beyond the call of duty, and James Steinbauer for his extensive research and trips to the California State archives. Thank you to McKenzie Funk for an early read that was both thoughtful and game-changing.

Thank you to *The New York Times Magazine* and the people who make it every week. In the decade I've known him, my editor Dean Robinson has taught me more about writing than anyone. (Sorry, Mom!) The article that inspired this book took a year and a half of reporting, editing, and writing, and he was patient enough to hold my hand and demand more when it required more.

Thank you to my family, friends, and anyone else instrumental in getting this done. You know who you are. In case you don't, here's an alphabetical list! I love you all for reasons I won't get into. Just know you are loved.

Aaron Fili, Aaron Mann, Aaron Mishel, Adam Gomolin, Adam Wright-Chisem, Adnan Khan, Adrian Nicole LeBlanc, Adrienne Kafka, A.J. Daulerio, Alex Kafka, Allison Koch, Allison Tray, Amy Osburn, Andrew Benard, Andrew Nolan, Andrew Peacock, Arkadi Gerney, Autumn Bernstein, Avery Fisher, Barbara Barschak, Betsy Beers, Bill Vourvoulias, Bill Wasik, Bob Metzger, Brenda Ann Kenneally, Bruce Cormicle, Bruce Crownover, Caitlin Roper, Caity Weaver, Carly Wray, Carol Salzman, Carrie Odell, Charles Heath, Charlotte Lowe, Christine Walsh, Christopher Federico, Christopher Isenberg, Chuck Eddy, Cindy Zaplachinski, Clarice Gillis, Clarity Haynes, Corene Kendrick, Craig Melzer, Damon Tabor, Dana Nelson, Dana Shapiro, Daniel Swain, David Lederer, David Lowe, David Mishel, David Shear, Debbie Peacock, Debra Kaysen, Dee Golles, Denise Thomas, Dorothy Mazumdar, Drew Smith, Effie Philips, Elizabeth Weinstein, Emily Bazelon, Emily Hass, Emma Carmichael, Emma Lantos, Emma Mann-Meginniss, Ereni Katsaggelos, Erin Stack, Ethan Lipton, Eva Fisher, Fariyah Farah, Francesca Mari, Fredo Miccoli, Gail Isenberg, Gavin Bulmash, Gavin Peacock, Glenna Gordon, Greg Seibert, Hal Bulmash, the Hamilton family, Hamilton Nolan, Hana Elwell, Hannah Lantos, Hardy Fisher, Harvey Chernack, Helen Tannenbaum, Henny Lowe, Henry Schwartz,

Henry Weinstein, Hernan Diaz, Huck Hodge, Hugh McCallum, Ira Glass, Irving Tannenbaum, Jack Kerr, Jackson Mishel, Jake Gilchrist, Jake Mishel, Jake Silverstein, James Lochart, Jan Lowe, Jan Mishel, Jason Brand, Jason Frankel, Jason Levine, Jay Kang, Jebediah Reed, Jeff Brand, Jeff Lantos, Jeff Levin, Jeff Sharlett, Jennifer Romolini, Jenny Engel, Jeremy Engel, Jessica Lantos, Jessica Lustig, Jia Tolentino, Jill Frankel, Jim Isenberg, Joanna Shear, Jon Caldwell, Jon Mooallem, Julian Kafka, Julianna Roosevelt, Julia Schwadron, Julie Frankel, Juno Elwell-Higgins, Héctor Tobar, Karen Spira, Karey Green, Kate Judge, Katherine Mann Lederer, Kathy Ryan, Katy Scogin, Kim Monda, Kyle Chernack, Kyle Peacock, Laura Levin, Lauren Lantos, Laurie Becklund, Leah Mann, LeeAn Lantos, Levi Elwell-Higgins, Lia Miller, Linda Diamond, Lindsay Fram, Lisa Kearns, Lizzie Simon, Lorna Frankel, Luci Lantos, Lynn Franco, Lynn Frankel, Madeleine von Froomer, Madeline Elwell, Madeline Lowe, Maer Roshan, Margot Lederer, Margot Robbie, Marilyn Levin, Mark DeAntonio, Mark Lowe, Marlena Lantos, Martha Montello, Mason Pettit, Matthew Desmond, Matthew Lowe, Max Hart, Maya Fisher, Meredith Mishel, Mia Bulmash, Michael Diamond, Michael Lowe, Michael Mann, Michael Romano, Michelle Memran, Michelle Reynolds Lowe, Mike Casalett, Mike Davis, Mira Elwell, Miriam Kramer, Mitchell Lederer, Monserrat Fontes, Nancy Fritz, Nancy Kaye, Nancy Meakem, Nandi Rodrigo, Naomi Glauberman, Nate Kaufman, Niko Higgins, Noah Sneider, the Nolan family, Nora Mann, Oliver Staley, Pam Mann, Patrice Evans, Patrick Hoffman, Paula Littauer, Peter Lowe, Philip Montgomery, Phyllis Peacock, Preston Marin, Rachel Benoff, Rachel Brand, Rachel Lowe, Rebecca Peacock, Rebecca Traister, Reuben Jonathan Miller, Reyhan Harmanci, Richard Frankel, Richard Gurwitz, Romeo Ymalay, Rosie Goldensohn, Russell Jacoby, Sally Tannenbaum, Sam Jacoby, Sarah DeLappe, Sarah Jacoby, Sarah Lederer, Sarah Poulter, Sasha Lilien, Scott Budnick, Scott Wofford, Seth Fletcher, Sharif Corinaldi, Simon T., Sofia Katsaggelos, Sophie-Claire Hoeller, Stefanie Grutman, Stephanie Haren, Stephen Elwell, Stephen Lowe, Steve Brown, Stuart Bakal, Stuart Bulmash, Stuart Seaborn, Sue Elwell, Sue Kalinowski, Susan Baskin, Susan Brand, Susan Burton, Taylor Berman, Terry Meginniss, Tess Lantos, Tom Lantos,

Tommy Thomas, Tony Grutman, Tony Migliaccio, Tyler Chernack, Walter Lowe, Will Peacock, Zack McDermott, Zan Strumfeld, Zerline Goodman, Zoe Ani, and Zoe Katsaggelos.

Thanks to MacDowell for providing a space to work, blank walls to plot chapters, and fellow fellows to provide feedback, inspiration, and camaraderie; and to the Logan Nonfiction Fellowship at the Carey Institute for Global Good for gathering a cohort instrumental to the development of this book. And to the Quincy Street residency.

Finally, thanks to my mom and Jeff; my dad and Marilyn; Matt, Romeo, and Maggie; David, Laura, and Frankie—the best family a girl could hope for.

INDEX

Lynwood, Century Regional
Detention Facility at, 90–99, 113,
178; Alisha at, 199, 200, 264–66;
Carla at, 94–95; food at, 94–95;
Hilton at, 92; Laurie at, 106;
Moore at, 95–96, 98; Scotti at,
97–98; Selena at, 15; sexual assaults
at, 97–98; Shawna at, 42, 44, 95,
98–99; Yelp reviews of, 92–93

MacArthur Park, 175–78, 252
Maddy, 112
Malibu Conservation Camp #13, 21,
31, 49–75, 89, 118, 122, 129, 153,
184–85, 189, 190, 218, 234, 263,
268; Bailey as Crew 13-3 foreman
at, 4–6, 9–11, 16–18, 21–22, 24, 27,
32, 36–37, 82, 274; Crew 13-1, 75;
Crew 13-3, 3–27, 31–38, 153, 187,
269; Crew 13-4, 69–70; hikes of,
68; Mulholland Fire and, 3–27, 28,
31–37, 47–48, 49–52, 169; Selena
at, 175, 178–82, 187; Shawna's
death while working with, 26–27,
28–37, 47, 48, 49–53, 56, 62, 63,
75, 81–82, 84, 141, 169, 269, 274;
Woolsey Fire and, 250–51
Maltese Falcon, The, 279
Maria, 16, 24, 27, 36, 269–71
Mariposa Valley, Calif., 187
Marquet, 108–109, 129–35, 224–31,
258–60, 275; arrest of, 135; at
CCTRP, 224–25; children of, 134,
138, 230–31; at Chowchilla, 108,
129, 130; at CIW, 47, 130; in CIW
fire program, 107–108, 225; drug
use of, 134–35, 139; in fire school
at Miramar College, 227–30; fire
work of, 139–42, 229–30; in foster
care, 131–33; jobs of, 227, 231,
258, 260; at Rainbow, 107, 129–30,
138–44, 224, 227, 228; religious
faith of, 108, 109, 138–39, 141,
224–27, 258–59; on search and
rescue mission, 143–44

Matchbox Twenty, 30
Mendocino Complex Fire, 220–21,
239
Mendocino National Forest, 158
mental health care, 194–95, 262
Mexicans, 156
Michael D. Antonovich Antelope
Valley Courthouse, 117–18
Miguel, 160–61, 171–74
Mike, 19–20
Miller, Reggie, 69
Moore, Unique, 95–96, 98
Mormons, 80
Muir, John, 236–37
Mulholland Fire, 3–27, 28, 31–37,
47–48, 49–52, 169

Napa Valley, 127
Native Americans, 80, 154, 156, 236
Newsom, Gavin, 249, 262, 264, 280,
281, 283
New York City Fire Museum, 150
Nichelle, 17, 23, 33, 62–63, 275
Nixon, Richard, 136
Noeli, 269–71
North Complex Fire, 280
North Fire, 179

Oakland Hills Fire, 54–55
O.C., The, 100
Okamoto, Vincent, 200, 202, 203,
210, 213, 215
Osby, Daryl L., 185

Pacific Coast Highway (PCH),
157–58
Pala Fire, 139–40
Palmdale, Calif., 80, 87, 185
Palomar mountains, 120, 125
Patagonia, 64, 66
Pechango Resort Casino, 120
Personal Fitness Training (PFT), 47,
106–108, 110, 112

A NOTE ABOUT THE AUTHOR

Jaime Lowe is the author of *Mental*, a memoir about lithium and bipolar disorder, and *Digging for Dirt: The Life and Death of ODB*, a biography of Ol' Dirty Bastard, a founding member of the Wu-Tang Clan. She is a frequent contributor to *The New York Times Magazine* and other national and international publications. Lowe has contributed to *This American Life* and *Radiolab*, and has been featured on NPR and WNYC. She was born and raised in California.